HYPER-LEARNING

HYPER-LEARNING

HOW *to* ADAPT *to* *the* SPEED *of* CHANGE

EDWARD D. HESS

Berrett–Koehler Publishers, Inc.

Berrett-Koehler Publishers, Inc.
1333 Broadway, Suite 1000
Oakland, CA 94612-1921
Tel: (510) 817-2277   Fax: (510) 817-2278   www.bkconnection.com

Ordering Information

Quantity sales. Special discounts are available on quantity purchases by corporations, associations, and others. For details, contact the "Special Sales Department" at the Berrett-Koehler address above.

Individual sales. Berrett-Koehler publications are available through most bookstores. They can also be ordered directly from Berrett-Koehler: Tel: (800) 929-2929; Fax: (802) 864-7626; www.bkconnection.com.

Orders for college textbook / course adoption use. Please contact Berrett-Koehler: Tel: (800) 929-2929; Fax: (802) 864-7626.

Distributed to the U.S. trade and internationally by Penguin Random House Publisher Services.

Berrett-Koehler and the BK logo are registered trademarks of Berrett-Koehler Publishers, Inc.

Printed in Canada

Berrett-Koehler books are printed on long-lasting acid-free paper. When it is available, we choose paper that has been manufactured by environmentally responsible processes. These may include using trees grown in sustainable forests, incorporating recycled paper, minimizing chlorine in bleaching, or recycling the energy produced at the paper mill.

Library of Congress Cataloging-in-Publication Data

Names: Hess, Edward D., author.
Title: Hyper-learning : how to adapt to the speed of change / Edward D. Hess.
Description: Oakland, CA : Berrett-Koehler Publishers, [2020] |
    Includes bibliographical references and index.
Identifiers: LCCN 2020016545 | ISBN 9781523089246 (hardcover) |
    ISBN 9781523089253 (pdf) | ISBN 9781523089260 (epub)
Subjects: LCSH: Employees—Effect of technological innovations on. |
    Organizational change. | Learning. | Intellectual capital. | Human capital.
Classification: LCC HD6331 .H44 2020 | DDC 658.3/124—dc23
LC record available at https://lccn.loc.gov/2020016545

First Edition
26   25   24   10   9   8   7   6   5   4

Book producer: Westchester Publishing Services
Cover designer: Howie Severson

To Mother, Father, and Katherine

and

*To you—wishing you Inner Peace and
the joy of Hyper-Learning*

CONTENTS

PROLOGUE *1*

PART 1: HYPER-LEARNING REQUIRES A NEW WAY OF BEING

CHAPTER 1: Achieving Inner Peace *23*

CHAPTER 2: Adopting a Hyper-Learning Mindset *57*

CHAPTER 3: Behaving Like a Hyper-Learner *91*

CHAPTER 4: The Susan Sweeney Personal
Transformation Story *134*

CHAPTER 5: The Marvin Riley Personal
Transformation Story *152*

PART 2: HYPER-LEARNING REQUIRES A NEW WAY OF WORKING

CHAPTER 6: Humanizing the Workplace *165*

CHAPTER 7: Creating Caring, Trusting Teams *185*

CHAPTER 8: Having High-Quality,
Making-Meaning Conversations *205*

CHAPTER 9: EnPro Industries: Enabling the
Full Release of Human Possibility *227*

CHAPTER 10: Hyper-Learning Practices *250*

CHAPTER 11: The Adam Hansen Personal
Transformation Story *276*

EPILOGUE *290*

NOTES *295*

ACKNOWLEDGMENTS *301*

INDEX *303*

ABOUT THE AUTHOR *317*

HYPER-LEARNING

How to Adapt to the Speed of Change

Why should you read this book? Because it's about your future and the future of your children and grandchildren. The underlying question is: How will you and they pursue a meaningful life when smart technology takes over most of the jobs and skills that humans currently do? How will you and they keep up with the pace of technological change in order to stay relevant in the workplace?

The answer I propose is Hyper-Learning.

The word "hyperlearning" has been used by other people and organizations in the technology area and in the area of providing courses to students for standardized test preparation. It has also been defined in the education field as a categorical leap beyond artificial intelligence resulting from the uniting of technology trends. This book takes a different approach by creating a hyphenated word, Hyper-Learning, and defining it as the "human capability to learn, unlearn, and relearn continually in order to adapt to the speed of change."

Hyper-Learning is continual learning, unlearning, and relearning.

By *hyper*, I do not mean the modern connotation of being excitable, manic, nervous, or fidgety.

I use the term to reference the original Greek meaning of "over" or "above." Hyper-Learning is learning that is *over* and *above* what is typical. It is an overabundance of continual, high-quality learning.

Hyper-Learning requires a radical **New Way of Being** and a radical **New Way of Working** than you're probably used to.

This book explains *why* and *how* to become a Hyper-Learner. Before proceeding, please take out a notebook that you can use as a **Learning Journal** for recording thoughts, reflecting on the content, and completing included workshops while reading.

A CHALLENGING NEW ERA FOR HUMANS

We've been in the midst of the digital age arguably since the introduction of the personal computer, but much of the populace is only now beginning to understand and predict the consequences of the relentless technological progress that characterizes this era. The continuing advance of artificial intelligence, biotechnology, nanotechnology, genetic engineering, virtual and augmented reality, quantum computing, and big data is challenging humankind on a scale analogous to the species-altering habitat migration our ancient ancestors faced. Environmental destruction forced early humans to leave the relative safety of their African rainforest habitat for the much more dangerous open savanna.

While the savannas offered new sources of food in the form of meaty animals, they also made humans less hidden and more vulnerable as prey to those often faster and bigger meaty animals.

In effect, our ancestors had to learn how to survive and thrive in a completely new environment. Our ancestors had to unlearn and relearn. And I submit to you that that is what we all have to do in the digital age, over and over again.

I believe we can continue to have meaningful work in the digital age only if we can add value by doing the tasks that technology can't

do well. At least for the near future, those tasks are exploring the unknown and novelty by being creative, imaginative, and innovative; engaging in higher-level critical thinking; making decisions in environments with lots of uncertainty and little data; and connecting with other human beings through high emotional engagement and effective collaboration.

All of those tasks are heavily influenced by the uniquely human way we approach and engage in learning. Contrary to the bits and bytes fueling smart technology, human thinking and learning are driven by a complicated and integrated interplay of our minds, brains, emotions, and bodies. **How well we think, learn, and engage in the human tasks of the future depends on how well we manage and optimize what's going on with our minds, brains, and bodies**—for example, how well we leverage the power of our subconscious, imaginative, and creative minds and how well we connect emotionally to other humans through trusting, caring relationships.

A key human uniqueness as compared to smart machines is our emotional and social intelligence.

THE NEED TO EVOLVE

Our early ancestors survived being forced onto the open savanna by becoming hunter-gatherers—not alone but in cooperation with others. They survived by creating small teams that worked together to find food and safety and to care for offspring. They survived by sharing the bounty that individual team members found. They prospered because they collaborated, learned together, and shared resources.

Now we are on the leading edge of an era in which technology has the potential to both advance and destroy civilization. The McKinsey Global Institute predicts that by 2030 over 25 million jobs in the United States will be automated.[1] Research from Oxford University predicts that within 15 years there is a high probability that 47 percent of U.S. jobs—including professional jobs—will be automated.[2]

We now face an existential question. How do we live meaningful lives and have meaningful work in a world where familiar jobs and skills continue to be automated by smart technology?

I believe the dramatic changes our species will experience as the digital age continues to advance are akin to the changes our ancestors faced when they left their personal rainforests for the open savanna, and similarly, we will have to evolve. Over the next few decades, we will have to become the **digital age's hunter-gatherers**. Many of us will have to become entrepreneurs, selling our skills to people as they need them. Some of us will have to band together to earn money. Some of us will continue to have highly desired skills and full-time employment, but that security will last only as long as our skills stay ahead of the advancing technology. We will have to constantly adapt to ever-changing circumstances and excel at lifelong learning. We will have to become Hyper-Learners.

"Most important of all will be the ability to deal with change, learn new things, and preserve your mental balance in unfamiliar situations," says leading thinker and futurist Yuval Noah Harari. The point, he stresses, is "not merely to invent new ideas and products but above all to reinvent yourself again and again."[3]

Let's stop here for a moment.

Let's *make meaning* together. In your Learning Journal, please write down what Harari's words "reinvent yourself again and again" mean to you.

How do you interpret those words?

How would you reinvent yourself?

To me, Harari's words mean that I will have to constantly upgrade my approach to daily life—my mental models, scripts, and stories about how the world works—and learn new ways to add value and have a meaningful life. To me, having a meaningful life means having meaningful work that supports my loved ones and meaningful relationships, and that means continually learning new skills and knowledge, improving how I think and emotionally connect and relate to people, and adapting as technology continues to advance. I will have to work hard every day on becoming my **Best Self**. I will have to embrace a **New Way of Being** and **Working** to become a **Hyper-Learner**—a continual, high-quality, life-long learner.

Many of us working now may have been taught to believe that the most important learning occurs during the first 20 to 30 years of our lives. After that we can go out into the world, find a way of life that generally works for us, and do that thing over and over, maybe in different contexts, until retirement. That game is over.

As the digital age continues to advance, I think humans will have to spend their entire lives learning to become and maintain their Best Selves cognitively, morally, emotionally, and behaviorally.

Harari states:

> **"Change itself is the only certainty. . . . To stay relevant— not just economically but above all socially—you will need the ability to constantly learn and reinvent yourself. . . . As strangeness becomes the new normal, your past experiences, as well as the past experiences of the whole of humanity, will become less reliable guides."**[4]

Let's think about that last part: "your past experiences . . . will become less reliable guides." What does that mean to you? Let's make meaning again. Please write down in your Learning Journal what it means to you.

To me, these words mean:

- Change will be constant. What worked for me yesterday may not work for me today. I can't get complacent.

- I have to constantly ensure I am not missing something. I can't afford to believe that I know for certain what works.

■ I have to be very aware of how my environment is changing and figure out (with the help of people I trust) what I need to do to stay relevant in order to add value.

■ I have to be observant and seek out different perspectives. I have to become an explorer, seeking out the new and the different, looking for novelty.

■ I have to stay current—upgrading how I live my life and do my work. I have to constantly upgrade myself just like I upgrade my technology devices with new software. That means I have to be a proactive learner who is curious and aware.

■ I need to seek out the opinions of experts and thought leaders and new knowledge from lifelong learning opportunities and from smart people who are in different occupations than mine.

■ I have to look for and anticipate change. I have to ask myself each day, what is different or new here?

SO, WHAT'S THE PROBLEM?

Let's just adapt and become Hyper-Learners, you might say. Let's just get on with it.

Unfortunately, humans have two main obstacles to becoming Hyper-Learners. One comes from the way we're "wired" and the other comes from our typical work environments.

First, our wiring. The **science of adult learning** shows that our brains and minds are geared to be efficient; confirm what we expect to see, feel, or think; protect our egos; strive for cohesiveness; and operate much of the time on autopilot. We are creatures of habit. As for our thinking, psychologist and Nobel laureate Daniel Kahneman says, "Laziness is built deep into our nature."[5]

As a consequence, we have many ingrained biases that guide our thinking, and most of us are cognitively blind—we won't even process information that disagrees with our mental models. We have confirmation biases, meaning we automatically prioritize information that confirms what we think we already know, and we rarely look for reasons why we may be wrong. We also have cognitive dissonance, which means that even when we do let contradictory information into our minds, we rationalize it to fit within our existing beliefs.

And we all struggle to manage two big inhibitors of human learning: our *egos* and our *fears*. We underestimate the magnitude of our ignorance, and we have been educated to avoid making mistakes, which means we tend not to take risks in exploring what is new or different.

Ego can get in the way of learning because it can lead to closed-mindedness, arrogance, defining oneself by what one knows, poor listening skills, and viewing collaboration as competition.

Fear hinders learning because people are fearful of making mistakes, fearful of being wrong, fearful that they will look bad or not be liked or offend someone by asking hard questions. Many people are scared of working on any new project or engaging in discovery and experimentation because they've been taught that making mistakes is how you lose your job. And many people are fearful of speaking to power. In many work environments, it might be wise to fear these things. But going forward, organizational leaders and every individual will need to get over these fears to stay relevant and engage in Hyper-Learning.

The science is compelling. We are all suboptimal learners.

Yes, some of us are better than others, but few if any of us can reach the level of excellence increasingly needed in the digital age by ourselves. As Chris Argyris, a renowned expert on organizational learning, says, "Defensive reasoning encourages individuals to keep private the premises, inferences, and conclusions that shape their behavior and to avoid testing them in a truly independent, objective fashion."[6]

As a result, we need others to do our best learning, because others help us to:

- See what we don't see

- Challenge our thinking

- Update our mental models (a necessity for learning) by bringing forth their own mental models and differing interpretations, concepts, and data

- Pick up emotional cues we might have missed

My psychology mentor of almost 40 years, Dr. Lyle Bourne Jr., said to me a few years ago:

> **"All learning occurs in conversations with yourself (deep reflection) or with others."**

Think about that statement. Conversations are how we make meaning of the need to change—to learn—to do something new or different. They are how we verbalize a new story and begin to embed it into our cognitive and emotional systems. It is how we rewire our brains by creating new associations that expand the connectivity of our internal databases.

If you want to be a Hyper-Learner, you'd better excel at having meaningful learning conversations with others, and you'd better excel at listening. You'd better learn to listen in a way that leads to understanding a speaker's position and consider his or her views rather than automatically judging or arguing against them or automatically defending your own view or ego.

Dr. Barbara Fredrickson's positive psychology research, which is highlighted in her books *Positivity* and *Love 2.0*, is foundational to higher levels of human performance. She has said,

> **"It is scientifically correct to say that nobody reaches his or her full potential in isolation."**[7]

What this means is that all of us need to learn from others, from people who have different backgrounds, training, and experiences. We need the input of people with different mental models to help us challenge our own views. That is why as the digital age continues to progress most cognitively based human work increasingly will require collaboration among small teams or groups (just like the hunter-gatherers).

In other words, Hyper-Learning is a team sport in which every person is a Most Valuable Player.

So we humans have to accept the science that our default way of being is suboptimal for learning and that we need the help of others to truly become Hyper-Learners.

Note the two crucial implications of this. We need to learn *how to learn* and *how to collaborate* better. Both of those things require us to better manage our thinking and emotions, take experimental risks, and be vulnerable. They require us to be open-minded, manage our egos and fears, have candid and difficult conversations, be authentic and transparent, reflectively listen, and connect, relate, and emotionally engage in positive ways with team members.

Let's pause here.

Do you accept the science?

On reflection, do you accept or agree that you are a suboptimal learner?

Can you say out loud, "I am a suboptimal learner"?

Did you do it? How did it feel?

Weird? Liberating? Uncomfortable?

Think about this. Each morning when you wake up, consider practicing the following statement:

I am a suboptimal learner, but I will optimize my learning opportunities today in every human engagement.

To rehash, our brain prioritizes and seeks, and our organizations and social and cultural norms and structures support and reinforce:

■ Efficiency

■ Speed

■ Confirmation of what we believe

■ Affirmation of our egos through cognitive and emotional self-protection

■ Cohesiveness of our inner stories (mental models)

All of that hinders Hyper-Learning.

As the relentless changes of the digital age continue, we must learn to manage our minds and brains to enable Hyper-Learning by:

■ Seeking novelty, exploration, and discovery

■ Asking questions: The three Ws (Why? What if? Why not?)

■ Deferring judgment: a "Yes, and" not a "Yes, but" approach

■ Embracing ambiguity and not rushing to the safety of making premature decisions

■ Having High-Quality, Making-Meaning Conversations with others

■ Taming our egos and our fears

■ Generating and sharing positive emotions

For most of us to do all of that, we need to adopt a New Way of Being and a New Way of Working.

A NEW WAY OF BEING

Hyper-Learning is cognitive, behavioral, and emotional.

Managing your thinking, behaviors, and emotions in order to engage in Hyper-Learning is about becoming your **Best Self** cognitively, behaviorally, emotionally. Operating at your Best Self requires three main steps.

Step 1: Achieving Inner Peace

Inner Peace is based on science and ancient philosophies and is the foundational building block to becoming a Hyper-Learner. What I mean by Inner Peace is a state of inner stillness and calmness that enables you to embrace the world with your most open, nonjudgmental, fearless mind. For many people the ability to enter a state of Inner Peace requires a significant personal transformation.

Inner Peace comprises four key elements: a **Quiet Ego**, a **Quiet Mind**, a **Quiet Body**, and a **Positive Emotional State.**

By cultivating these four elements, you are better able to manage your thinking, behaviors, and emotions; engage with the world outside of you with more open-mindedness, awareness, and willingness to see other perspectives; and change your mental models in order to learn.

A state of Inner Peace does all this by mitigating the two big inhibitors of learning: ego and fear.

Inner Peace enhances your ability to tap into the power of your subconscious, reflectively listen, and positively connect and relate to others.

Chapter 1 explains the science and philosophy behind cultivating Inner Peace through those four elements. It explores research on self-mastery and self-control, mindfulness and loving-kindness meditation, the power of generating positive emotions and managing the kinds of emotions that inhibit Hyper-Learning, emotional synchronicity with others, and the importance of deep breathing.

With the included workshop you have the opportunity to create a checklist of Daily Intentions for cultivating a state of Inner Peace and your Best Self.

Step 2: Adopting a Hyper-Learning Mindset

Behaviors are how people make their priorities and intentions known to the world. But in most cases changing behaviors requires changing your mindset first—your internal story of who you are and how the world works. Before you can change your behavior in ways that enable you to become a Hyper-Learner, you have to create the right mindset—a personal story of *why* you should change.

In chapter 2, to help you begin to cultivate a Hyper-Learning Mindset, I share ideas and theories from ancient and modern philosophers, psychologists, social scientists, leading academics, and noted business leaders that align with underlying principles of Hyper-Learning.

This chapter ends with two workshops. First, I invite you to take your learnings from chapters 1 and 2 to discover your own reasons for *why* you need a Hyper-Learning Mindset. Then you have the opportunity to create a personal list of Hyper-Learning Mindset principles that you can easily refer to daily to help reinforce your Daily Intentions toward Hyper-Learning.

Step 3: Behaving Like a Hyper-Learner

This book focuses heavily on behaviors. It is through behaviors that we engage with the world and others. It is through behaviors that we truly become Hyper-Learners. Behavior change requires the utmost self-discipline and daily effort and vigilance. The advancing digital age will test you, but it will also give you a choice. Will you take your way of being and learning to a higher level or will you be left behind?

What are key Hyper-Learning Behaviors? In my experience there are too many for any organization or person to work on at any given time.

One must prioritize down to a manageable number—seven or eight behaviors that are the foundational building blocks of your Hyper-Learning activities. That is the start.

Then those Hyper-Learning Behaviors must be *precisely defined* so you can assess your current state of competence and what aspects of that behavior you need to work on. Very importantly, you then have to assess your performance daily by getting feedback and measuring your rate of improvement. And when you have improved those behaviors, you should pick two more to improve and so on.

Precisely defining behaviors is drilling down to and identifying observable sub-behaviors that evidence the desired behavior and observable sub-behaviors that evidence the lack of the desired behavior. Getting this granular is key. **It gets at how you talk, the words you use, your tone, how you connect to people, your facial expressions, your presence, how you listen, how you collaborate, how you think, and how you deal with emotions and disagreements**.

Chapter 3 includes a workshop on identifying **Hyper-Learning Behaviors** and a case study concerning W. R. Berkley Corporation, a very successful public insurance company that used this same behavioral approach to empower all employees to become innovators. The chapter ends with an opportunity to take a **Hyper-Learning Behaviors Diagnostic**, which I have used with over 3,000 executives and leaders, and to create a Hyper-Learning Behaviors Development Plan. Through this exercise you can choose the Hyper-Learning Behaviors you want to work on and determine an objective way to measure your progress toward becoming a Hyper-Learner.

Another crucial step in developing and making Hyper-Learning Behaviors habitual is to engage in **Hyper-Learning Practices** on a daily basis. Chapter 10 provides guidance on how to do that. It discusses activities that you as an individual can infuse into your daily life to help you become a Hyper-Learner and that organizations can facilitate and embrace to enable all their people to Hyper-Learn.

Personal Transformation

To see many of these steps in action, this book introduces you to three senior executives—Susan Sweeney, Marvin Riley, and Adam Hansen—who share their amazing personal transformation stories in the pursuit of their Best Selves and Inner Peace.

A NEW WAY OF WORKING

To be a Hyper-Learner requires not only a New Way of Being but also the ability to work in an environment conducive to Hyper-Learning. Unfortunately, many of our workplaces were designed in ways that inhibit Hyper-Learning. That is not good. That has to change. The digital age increasingly will require it.

Hyper-Learning requires a humanistic and emotionally safe and emotionally positive work environment. Hyper-Learning requires an environment in which people can be fully engaged cognitively, emotionally, and behaviorally and that requires an emotionally positive environment where people feel safe and valued; have caring, trusting work relationships; and can bring their uniqueness to the pursuit of meaningful work.

Recent research by Gallup showed that 85 percent of global employees are not engaged in their work or appear not to have great jobs.[8]

That is a WOW! Let that one sink in.

Are you in the 15 percent or the 85 percent?

Admitting to being in the 85 percent is nothing to be ashamed about. Likely it says nothing bad about you personally. Likely it's the fault of the business environment you find yourself in—one that devalues and fails to meet the emotional needs of workers and isn't conducive to people bringing their Best Selves to work or finding meaning and purpose. An environment like that will not have engaged employees or Hyper-Learners.

Hyper-Learning happens in *idea meritocracies*—environments where the best idea wins and where people feel safe to speak to power. It happens in environments that minimize internal competition, elitism, political games, hierarchy, and a survival-of-the-fittest mentality. In other words, Hyper-Learning occurs best in environments free of the two big inhibitors of learning: ego and fear.

Humans Are Not Machines

Most organizations today strive to be rational, anti-emotional machines. By definition, organizations are designed to drive predictable, standardized results by turning human resources into human machines.

We now know that as the digital age continues to progress, most tasks requiring predictable, standardized results and operational excellence will be automated. Smart machines eventually will replace all the human machines.

The whole concept of managing others must change to produce the higher levels of human performance increasingly demanded by the digital age. Command/control and directing others will, in most cases, be obstacles to success. **You cannot effectively command and control or direct a person to do the kinds of jobs and tasks that will be left for humans, which require innovation, creativity, and emotional engagement with others.**

Gary Hamel, one of the giants in the field of business management thinking, says,

> **"Humanizing the language and practice of management is a business imperative (and an ethical one)."**[9]

And

> **"Put simply, you can't build an organization that's fit for the future around an ideology that *preemptively* and *structurally* empowers the few while disempowering the many."**[10]

This New Way of Working is illuminated in chapters focusing on Humanizing the Workplace; creating and being a part of Caring, Trusting Teams; engaging in High-Quality, Making-Meaning Conversations; and adopting Hyper-Learning Practices as the daily way of working.

Humanizing the Workplace

It is time for the old ways of working to die, because our traditional workplaces, cultures, and policies inhibit Hyper-Learning, and they inhibit employees becoming their Best Selves at work.

Chapter 6 explains how this New Way of Working requires a new way of organizing, managing, leading, and behaving that maintains organizational rigor and discipline but is significantly more caring, compassionate, and emotionally positive.

It explains why the old ways must be replaced by a **humanistic system that liberates people** to think and emotionally engage at their highest levels, that gives them the courage to innovate and create, and that allows them to thrive in an idea meritocracy. And that system must enable continual human development cognitively, emotionally, and behaviorally because Hyper-Learning requires it.

Caring, Trusting Teams

The highest levels of human performance in the digital age increasingly will come from what I call Caring, Trusting Teams.

Studies show that the highest levels of human performance occur on teams in which all members have a common purpose and values, deeply care about each other as unique human beings, have compassion for each other, and trust each other. Trusting each other means believing that no one on the team will do harm to the others and that everyone is totally invested in each other's personal development and success.

With trust, teams can cultivate candor, mutual respect, exploration, making-meaning conversations, and open dialogue in search for the truth or in search of the new and different. Only then will the two big inhibitors of learning (ego and fear) be mitigated.

With a Caring, Trusting Team, people can bring their Best Selves to the conversation and the highest levels of human thinking can occur. Each team member can bring his or her creativity, imagination, and unique human value to the conversation and contribute to meaningful and purposeful work. As Irish poet and philosopher John O'Donohue says in his book *Anam Cara*, **"Imagine how lovely it would be if you could be yourself at work and express your true nature, giftedness, and imagination."**[11]

Chapter 7 provides guidance on how to create a high-performing Caring, Trusting Team, how to become a valuable member of one, the biochemistry of generating positive connections and emotions with others, and the science of collective intelligence.

High-Quality, Making-Meaning Conversations

One of the processes crucial to Hyper-Learning and the journey through this book is the making-meaning process. Making meaning with other people goes back at least to our species' early days as hunter-gatherers, when after the discovery of fire people would sit around those fires and talk. Talking was how learning was shared. Talking was how people came to understand each other. Talking was how social and behavioral norms were created.

High-Quality, Making-Meaning Conversations are not about advocacy, self-promotion, or competition. They are about seeking mutual understanding.

In such a conversation you are seeking to understand others, and you are seeking to be understood by others.

It is through having High-Quality, Making-Meaning Conversations that we can explore, discover, and resolve misunderstandings and differences. It is through making meaning that the real purposes of the meeting or the conversation, the meaning of key words, and the real reasons people are espousing the positions they are espousing are illuminated for all to consider.

It is through High-Quality, Making-Meaning Conversations with Caring, Trusting Teams that we can have a chance of experiencing what I call *collective flow*, which I believe to be the highest level of team engagement.

Collective flow reflects a team becoming one—an emotionally integrated group of people devoid of fear and self-centeredness, totally engrossed in the common task. It is then that individual contributions can emerge leading to "wow" engagement, innovation, creativity, critical thinking, and problem solving. It is then that the unique strengths of people can flourish because of the chemistry among them and the interaction of their hearts and minds (not just minds). **Collective flow is magical!**

Chapter 8 discusses how to cultivate High-Quality, Making-Meaning Conversations.

EnPro Industries: Enabling the Full Release of Human Possibility

To see an example of this New Way of Working in practice, chapter 9 discusses EnPro Industries, Inc., a global, engineering-based, special-component manufacturing company that has adopted the following dual bottom line philosophy:

Dual Bottom Line

"Our purpose is to enable the full release of human possibility.

"As a Dual Bottom Line company, human development carries equal importance to financial performance.

"There is no trade-off between the two, and we measure both. People who are focused on developing themselves pursue excellence, and when excellence is pursued, financial results are superior.

"Our human development philosophy is evident in our daily behavior and supported by an education system built on everyone teaching and learning from others. We recognize people learn and change from the inside of themselves on their terms, consistent with their beliefs."[12]

Chapter 9 brings to life how EnPro promotes and operationalizes this philosophy through its stated values, corporate mindset, emphasized behaviors, and 25 company practices.

PRACTICAL GUIDANCE

This is a *how-to* book.

It is an active-learning book. It is a behaviors-based book.

I want you to walk away with a personal, implementable plan for becoming a Hyper-Learner, including a way to measure your progress and get feedback from trusted others.

Through Reflection Times and workshops, you have the opportunity to begin your own Hyper-Learning journey. As advised earlier in this prologue, I highly recommend that you start a Learning Journal for completing the exercises and taking notes while reading the book and for continued use and reference after.

This book and the model of Hyper-Learning I developed are based on the best relevant research and applied sciences from 500 leading academic articles and more than 180 books, and from 17 years of my own work in the areas of organizational and individual performance and leadership. I have primarily focused my time in academia on cracking the code of human excellence. This book is a continuation of that professional journey and my personal journey in striving to become my Best Self (I am still on it).

At its core, this is a book about how to continually learn, unlearn, and relearn.

It is a book about how to optimize your uniqueness as a human being—what makes you different from the smart machines—so you can continue to stay relevant in the digital age.

It is a book about the power of human emotions, choices, and behaviors that enable the highest levels of human cognitive, emotional, and behavioral performance.

You cannot take comfort in the experience and skills that you now have. You will have to continually reinvent yourself, and that requires Hyper-Learning.

Having to become your Best Self to engage in Hyper-Learning is not just about virtue—it's not just a nice thing to do once you've become successful—it's necessary to continually hone relevant and valuable skills.

OUR LEARNING JOURNEY

I invite you to dive in, and just like being in the ocean, you may feel battered by the waves of the new, the different, and even the weird. But just as in the ocean, when you dive down under the waves, you will find calmness when you reflect deeply about the key points in this book and have High-Quality, Making-Meaning Conversations with trusted others.

I hope you embrace the learn-by-doing Reflection Times and workshops included in the chapters. May your read be joyous and liberating, and may it propel you on a meaningful journey toward becoming a Hyper-Learner.

PART 1

Hyper-Learning Requires a New Way of Being

CHAPTER 1

Achieving Inner Peace

Inner Peace is the foundational building block of becoming a Hyper-Learner. To engage in Hyper-Learning requires your Best Self—your highest-quality performance emotionally, cognitively, and behaviorally—and you cannot operate at that level until, as a baseline, you cultivate a state of Inner Peace.

Inner Peace is an internal quietness or stillness, which I define as being fully present in the moment with an open and nonjudgmental mind and a lack of self-absorption. It's a state of positivity with limited stress and fear. **With those internal qualities, you are more open to**:

- Learning

- Stress-testing your beliefs (not values)

- Listening to learn, not to confirm

- Embracing opportunities, differences, novelty, and the unknown

- Considering opinions that differ from yours

- Building caring, trusting relationships

- Having High-Quality, Making-Meaning Conversations

- Attaining states of flow and collective flow with colleagues

- Cultivating openness and trust with others

- Managing your fears and insecurities

With Inner Peace, you're more able to exercise choice in your thinking, emotions, and behaviors.

You can decide between allowing your mind to wander and being present.

You can either engage with the negative emotions that hinder learning or take steps to mitigate their impact by taking deep breaths to relax or by actively thinking about something else or by reframing the situation. For now, the key point to recognize is that you can *choose* to let emotions control you, or you can *choose* to manage your emotions. You can choose to actively generate positive emotions and "own" your emotions, or you can give others the power to determine your state of mind or state of heart by allowing their behaviors to heavily influence you for long periods of time.

Inner Peace can help you mitigate natural tendencies that can get in the way of Hyper-Learning, such as:

- Being risk-adverse and insecure

- Wanting to be liked and fearing exclusion from the "right" groups

- Wanting too much to win and generally viewing others as competition in a zero-sum game

- Being heavily influenced and consumed by your ego and constant mind chattering

- Overestimating the importance of "smarts" and underestimating the power of the heart

- Overvaluing logic, speed, and efficiency

- Undervaluing slowing down to really engage and really listen with a nonjudgmental, open mind

- Undervaluing the power of emotions and the power of your subconscious

- Undervaluing just being rather than always doing

- Dismissing the need to master self and emotionally invest in building trusting relationships

Another way to think about Inner Peace is as the foundation of certain powers.

The 10 Powers of Inner Peace

- The Power of Serenity

- The Power of Humility

- The Power of Slowing Down

- The Power of Presence

- The Power of Reflective Listening

- The Power of Positive Emotions

- The Power of Reflection

- The Power of Emergence

- The Power of Being

- The Power of Owning You

Cultivating Inner Peace can help you remove internal noise and distraction and help you align your inner world—your mind, body, brain, and heart—so you can better engage with the outer world. From this quiet state, you can allow your uniqueness to emerge.

This chapter describes the four underlying elements of Inner Peace—a **Quiet Ego**, a **Quiet Mind**, a **Quiet Body**, and a **Positive Emotional State**—and provides practical guidance on how to cultivate them.

Reflection Time

Reflection Time means taking your time to think deeply—reflect and illuminate, illuminate and learn.

Please take your time and reflect on the questions I pose below.

Please think back to a recent time when you had back-to-back work meetings. Did you walk into each meeting with a calm, quiet mind?

Were you fully present or were you thinking about something that occurred earlier in the day or about what was coming next?

In each meeting, were you in a listening mode? Or were you critiquing or making judgments while another person was talking?

Was your body relaxed or did you feel tightness? Did you feel some nervousness, fear, or anger? Were you even aware of your body? Your breathing?

Did you spend time thinking about whether you looked good or appeared smart or were well liked by the others?

What does internal noise mean to you? Does your mind "talk" to you? Does it critique your performance? The performance of others? Does your mind like to judge others?

Did you know that with training you can quiet your mind?

Did you know that with training you can influence
how you feel?

Did you know that your mind, heart, and
body are all influencing each other?

THE SCIENCE OF US

To fully understand the power and necessity of Inner Peace for Hyper-Learning, you need to have a basic understanding of how the human brain, mind, and body work together. It's beyond the scope of this book to explain in detail the science of human thinking, emotions, perceptions, and behavior, but the following is a high-level summary of what the research says and how it challenges common beliefs. Making you an expert on brain science is not the object of this book. The purpose is to give you some background on how your thinking, emotions, and perceptions emerge so you have a sense of your starting point.

Each human being is a complex adaptive system influenced materially by his or her genes, social environment, and past experiences.

Humans are wired to seek safety and to *fight or flee* when survival is threatened, but we're also wired to make meaning and connect with others.

Evolutionary science and psychology have also shown that we are social animals at our core. We survived as a species because we learned how to work together to adapt to volatile changing circumstances.

Research into our history and biology shows that we are not primarily competitive but have deeply ingrained tendencies to cooperate with others.[13]

We have our brains and our bodies—made up of physical matter, chemicals, and electrical parts. And we have our minds—mental phenomenon and experiences created by complex neurophysiological processes.

Our Brains and Our Bodies

The human brain makes up only about 2 percent of the body's mass but uses 20 to 25 percent of its energy. For that reason, it has to work efficiently. Rather than lying dormant until triggered by stimuli to react or perceive the world, your brain is intrinsically active at all times, predicting what to do next to keep you alive and well.

It is constantly guessing which combination of past experiences and prior knowledge this current situation or sensation is most like in this context and what should be done about it. Neuroscientists describe this process as one of *active inference* according to Bayesian probability.[14]

Your brain isn't just making predictions about what you will experience, however—it's actually constructing your every experience. Because the brain can't experience the world directly, it has to constantly create a simulated model of those experiences based on the bits of information it receives from internal and external sensations. Your brain makes meaning of that information—both anticipates it and explains the consequences of it—based on the data it already has from your past experiences and social and cultural learnings.

In other words, your brain is always predicting what you will see, feel, and do well before you have conscious awareness of those predictions, and then based on those predictions, your brain actively constructs every thought, perception, and emotion you experience.

Put simply, your brain does not experience reality, it constructs it.

As neuroscientist Lisa Feldman Barrett explains it, "Your brain is wired for delusion: through continual prediction, you experience a world of your own creation that is held in check by the sensory world. Once your predictions are correct enough, they not only create your perception and action but also explain the meaning of your sensations. This is your brain's default mode."[15]

To keep you alive and well, your brain has to anticipate and make sense of what's happening externally (in your environment) and internally (what's happening with your organs, tissues, nervous system, heart, hormones, immune system, etc.). The state of your physical body and the accompanying sensations (what is called *interoception*) are key to your brain's predictions and thus key to every thought, perception, and emotion you have.

Most of the time your brain makes the right predictions about internal and external sensations. When actual stimuli do conflict with a prediction, however, your brain can either update the prediction (i.e., it can learn or update its mental model) or it can ignore the conflict. The latter happens far more often than you're probably aware of, because your brain likes cohesive stories that fit within the mental model it already has.

Your brain likes efficient shortcuts and assumptions and is operating mostly outside of your awareness, so it takes immense motivation and effort to update your mental models—to recognize your own biases, challenge your own assumptions, think outside of the box, and learn something new. **This is why scientists say that we actually "see what we believe" rather than the reverse.**

In fact, research suggests that because children have fewer prior experiences and assumptions to draw from, they are better learners of novel information than adults and are more receptive to updating their beliefs.[16]

Because of brain plasticity, however, the opportunity exists for all of us to continually rewire our brains, update our mental models, and improve our thinking.

For example, you can expand the range of experiences your brain draws from to interpret and predict what you perceive, think, and feel. Expanding your perspectives and knowledge is one of the purposes of Hyper-Learning.

Our Subconscious and Conscious Minds

If our brains and bodies are our hardware, then our minds are our software, and many of us have an unrealistically positive view of our software's ability to process information. Our conscious minds can only process about 40 bits of information per second—about a short sentence. Our visual system can process 10 million bits per second, but only a small portion of that goes into our conscious minds.[17]

As Edward O. Wilson says, "In our daily lives we imagine ourselves to be aware of everything in the immediate environment. In fact, we sense fewer than one thousandth of one percent of the diversity of molecules and energy waves that constantly sweep around and through us."[18]

The subconscious mind processes far more information than the conscious mind and plays a large role in every conscious thought, perception, and feeling. Contrary to dualistic perspectives, however, the distinction between our conscious and subconscious minds is not clearly delineated, nor can we say that one is better than the other. We actually operate at multiple fluid levels of awareness, and we engage in various types of thinking. For example, we can have highly focused, task-oriented conscious thoughts, and we can have spontaneous, meandering, and imaginative mostly subconscious thoughts, such as when we're daydreaming or dreaming while asleep.

Our minds actually wander a lot—according to research, about 50 percent of the time. When our minds are wandering, we aren't focused on the present moment, and we can get stuck ruminating about the past or obsessing about the future. As a result, mind-wandering can inhibit learning, reflective listening, emotional engagement, and effective collaboration. We all have an inner chatterbox—a constant self-talker, self-evaluator, or commentator of whatever is going on in our lives. It is this "monkey mind" that is constantly worrying about what other people think of us. (Well, they are probably not thinking about you because they are thinking about what you think of them. That is how the self-referential monkey mind plays.)

But mind-wandering can also be a great aid in thinking of new ideas, imagining different futures, and sensing new insights from data. Have you ever awoken in the middle of the night or in the morning with a cool new idea? I bet you have. Where did that come from?

Have you ever taken a break from work and gone for a walk outside in nature, just resting and enjoying the smells, the quiet, and the colors, and a new idea or an answer to a current problem you were working on pops into your mind? That is the power of your subconscious, which is key to your ability to create, innovate, and imagine.

Understanding the interplay between conscious and subconscious thinking and knowing how best to manage and leverage that interplay is becoming a very valuable human skill in the digital age.

Emotions

How do emotions emerge? It seems obvious, doesn't it? Someone acts in a certain way or something happens that automatically triggers an emotional response and then a certain behavior. That is what I was taught. According to the latest science of emotions, however, your brain constructs an instance of something you've learned to call a particular emotion based on your past experiences and knowledge and the social and cultural norms that you've internalized. It may feel automatic to you, but your brain is, in effect, guessing that the situation you are in now with this set of factors and these sensations is like another situation in which you'd constructed an instance of a particular emotion. But again, your brain is sometimes wrong, such as when it constructs an instance of anger but you're actually just hungry, or when you experience what you believe to be warranted frustration, but really, you're just sleep deprived.

Like most people, you probably experience your emotions as inevitable, but it turns out that you (your brain) orchestrates them. That means you can choose to drill down and consider if a particular emotion you're experiencing is in fact appropriate in this instance, and you can choose how to behave in response. **You can slow down, turn off auto-pilot, and prevent inappropriate or unproductive emotional reactions.** One way to regulate your emotions, according to research, is to get really granular about how you're truly feeling and to label that sensation—deconstruct it. You can also pause to ask yourself if the facts truly warrant the emotional response predicted by your brain. These kinds of steps can help you manage your emotions in the moment, but they can also help rewire your brain so that the next time the situation comes up, your brain has a better prediction.

Brain-Body-Mind Connection

What the science is clear on is that our brains, bodies, minds (including all our thoughts, emotions, and perceptions) are profoundly interconnected. When I studied cognitive psychology decades ago, I was taught that humans have a rational side of the brain and an emotional side and that being rational does not involve emotions. Well, modern science has proven that way of thinking to be wrong because our emotions are involved in every part of cognition—what we perceive, what we process, how we process it, how we file data, and how we recall data. Our emotions are integral to how we think. Our body is integral to our emotions and how we think. And vice versa. Later in the chapter, I'll explain the importance of positive emotions to thinking like a Hyper-Learner and to overcoming our often overactive physiological fight-or-flight response that can impede Hyper-Learning.

The body plays an integral role in how we make social connections as well. We communicate with other people through our facial expressions, tone of our voice, and body language. If we truly trust the person we are interacting with, we often mirror his or her body language and can sync up physiologically, releasing oxytocin, a neuropeptide that plays a role in social bonding and is often called the trust or cuddle hormone.

The brain-body-mind connection is why taking care of and listening to your body is so important to operating at your best. That brings nutrition, quality preventive healthcare, sleep, and exercise into the journey to your Best Self. Nurturing the body with sleep, taking work breaks (especially walks in natural settings), and not abusing the body in terms of food and drink are also crucial. You want a body that is sending positive signals to your brain.

~

I have posed the following questions to more than 2,000 senior executives:

- How do you think?

- How do you emotionally connect with others?

Very few can explain. Most say, "It just happens" or "I just do it."

Now is the time to truly understand how it happens and to actively manage your human hardware and software.

You can learn to take better control and more ownership of YOU—how you think, how you manage your emotions, how you behave, how you influence your body chemistry (I am not talking about drugs or alcohol), and how you overcome your ingrained automatic responses.

Reflection Time

What did you learn from reading the summary
about how your brain and mind work?

What did you learn about your emotions?

What did you learn about your body?

What did you learn about how your body, mind, brain,
and emotions are connected and integrated?

Please write down five key learnings in your Learning Journal.

Here are my five top takeaways from the summary above. I am not advocating, and I am most definitely not saying these points are the right answers. I am sharing solely to encourage you to think deeply about what new opportunities are available to take more ownership of how you behave. Also, please understand that I have a big head start in that I have been studying this for years and have had time to try out and adopt new practices regarding the science:

1. We have far more control over our emotions than we realize. That is a game changer in how we approach our day and how we come across to others.

2. We can interrupt the seemingly automatic link between our emotions and our behavior by slowing down to process and evaluate whether our feelings are warranted or justified and to choose the appropriate response.

3. We can impact our thinking and emotions by nurturing and calming our bodies and being more sensitive to body signals.

4. Our brain is a prediction machine. It is not perfect. It makes mistakes. That raises important questions for us. For example, when should we slow down and stop to evaluate what our mind is telling us to do? In what kinds of circumstances is our brain likely to be wrong? What do the facts say? What is the downside if our brain is wrong?

5. We tend to undervalue the power of our subconscious minds.

Regarding the last point, I have learned how to utilize my subconscious more and that has produced positive new ideas. A perfect example of that is this Reflection Time exercise. As I was writing this chapter, I thought I needed a break and so I went for a 20-minute walk in a natural setting and did not intentionally think—instead I focused on the colors of the leaves and flowers and the shapes of clouds, and I did deep breathing as I walked. I was resting my conscious mind and allowing my subconscious mind to work if it wanted to. Toward the end of the walk, guess what popped into my mind? The idea that I needed this Reflection Time in this part of this chapter. Yes, it just popped up and it immediately felt good and I felt a smile happening on my face—even my emotions predictor got in the game.

Now that you understand a little more about the science of how you operate, the necessity of cultivating Inner Peace should make a bit more sense. Now let's explore the four underlying components of Inner Peace.

A QUIET EGO

We know from neuroscience that there is no physical place in your brain that houses your ego. So, what is it? And where does it come from? Is it your self-image? Is it your story about who you are? Is it how you identify or define "you"? Is it the degree to which you are self-centered or self-absorbed? All of the above? Please take a minute or so to come up with your answer.

～

For our purposes, let's define ego as how you identify *who* you are—the thing you've linked your positive self-image to—the thing about yourself that makes you feel good or that you feel the need to defend.

Reflection Time

What is it that you've tied your positive self-image to?

Is it being a nice person?

A smart person?

A caring person?

A successful professional?

Knowing a lot?

Is it the size of your house?

The brands of clothing you wear?

The kind of car you drive?

The clubs you belong to?

Your job title? How much money you make?

Now let's challenge that self-image.

If you define yourself by being smart or successful in your work, how do you react when someone disagrees with you or challenges your position? Do you immediately attack the other person's reasoning? Why?

Does it make sense to get defensive or feel like your very sense of self is threatened if someone disagrees with your facts, premise, or assumptions?

Are you really defined by what you know or think you know?

Does it make sense to base your self-worth on your assumption about, for example, whether a customer likes a new product? Or your opinion that X is the best answer to solve a problem?

If you define yourself as being very smart, how open-minded will you be if someone sees a different way than you see to achieve an objective?

Now let's try a different approach. How would you describe someone with a "big" ego? Please take a few minutes to write out your answer.

Now think about your definition.

Did you describe a person with a big ego in a way that wouldn't implicate yourself?

How about asking someone you trust to honestly answer if he or she perceives you to have a big ego?

Then ask your significant other or your closest friend that question. What did he or she say?

Let's take another avenue. Think about a couple of recent times at work when someone challenged your view or disagreed strongly with your view. Can you visualize that?

What did you do?

Did you immediately respond and defend your position?

Did you experience uncomfortable emotions
like anger or frustration?

Did you deflect the questioner?

Are any of those responses the way a person
with a strong ego might react?

Okay, so how *should* you react?

How would people who have "quieted"
their egos react, do you think?

I believe people with Quiet Egos in most cases react to being challenged by first trying to understand other people's positions. For example, they ask questions about the data another person is basing his or her views on or about why the other person disagrees with particular points. Then people with Quiet Egos might share the data behind their beliefs and start an open-minded conversation about how to get to the best data-driven answer.

A Quiet Ego is crucial to Hyper-Learning because it enables open-mindedness, reflective listening, and the abilities to seek out discon-firming and novel information, emotionally connect and relate to others, and effectively collaborate.

To have a Quiet Ego, you first have to admit that you have a non-Quiet Ego!

As I've already said repeatedly, ego is one of the two biggest inhibi-tors of Hyper-Learning. Your goal, I hope, is to become a very good

Hyper-Learner, and if your ego gets in the way even a little bit, you will suboptimize your performance.

As I look back upon my career in the business world, I was very self-centered as an executive between the ages of 34 and 40. I was a kind, "big ego" guy. I was not brash or the type of person who filled a room or who had to be the center of attention. I was just self-absorbed in my work and focused on being the best at what I did. I was outstanding at knowing, and I was awful at not knowing. I listened to confirm what I already knew, and I viewed collaboration as a competition. I loved getting the right answer before anyone else.

Eventually I hit a wall personally, and that forced me to take a hard look in the mirror and get a professional coach to tell me the truth. I had to change how I measured myself. I had to change how I identified myself and what I valued as success. I had to quiet my ego and redefine myself.

I had to be much more appreciative of all the people who helped me do what I do.

Break Time

We have covered a lot of ground. In reading the final draft of this chapter, I felt like I needed a break here. Do you need a break? If so, please take one. We are not in a speed race. We are on a learning journey together. Why not take a short walk? I am going to take one.

Welcome back! Ready to go? I am refreshed. How about you?

Now that you understand the purpose of quieting your ego, how do you do it? There are at least three ways that I know of: (1) Make a conscious decision to change what you have invested your identity in, (2) practice mindfulness meditation, and (3) engage in acts of gratitude.

Change How You Define Yourself

For many people who've already experienced success, their self-worth goes back to elementary school when they were first told by a teacher that they were smart. The teacher probably told them they were smart because they got high grades on tests and made few mistakes.

Other successful people identify with the prestige of the schools they attended, the clubs or associations they've joined, or the employers for whom they work. Some people define themselves by their professional titles, rank, seniority, or income. Some identify with what they own (e.g., a fancy home, an expensive car, particular brands of clothing).

What makes you feel good about yourself?

If your ego is wrapped up in being smart or getting promotions and raises at work, how might that influence *how* you work?

Will it impact your willingness to be open-minded, stress-test your beliefs (not values), take on projects that have risk, or be a good listener and collaborator?

If your ego is all wrapped up in being liked by others or being part of the "in-group" or getting pay raises or not making mistakes, I invite you to think about whether having that kind of ego will enable or hinder you in becoming a Hyper-Learner.

Will it enable you to excel in new areas that are characterized by more unknowns than knowns and in which learning occurs by doing iterative experiments that in reality will fail most of the time?

We all have egos. What you must confront is the question of whether your ego is so loud that it impedes your ability to become a Hyper-Learner. If there is any risk that the answer for you is yes, then you need to work on cultivating a Quiet Ego.

If you have a loud ego, what should you identify with instead? How else should you define yourself?

This question is probed further in chapter 2. For now, I'll give you one possible answer based on the concept of NewSmart that co-author Katherine Ludwig and I wrote about in our book *Humility Is the New Smart*.

In a nutshell, a NewSmart identity would be reflected in the statement: **"I will no longer define myself by what I know or how much I know but rather by the quality of my thinking, listening, relating, and collaborating."**

Another answer could be: **"I will no longer define myself as being the smartest person in the room but rather as being the best Hyper-Learner I can be."**

Another answer could be to define yourself as: **"Striving to be my Best Self every day!"** (assuming you define Best Self as having a Quiet Ego, etc.).

Reflection Time

Please take some time to identify your ego—to describe how you define yourself. Please write it down. This will be a good starting point for building or iterating upon as you read the rest of this chapter and the next chapters.

Practice Mindfulness Meditation

In all, there are three kinds of wisdom: the wisdom of hearing, the wisdom of reflection, and the wisdom of meditation.
—Matthieu Ricard[19]

Meditation is thousands of years old and the fundamental practice of many Buddhist traditions. It is only in recent decades that Western scientists have begun to study the psychological and brain-based effects of certain kinds of meditation, particularly mindfulness meditation. Many of these effects are relevant to cultivating a Quiet Ego and a less self-focused approach to life.

According to Jon Kabat-Zinn, a physician and developer of the world-renowned Mindfulness-Based Stress Reduction program, "Mindfulness is awareness, cultivated by paying attention in a sustained and particular way: on purpose, in the present moment, and non-judgmentally."[20]

Mindfulness meditation is a way of bringing all of your awareness to something specific like your breath or a part of your body or an object or mantra and continually bringing your attention back to that thing every time your mind wanders off, which it inevitably will do.

William James, who is considered the father of American psychology, said, **"Voluntarily bringing back a wandering attention, over and over again, is the very root of judgment, character, and will."**[21]

When you are not focused on a particular task in the present moment, your mind typically reverts to the default mode of thinking—self-referential mind-wandering. Research suggests that certain types of meditation, including mindfulness, may quiet down our brain's default mode, leading to less self-referential mind-wandering. It also suggests that training in mindfulness can lead to an ability to let go of thoughts rather than fixate on or identify with them.

Kabat-Zinn says, "These arisings in the mind—whether they are thoughts or emotions or sensations—self-liberate, dissolve on their own. They don't lead to anything else, they don't capture us and pull us away, *if* we don't feed them."[22]

In their book *Altered Traits*, noted author Daniel Goleman and leading neuroscientist and meditation researcher Professor Richard J. Davidson of the University of Wisconsin explain that "our sense of self emerges as a property of the many neural subsystems that thread together . . . our memories, our perceptions, our emotions, and our thoughts" and that the goal of many meditation traditions is to make our relationship with all of that less sticky—to train attention away from self-reference and self-identification with thoughts.[23] That is what a Quiet Ego is.

It is somewhat ironic that in order to master ourselves, to become our Best Selves, our "selves" need to become more "selfless"—that is, we need to reduce the amount of time we are consumed by self-referential thinking in order to be more effective with the world outside of us and with others.

If you've never tried mindfulness meditation, you could start by practicing placing all of your attention on, say, your breath for two to three minutes without losing focus. If you are new to meditation you will probably struggle. Over and over again, your mind will wander off and you will need to practice not engaging with whatever thoughts it wanders off to (e.g., thoughts about how bad you are at meditating or how hard it is to stay focused) by bringing your attention back to your breath as quickly as possible. After a week or so of practicing, you'll probably be able to expand your practice to 5 minutes. If you practice daily for a couple of months, you'll probably be able to work up to meditating for 20 minutes at a time.

With enough practice, it's likely your monkey mind or mind chattering will start to diminish, and you will be more fully aware of and really present with whatever you are doing. Wouldn't it be amazing to be able to go into work meetings, one after the other, totally focused on what is happening with inner silence?

As you will see throughout this chapter, mindfulness meditation is actually Inner Peace "superfood."

Research shows that meditation helps you cultivate all of the qualities of Inner Peace—a Quiet Ego, Quiet Mind, Quiet Body, and a Positive Emotional State—by helping you:

- Enhance your ability to regulate your attention

- Enhance your awareness of subtle body activities

- Regulate your emotions

■ Be less self-absorbed and self-centered

■ Reduce emotional defensiveness and self-identification

■ Improve immune function

■ Increase positive emotions

■ Reduce reactivity to inner experiences

■ Enhance sensory awareness without judgment

■ Enhance cognitive functioning

■ Decrease heart rate, blood pressure, and breathing rate

■ Be calm

■ Reduce activity in the amygdala—the area of the brain involved in responding to emotional stimuli (e.g., anxiety and fear)[24]

Now I have a question for you. If you want to become a Hyper-Learner why in the world would you not take up mindfulness meditation?

~

Engage in Acts of Gratitude

All of us owe our successes to the help of mentors, teachers, parents, friends, and work colleagues—the people who opened doors for us, helped us learn, helped us get past difficult times, or unconditionally loved us by always offering support and positive encouragement.

Taking steps to express our gratitude for this help can reduce our tendencies to be self-centered and thus cultivate a Quiet Ego. Example steps include saying thank you in the moment, writing thank-you notes, keeping a gratitude journal, and every night reflecting back on—and thanking silently with exact words—the people who've had the biggest positive impacts on your life. All of these steps involve daily reminders that individual success is not all about "me," and that none of us got here all by ourselves.

Practicing gratitude regularly has other benefits too. According to gratitude researcher Robert A. Emmons, "Clinical trials indicate that the practice of gratitude can have dramatic and lasting effects in a person's life. It can lower blood pressure, improve immune function, promote happiness and well-being, and spur acts of helpfulness, generosity, and cooperation."[25]

Now let's move on to the second part of achieving Inner Peace.

A QUIET MIND

A Quiet Mind is a calm, silent mind focused on the present moment. There is no chatterbox or monkey mind self-talk going on. It is a quiet state in which you are not intentionally thinking. Let me share what it feels like as best I can. A person with a Quiet Mind has trained his or her mind to, for example, go to a team meeting and focus 100 percent of his or her mind on what the other person is saying without self-talk, without a wandering mind, without silently judging or critiquing what the talker is saying, and without thinking about his or her response while the speaker is speaking.

With a Quiet Mind, you can be in receiving mode—you can focus all of your attention on what another person is communicating—not just on the words being said but on the speaker's body language, tone, volume, and emotional cues so you can truly understand. A person with a Quiet Mind can go from meeting to meeting all day long with the ability to be totally present with that same calm, silent mind and to give his or her undivided attention to other people as they talk and respond.

A Quiet Mind is not a competitive mind. It is a mind that is trying to perceive the world as it is, not as we personally want it to be. It is totally focused on being fully present in the moment of perceiving—not judging or multitasking or ruminating about the last meeting or planning for the next meeting or worrying about how much longer this meeting is going to last.

The best way to train for a Quiet Mind is through that Inner Peace superfood: **mindfulness meditation**.

I first tried meditation more than 10 years ago, but I was not dedicated, disciplined, or patient enough to continue. Then I met Ray Dalio, founder of the largest hedge fund in the world, Bridgewater Associates, LP, and builder of a company culture designed to optimize learning and thinking by mitigating ego and fear. I spent a lot of time studying Bridgewater and writing a 50-page chapter on the firm in a prior book, *Learn or Die: Using Science to Build a Leading-Edge Learning Organization*. I spent time with Ray, and he talked about the big influence that meditation had on his life. Watching him conduct meetings and have conversations with colleagues, it was very noticeable that he had learned how to manage himself.

Because of those conversations and observations, I started my second meditation journey eight years ago. This time I was committed. I read some books and listened to Jon Kabat-Zinn's guided meditations. I started trying to do 3 minutes of mindfulness meditation every day. I worked up to 5 minutes, then 10, then 20, then 30 minutes. I experimented with focusing on my breath, then my heart, then a full body scan. Focusing on my breath works best for me. Today I do 20 to 30 minutes of mindfulness meditation every day. It has changed me and my life all for the better. Thank you, Ray!

Meditation was a big step in my journey to becoming my Best Self (I am still on that journey) and to Inner Peace. I can go through a full workday, from meeting to meeting or conversation to conversation, and have a Quiet Ego and a Quiet Mind. I am not bragging—I am sharing that this stuff works and is achievable. It has enabled me to become a much better listener and a much more open-minded thinker.

About four years ago, I started reading more about Buddhist and Stoic philosophy and Cognitive Behavior Therapy as I was exploring more deeply how I could help clients change behaviors. That led me to try other forms of meditation, including loving-kindness meditation (LKM), which involves cultivating a sense of warmth and goodwill toward others. Studies have linked LKM to increases in positive emotions, compassion, empathy, and social connection, among other benefits. Sharon Salzberg is a well-known LKM expert. Her wonderful book *Real Love: The Art of Mindful Connections* was my loving-kindness and compassion "coach." In LKM, instead of focusing on an object as you do in mindfulness meditation, you bring certain people into your awareness and imagine wishing them a life of ease, health, happiness, and the like. Traditionally, you start LKM by sending these wishes to loved ones and then you move on to neutral people and then all living beings.

In addition to mindfulness meditation, I've added 5 to 10 minutes of LKM to my daily practices. The words that have worked for me are "I wish you love, joy, peace, and happiness." I place my right hand over my heart when I do this. What did I learn? After doing this awhile, I found that I felt more kindness toward other people. I was more patient with others and more accepting of the reality of human frailty.

And it did not take long at all for it to help me see the need for more gratitude practice in my life. It brought my heart more to the front and center. Now, every night, right before turning out the light, I do a gratitude meditation, silently talking to people who have passed away without me being as grateful for their help as I should have been, and I do my standard LKM, wishing people I care about who are still alive much love, joy, peace, and happiness, person by person, visualizing them.

So far, we have explored a Quiet Ego and Quiet Mind. Now let's get our body into the game.

A QUIET BODY

A Quiet Body is a body at peace with itself. It is calm and running smoothly; it is not tense, chronically stressed, anxious, angry, fearful, or experiencing pain. A Quiet Body is key to cultivating Inner Peace and operating at the level of our Best Selves; therefore, it's key to Hyper-Learning.

To truly cover the complex interrelationship of our bodies, nervous systems, brains, minds, cognition, and emotions is beyond the scope of this book. Suffice it to say that our body is sending signals to our brain all the time and those signals impact us physically, emotionally, cognitively, and behaviorally. Our brains respond by triggering responses designed to alleviate what it perceives as potential harm or in ways that maintain the status quo or in ways that enhance our body's replenishment or enrichment.

Our bodies are constantly seeking energy efficiency and homeostasis, but several factors can upset the balance, including negative emotions, illness, attachment to past disappointments, negative experiences, insecurities and fears, poor diet, inadequate sleep, and generally not taking care of our bodies.

You can enable a Quiet Body by certain meditation practices and by deep breathing practices. These practices can help you calm your body and positively influence your heart rate. We have explored meditation in our discussions about a Quiet Ego and a Quiet Mind. Remember I said in the beginning of this chapter that meditation was a superfood for Inner Peace. Please let me share with you my recent experience with deep breathing.

In January 2018, I started practicing deep breathing exercises that the Navy SEALs do and monitoring my heart rate daily. Now I do my breathing exercises a couple of times a day to regulate the pace of my body—the speed at which I am doing things—in the pursuit of slowing down to be more in the moment. I have become very sensitive to my heart rate, body temperature, and stress. And when I experience a fast heart rate, rising temperature, or stress in parts of my body, I immediately do my deep breathing and my self-talk. I tell myself to slow my motor down, and I try to experience a micro-joy—feeling very positive about someone or nature or something positive in my life.

In October 2019, I added another breathing exercise—Coherent Breathing (breathing five breaths per minute)—which I learned from the book *The Healing Power of the Breath* by Dr. Richard P. Brown and Dr. Patricia L. Gerbarg. I now use their app for a five-minute breathing exercise in which you take five breaths per minute sitting with your feet on the floor, eyes closed, back straight, and hands resting on each other on your lap. I usually do this early in the morning before I read what I call my Daily Intentions for cultivating Inner Peace. And I do it during the day whenever I feel I am going too fast or being overreactive. Deep breathing, like meditation, is an effective tool for cultivating Inner Peace.

Besides my deep breathing exercises to regulate my body, I have become very disciplined about what and how much I eat. I eliminated alcohol, started exercising regularly, cut my TV watching time down to maybe an hour a week on average, and increased my daily reading time (not counting my research reading) to 60 to 90 minutes a day. Every week, I also listen to a couple of podcasts from thought leaders in a field or discipline that I know little about.

All of this came about because of meditation. I know it sounds like a lot. Some of my students, clients, and friends have argued that my work productivity must have decreased because of all the time allocated to "bettering myself" activities. I tell them that, believe it or not, my work has become more productive and more meaningful because a different me comes to my classes and consulting workshops, and a different me is doing the research and writing. That me is more present. I bring more of the real me to the table, so to speak. I am more able to generate positivity; regulate my emotions, attention, and inner motor; and give my subconscious time to work and do its thing. All of that increases the quality of my engagement as compared to my past. So, by investing in my journey, I am ahead in the game, not behind.

Likewise, I invite you to invest in yourself.

Now let's move on to the fourth component of achieving Inner Peace.

A POSITIVE EMOTIONAL STATE

Cultivating positive emotions is crucial to becoming your Best Self because the science is crystal clear: when you are in a Positive Emotional State, you are better able to learn and be creative and you have more positive interactions with other humans. While negative emotions like anger, frustration, and fear are known to narrow attention and inhibit prosocial behavior, **decades of research in positive psychology strongly correlate positive emotions with less rigid thinking and being more open to new ideas and disconfirming information. Positivity is also associated with better problem solving, better recall of neutral or positive stimuli, and mitigation of ego defenses. This means generating positive emotions is key to Hyper-Learning.**

Barbara Fredrickson is a professor and renowned researcher of positive psychology. In my estimation, she is the mother of *positivity*—the science of positive emotions. She has stated: **"In fact, science documents that positive emotions can set off upward spirals in your life, self-sustaining trajectories of growth that can lift you up to become a better version of yourself."**[26]

Fredrickson is an expert on what she calls *positivity resonance*, which is the highest level of human connection that results from the sharing of one or more positive emotions between you and another. It is a synchronicity between your and another person's biochemistry and behavior that reflects mutual care and a motive to invest in each other's well-being. It is clear that the strongest human connections are dependent upon positive emotions, biobehavioral synchrony, and mutual care.

Positivity resonance is highly relevant to Hyper-Learning because, as we have discussed, the types of thinking that humans increasingly will be needing to do in the digital age require the assistance of small teams, and the effectiveness of those teams depends in large part on those teams attaining positivity resonance.

It is not possible for any of us to be in a Positive Emotional State all the time. Nonetheless, the science is clear that we can learn to generate more positive emotions. Since positive emotions are so important as a learning enabler, I have included a Positive Emotional State as a key component of Inner Peace. Positive emotions bring joy and happiness to us, and that is a different kind of peace than is needed for a Quiet Ego, Quiet Mind, and Quiet Body.

Here are some ideas for how to **generate more positivity**:

- Start with deep breathing—taking slow breaths in and letting your breath out slowly for a couple of minutes.

- Think of a loved one and your last joyous time together and wish him or her joy, peace, and happiness or practice LKM.

- Smile at people—big honest smiles—and wish them a good meeting or a good day. Smile a lot. Smile at people you do not know and say, "Have a good day" (and really mean it).

- Engage in acts of gratitude. You cannot say thank you enough.

- Think of a joyous experience you've had.

What has worked well for me is creating micro-joys during my day. For me some micro-joys are focusing mindfully on the beauty of nature, the beauty of colors, the joy of a young child, the unconditional love of a pet, watching a young couple holding hands, seeing a friend in passing and wishing them a good day, thanking a custodian for keeping the bathroom so clean at work, and going out of my way to smile and express gratitude to fellow workers for specific things I have witnessed.

Being kind to others, caring about others, being thankful for what you have, and experiencing simple daily joys all contribute to having a Positive Emotional State.

To raise your positivity, you can also focus on limiting your negative reactions and emotions. I am not talking about avoiding sadness, grief over a lost friend, or the worry that accompanies your own or a loved one's health crisis. I am talking about actively regulating negative emotions in the workplace when, for example, a co-worker hurts your feelings. You have a choice over how long to allow those kinds of negative emotions to fester. The easiest way to take your mind off a negative emotion is to actively think about something other than your hurt feelings. Rather than ruminating on the negative thoughts, think about a project or your next meeting. Another way is our friend deep breathing. Breathe it away. Another way is positive self-talk.

SHOWING UP WITH INNER PEACE

The day I was finishing this chapter, I spent the morning consulting with a global organization, talking with 70 leaders about Hyper-Learning and the themes in this book. During a break, a senior leader came up to me to discuss a workplace example I gave about Inner Peace, enabling something called *emergent thinking* (which you will learn more about in part 2). She asked me how she could make emergent thinking happen more often at her place of work. I invited her to consider showing up at more meetings in a state of Inner Peace. She got this sparkle in her eye and said, "That means I need to bring my best self to work every day." I gave her a big heartfelt smile as my answer. And she returned that smile.

Reflection Time

If we were together physically, I would ask you if
we each had permission to speak freely and were in
a psychologically safe place with each other.

I assume your answers would be yes. So, let's be vulnerable.

Nobody taught me how to master myself. Thinking used to just
happen for me. Stuff used to just pop up in my mind or I created
it intentionally by thinking about something. My chatterbox
mind used to talk a lot when I was not actively thinking. It liked
to critique and judge other people, and it liked to say stuff that

I was not willing to say publicly. It also bugged me about my insecurities, not letting me forget them. I had no idea where emotions came from or what to do with them. And my body was just there—I did not know I could use my breathing to calm myself down. I was just going with the flow of what was going on inside of me—my chatterbox mind owned me. My feelings owned me. I just wanted to be successful and accepted by the in-crowd.

I did not have a Quiet Ego or a Quiet Mind. I knew nothing about my body chemistry and how it impacted my behavior. I knew nothing about the science of emotions, and I was pretty self-centered. I flunked all four of the Inner Peace qualities. So I started on my journey to Inner Peace from ground zero at age 34.

How about you?

Do you control your inner chatterbox or monkey mind?

Do you manage negative emotions?

Do you generate positive emotions?

Can you be fully present without your judgmental or competitive mind?

Do you listen to others without critiquing them or creating your answer while they are talking?

Do you use deep breathing to calm your body, your emotions, and your mind?

Do you know how to quiet your ego so you can be more open-minded?

Please do not be discouraged if your answers are not what you would like them to be. I assume that, like most readers, you were not taught how to manage yourself unless you majored in psychology or philosophy or the arts.

I invite you to join the journey to your Best Self.

The personal stories in chapters 4 and 5 are about Susan's and Marvin's journeys to their better selves.

That is the journey I am inviting you to join. It begins with a journey to Inner Peace, which is the foundation to becoming a Hyper-Learner.

Are you in?

WORKSHOP: CREATE YOUR DAILY INTENTIONS

I learned from reading one of the Dalai Lama's books to write out my Daily Intentions—key behaviors I want to model. I spend 15 minutes or so reviewing them every morning . That has been very helpful because it helps me start my day with the right mindset. I also write down in a notebook the possible meanings of the dreams, ideas, thoughts, or feelings that come into my head from my subconscious mind first thing in the morning.

Assuming you want to be on a journey to your Best Self, I invite you to reflect on this chapter and create a short list of how you want to approach and live each day.

How do you want to be?

How do you want to behave?

How do you intend to achieve a Quiet Ego? Quiet Mind? Quiet Body? A Positive Emotional State?

How do you need to manage your self?

Please create your Daily Intentions list in your Learning Journal.

~

Here are my Daily Intentions. I am sharing only to give you an example. I am not saying to do it my way. My way is not your way.

First, I start each day by saying, "Thank you for this day and may I use it wisely."

Then I read an excerpt from the poem "Matins" by John O'Donohue from his book *The Space Between Us: A Book of Blessings*.[27]

And then I reflect on my **Daily Intentions**:

- Be kind and caring.

- Smile.

- Be compassionate.

- Generate positive emotions.

- Be a positive life force.

- Manage my self.

- Slow down.

- Engage in deep breathing.

- Be really present.

- Let negative emotions pass.

- Have courage—embrace fear.

- Leap over my insecurities.

- Exercise CHOICE (over how to react and behave and what to attend to).

- Take ownership of the day. ("I will not give anyone the power to hurt me or ruin my day.")

- Be slow to judge.

- Really listen.

- Eat healthy.

- Experience micro-joys.

Each morning, while reflecting on my Daily Intentions, I review where I faltered yesterday and determine whether I need to make amends with anyone. I put that on my to-do list and check it off when I have done so.

My friends, there is JOY in this journey.

CHAPTER **2**

Adopting a Hyper-Learning Mindset

To engage in Hyper-Learning, it is likely that you will have to change fundamental behaviors related to how you learn, how you manage your thinking and emotions, and how you relate to others. Before you can do that, however, you have to change your mindset, your deeply ingrained attitude about those things. **According to renowned developmental psychologist Robert Kegan, "Mindsets shape thinking and feeling, so changing mindsets needs to involve the head and the heart."**[28]

To identify possible qualities of a **Hyper-Learning Mindset**, we're going to explore the science of mindset, relevant psychological theories, ancient and modern philosophies, and the advice of leading thinkers and successful business leaders. What you will discover are fascinating overlaps in this wisdom across history and discipline about how the world works and how best to learn, manage the self, and relate to others.

This exploration will help you unpack your own assumptions and beliefs about relevant questions so you may start to cultivate an attitude more conducive to Hyper-Learning. The chapter prompts you to identify your own reasons for becoming a Hyper-Learner and to create your own **checklist of Hyper-Learning Mindset principles to refer to every day in the pursuit of Hyper-Learning.**

This chapter is designed for active learning, not just reading.

It is a learning by *doing* chapter.

This chapter is the hardest chapter in the book because of the breadth of content. It will not be a quick read.

Its purpose is to help you adopt a foundational mindset that will help you become a Hyper-Learner.

I know that this approach will work if you put in the effort. You do not have to do it all at one time. In fact, I recommend you do it over a couple of days. Approach this entire chapter as an exploration and discovery exercise during the course of which you will craft and describe for yourself the Hyper-Learning Mindset you desire.

I want it to be a JOY for you—a joyous learning experience. I truly mean that.

The psychologist Carl Rogers, who developed client-centric counseling, believed that "the only learning which significantly influences behavior is self-discovered, self-appropriated learning. Such self-discovered learning, truth that has been appropriated and assimilated in experience, cannot be directly communicated to another."[29]

Think deeply about each theory and approach that I present. Please take notes as you go in your Learning Journal.

Look for consistencies. Be open-minded. Which belief or principle might be a game changer for you?

As you read, make a list of principles or approaches that feel right for you.

Please take into account how many times each of those principles appears in the readings.

You should find overlap among the principles espoused by ancient philosophers and modern thinkers. I find that fascinating and so helpful!

Why would I find that so helpful?

Why would consistency or longevity of a principle be valuable or important? What does that say to you?

To become a Hyper-Learner, you must engage in the making-meaning process that is so vital to behavior change. The method here is the same one I have successfully used in my consulting practice for years. It works. Trust me.

The Inner Peace that you learned to cultivate in the last chapter will make you more receptive to changing your mindset in this manner, and it is a virtuous circle. Actively cultivating a Hyper-Learning Mindset will further enable Inner Peace and ultimately, as you'll learn in the next chapter, the behaviors needed to engage in Hyper-Learning.

MINDSET THEORIES

As a foundation, we start with two mindset theories that all of my consulting clients have found helpful. Both are designed to enable personal growth and learning throughout one's life. One could call these two mindsets **lifelong learning mindsets**.

Growth Mindset

A great starting point for mindset change is to consider Carol Dweck's landmark *growth mindset* theory.[30] Dweck is a Stanford psychology professor and a researcher of human motivation. Her work delineates what it means to have a *fixed* versus a *growth* mindset. I love her work. It is so powerful yet so simple.

According to her theory, you have a *fixed* mindset if you believe that intelligence is innate and fixed, that the level of intelligence you are born with is your destiny and can't get any higher. According to Dweck, a fixed mindset limits your motivation and, thus, your ability to learn. If you have a fixed mindset you might say, "I have reached my potential, so why should I try?"

If you adopt a *growth* mindset, however, you believe your intelligence is not fixed at birth and that you have the capacity to learn and get smarter. According to Dweck, a growth mindset motivates you to learn and persevere even when you struggle or fail.

We now know that intellectual capacities are not fixed in stone at birth because the human brain has plasticity. Everyone has higher potential and can learn more, improve their skills, and grow. It makes more sense to have a growth mindset because then you rightfully believe that you can develop new skills and new ways to think and that you can learn from your mistakes. If you believe you can be better, then it will be easier to motivate yourself to do the work required to be better.

You can learn no matter what your IQ score is.

What do you think? Are you going to adopt a growth mindset?

If you do not currently have a growth mindset belief, should you add a sentence about having a growth mindset to your Daily Intentions and reflect on it every day?

Should you record what you learned yesterday in your Learning Journal? That journal could be your evidence that you can grow and continue to learn.

NewSmart Mindset

The next idea to consider in cultivating your own Hyper-Learning Mindset is a concept called NewSmart that I put forward in my last book along with my co-author, Katherine Ludwig. The idea is to reframe what it means to be smart in order to mitigate the learning inhibitors (closed-mindedness, emotional defensiveness, and ego) that accompany an old-school understanding of smart.

Think about it.

How did you learn in school that you were smart?

In what grade did you learn you were smart?

Who told you? How did it feel? How was your smartness determined?

For most people I have talked to, it happened in early elementary school when their teachers told them they were smart because they made very high grades on tests or projects. That was evidence that they knew a lot and made few mistakes. As a young student, it probably felt good being singled out as smart. That reinforcement can put people on a journey to achieving high grades by knowing the most and making the fewest mistakes in school and at work.

Quite likely, your definition of smart fits into that story. It's a definition based on quantity methodology—knowing more and making fewer mistakes than other people. In many cases, when people identify themselves as smart in this way, their egos get tied up in those high grades and making few mistakes, and they identify or define themselves by what they know and how much they know. Well, that is a problem for Hyper-Learning.

First, as the digital age advances, smart technology will come to know much more information than any human being and be able to continually update and recall that information quickly and accurately.

As the digital age advances, humans won't be needed for knowledge accumulation and recall but for thinking in ways that computers can't think—ways that involve exploration, discovery, imagination, morals, creativity, innovation, and critical thinking when there are lots of unknowns or little data.

To be good at those tasks, you have to be open-minded, a good reflective listener, and an outstanding collaborator. You have to adapt and believe that healthy debates generate better answers. You have to believe in an idea meritocracy.

Think about that for a minute. How does innovation occur? Innovation in most cases comes about from an experimental process of testing an idea and learning from the results. Rarely is an innovation or a new scientific experiment right on the first trial. You experiment to learn and then you modify your idea and retest it. Mistakes are learning opportunities in the real world, so long as you do not make the same mistake over and over, because that would not be learning.

How would you define what it means to be smart in that environment?

Will your old-school definition based on knowing more than others work in that environment or will it impede your success?

Do you need a new definition of smart?

I believe many people do. That is the purpose of NewSmart.

Let's look at the five principles of NewSmart.[31]

1. **I'm defined not by what I know or how much I know, but by the quality of my thinking, listening, relating, and collaborating.**

2. **My mental models are not reality—they are only my generalized stories of how my world works.**

3. **I'm not my ideas, and I must decouple my beliefs (not values) from my ego.**

4. **I must be open-minded and treat my beliefs (not values) as hypotheses to be constantly tested and subject to modification by better data.**

5. **My mistakes and failures are opportunities to learn.**

Underlying these principles is the work of Richard Paul and Linda Elder as set forth in their book *Critical Thinking: Tools for Taking Charge of Your Professional and Personal Life*; learnings from Ed Catmull of Pixar Animation Studios as described in his book *Creativity, Inc.*; the well-known scientific method; and Ray Dalio's approach to seeking the truth as set forth in his book *Principles.*

Reflection Time

What do the NewSmart principles mean to you?

Which principles enable open-mindedness?

Which ones would make it easier to have thoughtful debate?

Which ones could mitigate ego? Why?

Which ones could make you a better learner?

How could you combine these principles with Carol Dweck's *growth mindset?*

Which principles are made easier by having a Quiet Ego?

A Quiet Mind?

A Positive Emotional State?

I invite you to reflect on each principle and visualize how you would operationalize each principle in a work meeting.

The primary reason for developing the idea of NewSmart was to help people not personally identify with or have their self-worth and ego all wrapped up in what they think they know. If you do that, it is very hard to constantly update your mental models. It is very hard to become a Hyper-Learner. In fact, it is nearly impossible.

One big change for many of us will be this: we need to be good at *not* knowing as opposed to being good at knowing.

MODERN THINKERS AND ANCIENT PHILOSOPHERS

Now we are going on a learning journey across thousands of years and many disciplines. I have assembled principles, theories, and ideas about how the world works and how to manage ourselves from leading psychologists, scientists, business leaders, and ancient and modern philosophers. I believe all of these ideas are relevant to and persuasive in creating a Hyper-Learning Mindset.

In presenting the philosophers and thinkers below, I provide only short lists of quotes and brief, bullet-pointed descriptions of what I've learned from them. That's because your processing and interpretations of the philosophies and theories will be much more effective than any analysis I could provide.

You must evaluate the core concepts on your own. You must "try them on" to see how they feel to you and visualize using them to truly inform or change what's in your head and heart.

Remember the purpose here: to learn how deep thinkers and wise people approach the world (i.e., their mindsets). How do they view learning and how do they approach managing self?

I've included some direct quotes from these wise thinkers, but most of the bullet-pointed content amounts to paraphrases or my own descriptions of core concepts learned from each authority. You will find the original sources for all such paraphrases and descriptions in a general note for each authority and for all direct quotes in a specific note with page number. A couple of times, I synthesized the authority's work into an even higher-level interpretation, and I clearly identify when I have done so.

HOW TO MAKE MEANING OF THIS CHAPTER

For each entry below, ask yourself how the quotes and concepts relate to cultivating a Hyper-Learning Mindset. Consider which ones are worthy of your further reflection.

Please put a checkmark next to those quotes and concepts that most resonate with you.

Treat each authority as a stand-alone read—by that I mean if you like a belief or concept in one part and see the same concept or belief in a latter part, put a checkmark every time you see that concept.

After you read all the authorities, please make a master list of your checked beliefs or concepts—with the number of times that the specific belief was checked by you.

You will use that information to define your Hyper-Learning Mindset by identifying 10 to 15 underlying principles.

Please note that I have taken the liberty of making various quotes non–gender specific because they apply to everyone.

ALBERT EINSTEIN

Albert Einstein[32] was a Nobel laureate and physicist who developed relativity theory and created the equation for energy.

According to Einstein:

- The most important thing is to continually ask questions. Curiosity is a requirement for learning.

- Imagination is more important than knowing. Rational thinking does not lead to new discoveries.

- "The true value of a human being is determined primarily by the measure and sense in which he has attained liberation from self."[33]

- "Only if outward and inner freedom are constantly and consciously pursued is there a possibility of spiritual development and perfection and thus of improving man's outward and inner life."[34]

- Our consciousness can be a prison for us, restricting us to our personal desires and to affection for a few loved ones. Free yourself from the "prison of your mind" by having compassion for all living creatures and the innate beauty of nature.

■ The measure of your intelligence is determined by your ability to continually change.

■ We need to think differently to solve our problems.

Did you reflect on each point?

Did you put a checkmark by the ones that resonate with you?

CARL ROGERS

Carl Rogers[35] developed and advocated for what he called client-centered therapy and is one of the founders of humanistic psychology.

According to Rogers:

■ "We cannot change, we cannot move away from what we are, until we thoroughly accept what we are."[36]

■ Understanding another person requires us to listen to understand as opposed to listening to critique or judge. Do I understand what he or she truly means?

■ "Life, at its best, is a flowing, changing process in which nothing is fixed."[37]

■ "The only [person] who is educated is the [person] who has learned how to learn; the [person] who has learned how to adapt and change; the [person] who has realized that no knowledge is secure, and that the process of seeking knowledge gives a basis for security."[38]

■ Our goals should be to liberate ourselves—to be curious, ask questions, discover, and embrace the fact that life is change, that life is an ongoing process and a journey of learning that should never end. That journey requires an open mind, not a closed mind, and it requires being fully present.

Did you reflect on each point?

Did you put a checkmark by the ones that resonated with you?

I will not remind you every time to reflect and put checkmarks, but that is your task.

WILLIAM JAMES

William James[39] was a philosopher and psychologist and is considered by many to be the father of American psychology.

According to James:

- ◼ "There is an everlasting struggle in every mind between the tendency to keep unchanged, and the tendency to renovate, its ideas."[40]

- ◼ "Objects which violate our established habits of 'apperceptions' are simply not taken account of at all."[41]

- ◼ The genius is a person who has learned how to think with an open mind and has freed himself or herself from his or her habitual ways of thinking.

WARREN BENNIS

Warren Bennis[42] was a pioneer and legend in the development of leadership studies.

According to Bennis:

- ◼ Great effective leaders will be those who treat people not as underlings but rather as valued associates and collaborators.

- ◼ "But the one competence that I now realize is absolutely essential for leaders—the key competence—is adaptive capacity."[43]

- ◼ "That is why true learning begins with unlearning—and why unlearning is one of the recurring themes of our story."[44]

■ Writing is the best way of learning who you really are and what you truly believe.

Please remember your checkmarks.

CHARLIE MUNGER

Charlie Munger[45] is vice-chairman of Berkshire Hathaway and a legendary investor.

According to Munger:

■ "In my whole life, I have known no wise people (over a broad subject matter area) who didn't read all the time—none, zero."[46]

■ "Develop into a life-long self-learner through voracious reading; cultivate curiosity and strive to become a little wiser every day."[47]

■ Use a "lattice-work of mental models," such as the redundancy/backup system model from engineering, compound interest from mathematics, the breakpoint/tipping-point/autocatalysis models from chemistry and physics, the modern Darwinism synthesis model from biology, and cognitive misjudgment models from psychology.[48]

■ If you want to get smart, continually ask why; seek out and reconcile disconfirming evidence.

■ Think forward and backward.

■ Continually update your mental models as new good information dictates.

Break Time

I suggest you take a break now. This chapter will take longer for you to digest than any other chapter. You need to take your time. You can only learn so much at any one sitting. If you can, go outside and take a walk.

Let the wisdom of these people sink in.

When you come back, I invite you to continue taking notes as you read. What makes sense to you? Which stated beliefs would it be helpful to read on a daily basis?

Continue making checkmarks for concepts that feel right for you.

Now I want to introduce you to another amazing person because I believe his approach to personal and institutional transformation is powerful. Notice his key principles and themes.

JOHN L. HENNESSY

John L. Hennessy is a computer scientist who has been an Endowed Professor of Electrical Engineering and Computer Science, chair of the Department of Computer Science, dean of the School of Engineering, and provost and president of Stanford University. In addition, he started two technology companies and now serves as chairman of the Board of Alphabet, Inc., and serves on other Silicon Valley boards. He has been honored with many awards. He has been an academic, entrepreneur, and business leader.

An amazingly successful diverse career. Would you agree?

He wrote one of the best leadership books: *Leading Matters: Lessons from My Journey.*[49] The book is about the leadership principles he believes are necessary to be a transformative leader. I want to share with you the table of contents from that book because I believe it provides a lot to learn.

His first chapters are about the foundational building blocks of leadership:

- Chapter 1: Humility: The Basis for Effective Leadership

- Chapter 2: Authenticity and Trust: The Essential Ingredients for Effective Leadership

- Chapter 3: Leadership as Service: Understanding Who Works for Whom

- Chapter 4: Empathy: How It Shapes a Leader and an Institution

- Chapter 5: Courage: Standing Up for the Institution and the Community

He then focuses on the methods to create transformational change:

- Chapter 6: Collaboration and Teamwork: You Cannot Do It Alone

- Chapter 7: Innovation: The Key to Success in Industry and Academia

- Chapter 8: Intellectual Curiosity: Why Being a Lifelong Learner Is Crucial

- Chapter 9: Storytelling: Communicating a Vision

- Chapter 10: Legacy: What You Leave Behind

Are his chapters about behaviors?

Are his chapters an approach to living each day?

Could they be how he defines one's Best Self?

JONATHAN HAIDT

Jonathan Haidt[50] is a professor at New York University and a thought leader in social psychology.

According to Haidt:

- The Golden Rule is fundamental to engaging with others.

- We can't be happy without friends and meaningful relationships with other people.

■ Recent research finds that most people approach their work in one of three ways: as a job, as a career, or as a calling. If you see your work as a job, you do it primarily to support yourself and your family. If you see your work as a career, you generally are climbing the ladder to more pay, perks, prestige, and power. If you see your work as a calling, you find your work intrinsically fulfilling, purposeful, and meaningful in and of itself.

■ "Work at its best, then, is about connection, engagement and commitment. As the poet Kahlil Gibran said, 'Work is love made visible.'"[51]

■ *Vital engagement*, according to Mihaly Csikszentmihalyi, the psychologist who first identified the psychological concept of flow, and his student Jeanne Nakamura, is a "relationship to the world that is characterized both by experiences of flow (enjoyed absorption) and by meaning (subjective significance)."[52]

Is your work a job, a career, or a calling?

Please do not forget to put checkmarks by what resonates with you.

RAY DALIO

As previously discussed, Ray Dalio[53] is the founder of Bridgewater Associates, the largest and one of the most successful hedge funds in the world.

I met Ray Dalio in 2013 when he agreed to let me "inside" his hedge fund to study how he had designed a culture and behavioral system intended to mitigate ego and fear so that co-workers could engage in thoughtful disagreement in high-quality conversations that would lead to better thinking and better performance. What a journey that was, and it led me to write a 50-page chapter about Bridgewater in my book *Learn or Die* where I discussed in detail his "striving for truth and excellence with great people."[54]

Since then, Ray has described his approach to life and lifelong earning in his best-selling book *Principles*. He recently published a much shorter illustrated version called *Principles for Success*, and I highly recommend that you watch his 30-minute YouTube video in which he discusses his approach. You will find other talks by him on YouTube that are also very much worth your time.

Ray has also posted this link on LinkedIn that gives you access to his work, including summaries of his principles: https://www.linkedin .com/pulse/what-i-have-offer-you-ray-dalio-1f/.

I encourage you to accept Ray's offer in the link and to take the time to explore Ray's principles through his talks and links. Please do that before moving on. There are many learnings there for all of us. Please make a list of his principles that resonate with you. How would they influence your Hyper-Learning Mindset?

As you know from my meditation story, I believe Ray Dalio has created an amazing thinking and learning approach to life. He confronts head-on the two big learning obstacles: ego and fear. His book *Principles* is a wonderful learning journey. Dalio's principles are similar in many ways to some basic Stoic and Buddhist principles and practices. In my opinion, Ray is a modern-day Socrates.

WILLIAM B. TURNER

William B. Turner[55] was a servant leader, business builder, philanthropist, and corporate director.

Bill Turner's story involves a transformational lifelong learning journey. He served for decades on the board of the Coca-Cola Company, helped build three great companies, donated to tens of colleges and universities to fund servant leadership centers, and was a caring man dedicated to his family, his community, and his religion. Bill was instrumental in funding an experiential MBA student leadership development program that I created at the Goizueta Business School at Emory University, which still thrives today.

Bill was the most humble wealthy man I have ever met.

Here are two self-tests from Bill's book with Delane Chappell called *The Learning of Love: A Journey Toward Servant Leadership.* Why not take the opportunity to do some self-assessment? Please have your work behavior hat on when you take these tests.

For both of these excerpts, ask yourself this question: "Do I?"

The Deadly Ps

Pride	Do you have a hard time admitting you are wrong? Do you have to win every argument? Do you blame others when things go wrong? Do you take credit for the good things that happen?
Prejudice	Are there people whom you look down on and think are inferior? Are there people whom you fear?
Position	Do you want the choice position at functions? Do you want to be recognized? Do you name-drop? Do you want to meet and be associated with famous people?
Popularity	Do you hold back your thoughts, flatter, or curry favor with people? Do you act in ways to seek approval from others or act in a different way with different crowds?
Possessions	Do you judge yourself and others by their clothes, jewelry, cars, or house? Do you try to possess people rather than serve them?
Power	Do you want to be in control? Do you try to use power to coerce others?[56]

What do you think? With this list, is Bill asking us how we define ourselves?

Is he asking us what we have our ego invested in?

Is he asking us how we approach our day?

How can your answers help you create your Hyper-Learning Mindset?

I once met Bill in his office in Columbus, Georgia. He had a small office with furniture that was decades old, and it was filled with mementos from his engagement with many colleges and businesses. We were talking and I said to him, "You have built successful businesses, served for decades on the board of Coca-Cola, built leadership centers, and been a philanthropist in your home town and state. What is the secret of leadership?"

Bill rocked back in his chair and then leaned toward me and said,

"Son, it is simple. Everyone just wants to be loved."

I have replayed that conversation many times over the last 14 years because I think deeply caring about people is mission critical to creating a sustainable business.

Maybe Bill was right. Maybe it really is all about love. When you read the personal stories by Susan Sweeney and Marvin Riley, keep Bill's statement in mind.

Here is Bill's approach to love (at work) based on 1 Corinthians 13. **Again, please ask yourself, "Do I?"**

- *Love is patient.* Do you keep your cool when people disagree with you?

- *Love is kind.* Do you share your time and concern with others? Do you try to be thoughtful of those around you?

- *Love is not jealous.* Are you threatened by others' talents? Do you get upset when others are recognized for their performance?

- *Love is not conceited.* Do you focus attention on yourself or try to make yourself look good at the expense of others?

■ *Love is not proud.* Do you know your limitations and ask for help when you need it?

■ *Love is not ill mannered.* Is your conversation polite and supportive, or do you put others down to make yourself look good?

■ *Love is not irritable.* Are you touchy, defensive, or supersensitive? Or are you easy to approach?

■ *Love keeps no record of wrongs.* Are you quick to forgive when someone hurts you?

■ *Love is not happy with evil.* Do you delight when someone slips up or fails? Do you ignore evil unless it touches you?

■ *Love is happy with the truth.* Do you try to be an open, real person even if it shows your weakness? Are you willing to admit your mistakes?

■ *Love never gives up.* Do you continually look for ways to love, care, and help?[57]

I do not know about you, but I have some work to do in the love area.

Dear Bill, thank you for coming into my life and sharing your good soul with me. May you rest in peace.

What did you learn from Bill?

What did you learn about yourself?

How will you incorporate that learning into your Hyper-Learning Mindset?

Do you need to amend your Daily Intentions?

TWYLA THARP

Twyla Tharp is a renowned choreographer who created dances for her company as well as the Joffrey Ballet, New York City Ballet, Paris Opera Ballet, London Royal Ballet, Denmark's Royal Danish Ballet, and American Ballet Theatre. She has won Emmys and a Tony award, was a MacArthur Fellow, and was inducted into the American Academy of Arts and Letters. These lessons come from two of her authored books: *The Creative Habit: Learn It and Use It for Life* and *Keep It Moving: Lessons for the Rest of Your Life*. Her book on creativity is an outstanding read.

According to Tharp:

- "Creativity is a habit, and the best creativity is a result of good work habits."[58]

- "No one starts a creative endeavor without a certain amount of fear; the key is to learn how to keep free-floating fears from paralyzing you before you've begun."[59]

The person you will be in five years depends on whom you meet and what you read over those five years. It takes ideas—lots of ideas—to create, and creativity always involves more than one idea.

Remember checkmarks?

VIKTOR E. FRANKL

Viktor E. Frankl[60] was a Holocaust survivor who went on to create the psychology of logotherapy as espoused in his book *The Will to Meaning*. Because of his personal experience, he knew that humans could overcome severe situations by adopting the right attitude and response. His field of psychology is about choice and the search for meaning.

As you will read, the Stoic and Greek philosophers were on the same journey, trying to unlock how we imperfect human beings can find meaning through our way of being. We will see that many Buddhist traditions try to do the same. What is so fascinating to me is the consistency of approaches across the different philosophies.

Like Buddhists, Frankl's approach was to focus on human suffering. We all suffer. The difference is how and to what degree. Sometimes the pain comes from external events that are real. Sometimes the pain comes from how we think and how we deal with our emotions. Frankl was convinced that, in any event, how we respond to our suffering is the determining factor. He said, "Logotherapy teaches that pain must be avoided as long as it is possible to avoid it. But as soon as a painful fate cannot be changed, it not only must be accepted but may be transmuted into something meaningful, into an achievement."[61]

What did Frankl mean in that quote? Is he suggesting that we have a choice over how we react to pain and negative events? How can you transform pain into an achievement? How can you mentally conquer your pain?

ABRAHAM H. MASLOW

Abraham H. Maslow[62] is considered one of the fathers of humanistic psychology.

According to Maslow:

- "Only the flexible creative person can really manage [the] future, *only* the one who can face novelty with confidence and without fear."[63]

- A person "reaches out to the environment in wonder and interest, and expresses whatever skills he has, to the extent that he is not crippled by fear, to the extent that he feels safe enough to dare."[64]

MARY CATHERINE BATESON

Mary Catherine Bateson[65] is a noted author and cultural anthropologist. She is also Margaret Mead's daughter. Decades ago, I was given her book *Composing a Life* by an executive recruiter who had determined that I was one of the top two finalists to become CEO of a major private real estate company in Washington, D.C. He told me that I was the best candidate, but he could not recommend me because I was so ambitious that he did not think I would stay very long with his client. He said, "You will never be satisfied. You will always be wanting to climb a bigger mountain." I was floored. He gave me that book and said he would buy me lunch after I read it.

In her book, Bateson stated that women leaders do not invest all of their energy and being in one area but rather use a "patchwork quilt" approach: doing many different things to meet their needs for meaning and purpose. Most men leaders, by contrast, invest all of themselves in their work. The message resonated with me because I was so success oriented that I had lost my way from a personal viewpoint. I had defined myself by my work, my position, my salary.

Bateson wrote a follow-up book, *Composing a Further Life*, which has some ideas that I think apply to our journey together. In it she says:

> "I like to think of men and women as artists of their own lives, working with what comes to hand through accident or talent to compose and re-compose a pattern in time that expresses who they are and what they believe in—making meaning even as they are studying and working and raising children, creating and re-creating themselves."[66]

How does her statement relate to the one by Yuval Noah Harari included in the prologue, in which he says that we all will have to reinvent ourselves over and over again in the digital age?

Bateson goes on to state that wisdom is not a noun:

> "It may be that the word *wisdom* refers not so much to what one knows but to a quality of listening, both internal and interpersonal. In other words, the willingness to learn and modify earlier learning is itself a component of wisdom, and the word refers to a process rather than a possession."[67]

Is she in effect saying that wisdom is part of Hyper-Learning?

BENJAMIN FRANKLIN

Benjamin Franklin could be called a Master Hyper-Learner. He was one of our country's founders as well as a scientist, innovator, philosopher, writer, businessman, and more. His life is worth studying.

Benjamin Franklin asked himself two questions every day:[68]

- "The Morning Question: What Good shall I do this day?"

- "The Evening Question: What Good have I done today?"

Could one of your Daily Intentions be to answer Franklin's Morning Question? What underlying principle of a Hyper-Learning Mindset would help you do that?

Break Time

Before you move on to consider ancient philosophies, I suggest you take another break. You can only assimilate so much in each session. Are you really thinking about how this content is relevant to developing your Hyper-Learning Mindset?

Trust me, all this work will be worth it because as you define the qualities of a Hyper-Learning Mindset for yourself you will be basing it on beliefs and concepts that work—assuming you practice them.

You are writing a plan about how you want to be—how you want to behave so that you will have a high probability of flourishing as the digital age continues to advance.

ARISTOTLE

Aristotle[69] was one of the two greatest ancient Western philosophers. Aristotle is described by Arthur Herman in his wonderful book *The Cave and the Light* as a practical man and a man of science.

▪ Herman says, "On one side, Aristotle's starting point is the same as Plato's. The best life is the one in which we follow our reason, not our passions or emotions. But man's function is not just to *think*—which Aristotle admits to be the highest of all human activities—but also to *do*."[70]

▪ Describing Aristotle's philosophy, Herman says, "As human beings, we have the potential for both [bad habits and good habits]. It all boils down to a question of the choices we make: not just at the start of the journey, but at every point along the way."[71]

▪ Aristotle believed that life is dynamic change and motion and that the Golden Rule is a foundation of morality.

Anything resonate with you?

PLATO

Arthur Herman described Plato,[72] the other of the two greatest ancient Western philosophers, as an idealist, not a practical scientist like Aristotle.

Here's what I learned about Plato from Herman:

▪ Plato, through Socrates, tells us to constantly reach for the highest level of knowledge. Our goal should be: "Where there's a Good and a Better, there must be a Best."[73]

▪ Plato believed our thinking and reasoning models should keep us from becoming absorbed or overtaken by the daily ebb and flow of thoughts that come into our minds.

▪ "Plato was not the first Greek to see thinking as a kind of winnowing process: of asking questions in order to get rid of what we know is false, so that what is left must be true. However, he is the first to say that this process gets us to the one true Reality."[74]

Is this the first time you have read about the importance of finding the truth through asking questions?

Any checkmarks?

LAO TZU

Lao Tzu[75] was a Chinese philosopher, an older contemporary of Confucius and a teacher of Tao philosophy. Tao is based on the concept of oneness—adapting to and finding harmony with the world by eliminating self-absorption and an opaque way of being. Key themes in Tao philosophy are softness, suppleness, adaptability, and being one with your work as opposed to being rigid.

According to Lao Tzu:

- "Chase after money and security and your heart will never unclench. Care about other people's approval and you will be their prisoner."[76]

- Observe the world but trust the clarity of your inner vision. Do not grasp onto fleeting thoughts.

- Seek an empty, quiet mind and let your heart be at peace.

- "I have just three things to teach: simplicity, patience, compassion. . . . Simple in actions and in thoughts, you return to the source of being."[77]

- Not knowing is true knowledge.

- All things change.

- Failure is an opportunity to learn. Own your actions—don't blame others.

Any checkmarks?

Break Time

We are building up to a workshop at the end of this chapter in which you will define a Hyper-Learning Mindset in a way that most resonates with you. You will do this by creating a list of short bullet points that capture the elements, values, and beliefs that you've checkmarked. The idea is that you can read over these bullet points daily to put yourself in the proper frame of mind to have a great day as a Hyper-Learner.

EPICTETUS

Epictetus[78] was born a slave and was sent by his master to study with a Stoic philosopher. He was ultimately freed and became a well-known philosopher who trained Marcus Aurelius. His book *The Art of Living* as interpreted by Sharon Lebell is a philosophy of "inner freedom and tranquility as a way of living."

- According to Lebell, Epictetus's "prescription for the good life centered on three themes: mastering your desires, performing your duties, and learning to think clearly about yourself and your relations within the larger community of humanity."[79]

- Epictetus said, "Some things are within our control, and some things are not. . . . Within our control are our own opinions, aspirations, desires, and the things that repel us. . . . We always have a choice about the contents and character of our inner lives."[80]

- Both Epictetus and Viktor E. Frankl believed that when something bad happens to you, you can choose your attitude toward it and how you respond and let it impact you.

- According to Epictetus, our minds are constantly making assumptions, critiquing, judging, jumping to conclusions, and projecting. The choice we have is to learn how to tame our minds rather than let them own us. We are what we attend to.

- Epictetus said, "The first task of the person who wishes to live wisely is to free himself or herself from the confines of self-absorption."[81]

- Epictetus felt strongly that self-conceit, arrogance, self-importance, and a big ego inhibit one's effectiveness in the world. He believed in a "beginner's mind" and being willing to say you do not know.

What resonated with you?

Are you finding some consistent themes across the readings? They are there. That is what is so amazing. The answer to how to cultivate Inner Peace goes back thousands of years. The hard part is the execution—having the discipline to work daily on becoming your Best Self and achieving Inner Peace in order to enable Hyper-Learning.

Checkmarks?

SENECA

Seneca[82] was a Roman political leader and philosopher. He tutored Nero, who went on to become emperor of Rome.

Here are my interpretations of what Seneca believed in and advocated:

- Wisdom, courage, self-control, and justice are the important virtues.

- Be kind to others and care about others.

- Live each day as if it is your last day.

- Every day you wake up is a gift.

- Wisdom is a prerequisite for a good life.

- Mentally rehearse possible bad times so you will be prepared to act appropriately.

- Live the Golden Rule.

- You are what you think.

- Think positive thoughts to get out of a negative funk.

- Hold yourself accountable every day.

- Avoid being arrogant.

- Master yourself.

- Mentally rehearse—simulate your future course of action by simulating multiple possibilities.

Had to be some checkmarks here!

MATTHIEU RICARD

Matthieu Ricard[83] received a PhD in molecular genetics from the Pasteur Institute in 1972 but left the field of science after a few years to become a Tibetan Buddhist monk. He has written extensively on Buddhist philosophy. He is the author of *On the Path to Enlightenment*.

According to Ricard:

- "In all, there are three kinds of wisdom: the wisdom of hearing, the wisdom of reflection, and the wisdom of meditation."[84]

- "As it is said, 'The sign of being wise is self-control. . . .'"[85]

Short, to the point, and powerful!

Do you agree or disagree?

THE DALAI LAMA

Born in 1935, His Holiness the Dalai Lama[86] became the spiritual leader of Tibet in 1950 after the Chinese invasion. Since 1959, he has lived in India. He was awarded the Nobel Peace Prize in 1989.

Here are key aspects of Tibetan Buddhist philosophy that I learned from four books written by the Dalai Lama. (One major caveat: I find Buddhist philosophy more complex than Stoicism. I say this to further emphasize that I am not an expert and that the following interpretation and summary of Buddhist points of view are my own.)

- Buddhist philosophy is all about suffering and how to embrace and reduce your suffering and the suffering of others. Buddhist philosophy is as much other-focused as it is self-focused. One has to find one's inner peace in order to effectively embrace humanity with compassion and care by helping others reduce their suffering.

- Inner peace comes about by awakening, and awakening comes about through meditation and deep reflection that calms your mind and gives you control over how your mind impacts your daily life.

- "Our inner lives are something we ignore at our own peril, and many of the greatest problems we face in today's world are the result of such neglect."[87]

- Deep reflection in Buddhism involves mental visualization— actually seeing and feeling yourself in a desired future state or in a state such as death, which will come to all of us.

- Meditation, deep reflection, and mental visualization are essential tools for personal transformation in Buddhist philosophy.

- The end result is to become a kind, compassionate, and wise person. Compassion, altruism, and love for all of humanity is the goal.

■ Like the Stoics, Buddhists believe in impermanence—that everything is in motion and always changing—and that we have choices as to what we attend to, how we define ourselves, and what we let own us.

■ Human suffering comes from attachments (grasping onto ideas or things), desires, anger, and negative emotions, which we latch onto because we think they are part of who we are. They do not have to be.

■ The undisciplined mind is an ignorant mind and is a cause of much suffering. Wisdom overcomes ignorance.

■ "According to Prasangikas, ignorance is not simply a state of unknowing. It actively grasps or conceives things to exist in a way that they do not."[88]

■ Inner mental and emotional strength and balance do not depend on religion. They are part of our natural disposition to be loving, compassionate, kind, and caring human beings.

■ Inner self-regulation is necessary to optimize our basic humanness.

■ Moving beyond self-interest is how we find meaning and purpose in life.

■ Do no harm.

■ Managing our minds is a necessity.

■ "Mindfulness is the ability to gather oneself mentally and thereby recall one's core values and motivation."[89]

■ "What is obvious is that our experiences of pain and pleasure, happiness and unhappiness, are all intimately related to our attitudes, thoughts, and emotions. In fact, we could say that all of them arise from the mind."[90]

- Anger and exaggerated self-centeredness are our two biggest obstacles to achieving inner peace.

- Inner peace and tranquility require kindness and compassion, and that requires us to train our mind in daily practice to strengthen positive attitudes and minimize negative attitudes or mindsets.

- "The essential objective of daily practice is to cultivate an attitude of compassion and calm—a state of mind."[91]

- A blueprint for happiness is to live a wise and moral life, which is enabled by a practice of focused meditation that produces inner calmness.

- Approach life with a positive attitude. Minimize anger and negative emotions. Own your intentions and behaviors.

- Reflect and learn from your mistakes. As important, reflect upon when you have acted with compassion and kindness toward others and visualize how good that felt. That kind of positive reinforcement will make it more likely you will behave admirably in the future.

What did you think of this summary?

Did you notice any consistencies with the Stoic philosophers?

The modern thinkers?

What statements related to a Quiet Ego? Quiet Mind? Quiet Body? Positive Emotional State?

WORKSHOP: YOUR WHY

Well, we have been on quite a journey.

I applaud your work. This is the hardest chapter to work through because of the breadth of content.

Let's start with your **WHY**.

Why do you want to be a Hyper-Learner?

In your Learning Journal, please write your answer to that question. This is your time to make meaning—to reflect on how coming digital age advances will personally affect you.

After writing out the answer to WHY, please move on to the next workshop, Defining Your Hyper-Learning Mindset, which gets at the WHAT.

Thank you!

WORKSHOP: DEFINING YOUR HYPER-LEARNING MINDSET

Defining the specific characteristics of your desired Hyper-Learning Mindset is mission critical to helping you adopt Hyper-Learning Behaviors. Your Hyper-Learning Mindset is your philosophy of how you want to approach the world each day—your principles of how you want to live.

To me, it is a fascinating learning journey every time I read this chapter.

Think about it—there are learnings here from some of the greatest philosophers in history and some of the greatest modern thought leaders. In many cases, the essence of the messages is the same. What does that mean?

I hope you made notes as you read through the previous pages. If not, I hope you will.

As Carl Rogers argues, real learning occurs when you actively engage with the words, ideas, and concepts and make your own personal meaning of them.

Try on the ideas.

How do they feel?

How would you behave if you believed that idea?

Visualize yourself behaving that way.

How did that feel?

Please do the above when you do this exercise.

My goal is for you to define your own Hyper-Learning Mindset by making a list of 10 to 15 quotes, beliefs, values, concepts, and/or philosophies described above and through the book so far that you believe will help you cultivate the attitude to become a Hyper-Learner.

How should you proceed?

Are there common themes across the authorities you read? Yes, there are. What are they? What does that say to you?

In your Learning Journal, I suggest you make your master list of key points that you noted. Note how many times you checked the same point or concept. Does that say anything to you?

Ask yourself, what is foundational? A growth mindset? Impermanence? The scientific method? A Quiet Mind?

Did you note similar points from different thinkers or philosophies?

From that list, identify 10 to 15 that are relevant to your current mindset, strengths, and weaknesses.

Rank your list so that the first item is the most important key building block for you and so on.

You can write your list in your own words.

With that list, you have now defined your own Hyper-Learning Mindset!

What now?

First, go back to the Daily Intentions list that you created in chapter 1.

Do you need to add anything to or delete anything from your Daily Intentions to take into account your new Hyper-Learning Mindset? There should be consistency.

I invite you to start your day reviewing your Daily Intentions and your Hyper-Learning Mindset principles every morning and to reflect at night on how you performed during the day.

Then you will be on the journey!

CHAPTER 3

Behaving Like a Hyper-Learner

Hyper-Learning is behavioral. Good intentions are not enough.

Behaviors are granular. They are reflected in how you talk, your tone, your physical presence, your volume, how you connect with people, how you listen, how you think, how you manage your emotions, how you ask questions, and how you react. Behaviors have impact. Behaviors can be positive or negative. Behaviors are how you operationalize your values, beliefs, and purpose.

This chapter is about illuminating the key behaviors you'll need to adopt or improve upon to increase your ability to become a Hyper-Learner and stay relevant in this rapidly progressing digital age.

Let's reflect together. In the Prologue, we talked about how Hyper-Learning requires a New Way of Being and a New Way of Working that facilitates learning, unlearning, relearning, and continually updating your mental models to keep pace with technological change in the digital age.

I explained that I believe Hyper-Learning will be necessary for human beings to do the skills that technology will not be able to do well: higher-order thinking involving creativity, imagination, and innovation as well as critical thinking that is not linear or that involves moral judgments or little data. You also learned about the increasing importance of high emotional and social intelligence, not only because as the digital age progresses jobs requiring those skills will be even more prevalent but also because Hyper-Learning itself requires us to excel at socially and emotionally connecting with others who can help elevate our thinking and learning.

In chapter 1, we discussed the science of us—our typical way of being and the realities of how our minds and bodies interact and operate, much of which can compromise our ability to Hyper-Learn unless managed. We then discussed how to cultivate a state of Inner Peace as a first positive step toward Hyper-Learning.

In chapter 2, we discussed the need to change our beliefs and assumptions about how the world works and how best to manage ourselves in it to create a mindset conducive to Hyper-Learning. That chapter outlined certain theories and philosophies (e.g., about human existence, about how and why to manage one's mind) that are relevant to developing a Hyper-Learning Mindset.

This chapter's purpose is to drill down to the basic behaviors that enable Hyper-Learning and to give you the opportunity to actively participate in choosing the Hyper-Learning Behaviors that you believe are most crucial and important for you to adopt or improve upon to become a Hyper-Learner.

To do that, we are going to learn from a successful public company that specializes in the property and casualty insurance area, W. R. Berkley Corporation (WRBC). The leaders of WRBC decided that because of coming digital age advances, all employees must excel at continual innovation, and thus they developed a behavioral approach to innovation. You should walk away from this chapter with a plan for how you will improve your Hyper-Learning Behaviors and how you will measure your progress.

WHAT ARE LEARNING BEHAVIORS?

So far, you've read about how your brain, mind, body, and emotions are all interrelated and involved in *how* you learn, and you've also discovered that you learn best when others help you overcome your reflexive ways of being.

You've also read that as the digital age progresses, most human activities will be team-based, require collaboration, or involve the delivery of services that are emotionally laden.

You've learned how positive emotions are critical to effective collaboration and human engagement.

Learning behaviors, then, are broader than just linear thinking behaviors. They include the social behaviors that enable emotional engagement with others and high-performance collaboration.

They also include the behaviors that enable innovation, creativity, and emergent thinking (an activity you'll learn more about in part 2).

All of those types of thinking require exploration and discovery and, in many cases, going into the "unknown." Learning is much more than just memorizing facts or developing a skill.

WORKSHOP: IDENTIFYING HYPER-LEARNING BEHAVIORS

Step 1: Reflecting on the first part of this book and your experience as a learner, please make a list of behaviors that you think are necessary for you to become a Hyper-Learner. Yes, it could be a long list. Think of this as a brainstorming exercise. Don't evaluate or critique. Just generate your list of behaviors. Behaviors should be observable by a third party.

Here are some ways to think about this. We have defined Hyper-Learning as learning, unlearning, and relearning.

What behaviors would help you learn?

What behaviors would help you unlearn? Be granular and keep it simple.

For example, one learning behavior might be "asking questions in order to understand why something is true." Another learning behavior might be "refraining from being defensive when someone disagrees with you."

This is important. This exercise is your introduction into thinking behaviorally. It is not an easy task because most of us have not been trained to think behaviorally.

I suggest you take 15 to 20 minutes for this exercise.

$\sim$

Okay. Here is a short list I created of possible Hyper-Learning Behaviors. I am not saying it is inclusive. It is the list I use in my teaching and consulting. You probably have some behaviors on your list that I don't have and vice versa.

A Hyper-Learner exhibits these qualities and takes these actions:

- Curiosity, exploration, imagination

- Embraces uncertainty and ambiguity

- Open-mindedness

- Challenges the status quo

- Humility, a Quiet Ego

- Emotional and social intelligence

- Mindfulness, being fully present

- Stress-tests one's thinking

- Empathy

- Effectively collaborates

- Courage and candor

- Uses data-driven decision-making

- Resilience

- Reflectively listens

- Manages self (mind, body, emotions, ego, and behaviors)

- Trustworthiness and integrity

Step 2: How does your list compare to mine? Please consolidate them.
Step 3: Now assume you have been asked to lead a team that will recommend seven key Hyper-Learning Behaviors from your consolidated list for a new initiative at your work.

Which behaviors are foundational?

Look for key behaviors that can be defined by several granular sub-behaviors that are actually observable.

For example, say you choose *effectively collaborates* as one of your key behaviors. That would be a good choice because you could probably easily identify several granular sub-behaviors of effective collaboration that could be observable by a third party and measured. It also would be a good choice because of the importance that collaboration plays in team activities.

This will take you some time. It requires thinking deeply about how best to learn and considering what you have learned so far about Inner Peace and a Hyper-Learning Mindset.

I highly recommend that you do this exercise together with someone—a work colleague, friend, or loved one. Do the exercise yourself first and then share it with someone and collaborate. That would be a wonderful and fun learning experience.

Step 4: Once you have identified your seven Hyper-Learning Behaviors, I want you to get granular by identifying the observable sub-behaviors that would evidence each of those desired behaviors and

the observable sub-behaviors that would evidence the lack of each desired behavior. This is key.

Using my example *of effectively collaborates*, what granular sub-behaviors evidence that someone is an effective collaborator? Assume you say, "Being a good listener." That is a good start. But how can you tell that someone is a good listener? How does a good listener behave? What can you observe that tells you it is highly likely that someone is a good listener? How about, before responding, she asks questions to make sure she understands what the other person is saying. Is that observable? Yes. Is that a good sub-behavior that would enable effective collaboration? Yes.

Okay, let's come up with an observable sub-behavior that would indicate someone is an *ineffective* collaborator. Got one? Please write it down. Is it observable?

Here's one: a person who interrupts a speaker to tell the speaker why he or she is wrong would be an ineffective collaborator. What do you think? Is that an observable sub-behavior that evidences poor collaboration?

Why is this exercise and its granularity so important?

Because to change behaviors, you need to measure yourself and hold yourself accountable. To do that you must be able to objectively confirm the data (your behavior).

What I mean by getting granular is directly and objectively observing behaviors without making any assumptions or guesses about why you are behaving or not behaving the desired way. And granular means observing the details: how you talk, the words you use, your tone, how you connect to people, your facial expressions, your presence, how you listen, and so on.

Here is another example. Many clients choose *reflectively listens* as a key behavior, and they tend to state that making eye contact is an observable sub-behavior that demonstrates listening. I ask them how they know a person making eye contact is really listening. Could the person be daydreaming or thinking about what he or she will say next instead of listening?

To help you understand how to do this, here is the result of a similar exercise I conducted in consultation with WRBC. The company identified *courage* as one of its key behaviors and identified a set of granular sub-behaviors that would evidence courage and a set of sub-behaviors that would evidence a lack of courage.

COURAGE	
What observable actions evidence that the behavior is present?	**What observable actions evidence that the behavior is not present?**
■ Takes risk / willing to experiment / willing to fail	■ Unwilling to take risks—unwilling to try new things
■ Admits when wrong—good at not knowing	■ Guarded and closed lipped
■ Seeks out disconfirming views	■ Avoids difficult conversations
■ Willing to navigate ambiguity	■ Not open—non-transparent regarding beliefs
■ Volunteers for new projects	■ Does not stress-test thinking with others
■ Openly shares view/opinion	■ Does not frequently seek feedback
■ Challenges the Status Quo	■ Rarely speaks up to higher ups
■ Willing to have difficult conversations	■ Afraid of making mistakes, looking bad or disagreeing with higher ups
■ Challenges the views/opinions of higher-ups	
■ Asks for help	
■ Asks for feedback	
■ Willing to be vulnerable	
■ Transparent about one's thinking and reasons/why	
■ Embrace difficult conversations	
■ Be authentic, be transparent	

You will probably note that some of WRBC's observable sub-behaviors may not be as observable as they think. But this is hard, and it was a good start for them.

Now it is your turn.

This exercise will take you about an hour. Please use your Learning Journal.

Please list your top seven desired Hyper-Learning Behaviors. Then, for each of those behaviors, list seven observable sub-behaviors that evidence the desired behavior and seven observable sub-behaviors that evidence a lack of the desired behavior. Some people find listing negative behaviors easier and then inverting the negative behavior into a positive behavior.

I suggest you make your list and then explain the objective to a friend or loved one and have them stress-test the granularity of the observable sub-behaviors you identified to see if they are granular enough.

Please save your work product. This is the first step.

Reflection Time

What did you learn?

About yourself?

About defining behaviors?

Do you see how this all fits together?

Hyper-Learning = Inner Peace + Hyper-Learning Mindset + Hyper-Learning Behaviors

Why are behaviors part of the Hyper-Learning model?

If you need others to learn at your best, does that make behaviors important or not? Why?

Does how you behave with others in learning impact
the quality and quantity of your learning?

Does how you behave toward others impact the
willingness of others to help you and the quality
of the help others are willing to give you?

You will have the opportunity to reevaluate your desired Hyper-Learning Behaviors after you read the WRBC story that follows and take the Hyper-Learning Behaviors Diagnostic at the end of the chapter. Now let's look at how WRBC approached the need for every one of its 6,500 employees to become a Hyper-Learner. They took the approach that they would make "Innovation by All" a strategic business objective, and for that objective to happen, employees had to become, in effect, Hyper-Learners because innovation requires continual learning, unlearning, and relearning through experimentation. To operationalize "Innovation for All" they used the mindset and behaviors approach I've been describing.

THE WRBC STORY

W. R. Berkley Corporation was founded by Bill Berkley in 1967 when he was a student at Harvard Business School. In 2019, the company's estimated revenue was $7.7 billion, and it had a market capitalization of $13 billion. Bill Berkley is now the company's executive chairman, and his son, Rob Berkley, is president and CEO.

WRBC is an entrepreneurial company with a decentralized, parent holding company structure and 53-operating units—46 of which were created internally. Each operating unit has lots of autonomy over daily operations because its people are closest to the customer and the market.

WRBC's strong people-centric culture is common across all operating units. Two quotes from the company's 2018 annual report illustrate this:

> "The culture of our Company emphasizes that everything we do and every person who participates is important to our enterprise, and that always doing the right thing is the cornerstone of our success.

> "Our values and principles are demonstrated every day at each of our operating units in the way we conduct our business, engage with our team members and give back to our communities. We exist as part of a greater society and have always believed in being supportive of the communities that we are part of because, in the long run, our enterprise and all its stakeholders benefit."

In 2018, WRBC's leaders decided that because of the disruption likely to arise from continued technological advances, the company needed to develop a culture of innovation throughout the organization. This is the story of how they went about doing it, bringing to life the importance of cultivating an inclusive, people-centric culture conducive to Hyper-Learning. As you read, think about the autonomy given to WRBC's people and think about the invitation the company's leaders are making. Notice how they talk about "feeling safe" and the "failure of innovation ideas." Relate their words to what you learned from the first two chapters.

What the leadership is asking of everybody is that they embrace both a New Way of Being and a New Way of Working. Chairman Bill Berkley and CEO Rob Berkley explain as much in their own words below.

I suggest you now imagine yourself to be a WRBC employee reading or hearing these words from your chairman and your CEO.

I invite you to read slowly and savor each sentence.

Please underline phrases or sentences that resonate with you.

There is so much learning in their words. Let each sentence sink in and feel it. They are sharing with the entire company how they have made meaning of coming digital age challenges, and they are inviting every team member to join them on a journey to innovation as a core way of learning and staying relevant in the digital age.

THE *WHY*

Bill Berkley: Change is always a constant, and technology sort of put steroids in it because it makes change not only faster, it makes change in different ways. Artificial intelligence doesn't just change how you look at things, it totally speeds up the process for decision making. Innovation is something that is constantly going on, and the idea isn't necessarily to just try and be ahead of it, but try to recognize directionally—where things are going so you can be open-minded to understanding how things get built one upon the next.

Rob Berkley: I think as it's been said in the past by our chairman, we as an organization have to have a constant discontent or dissatisfaction with the status quo. In order for us to be the company that we want to be in the future, we need to not only accept disruption, but we need to find ways to create it for ourselves, which is a hard thing to do.

When you're a successful organization and what you've been doing, not just in the past but today, has worked well, trying to find ways to reinvent yourself, and challenge and question what you've been doing is not easy.

But, undoubtedly, just as sure as the world is changing, our industry is going to need to continue to change, and we as a company are going to need to find ways to change and innovate and disrupt what we've been doing in the past.

Well, certainly from our perspective, when people ask us, "What is the culture of W. R. Berkley Corporation?" our response is there are 53 different cultures, but our expectation is that throughout those 53 different cultures, there is a handful of common values that serve as a common theme or a common thread throughout.

Our view is one of those values needs to be innovation, that finding ways to reinvent one's self, finding ways to adapt your business model to a new reality that we're facing every day, that's part of the challenge, but that's part of the opportunity.

What Is Innovation?

Bill Berkley: I think innovation is solving problems in a new way, doing things that are required to meet your customers' needs in a way that is different using technology, using communications. It's doing things in ways that are different. That's really what innovation is all about. It's helping to meet those customers' needs, it's helping to fulfill their expectations, and doing it better, faster, more efficiently and effectively at a lower price.

Rob Berkley: The employees are a key to this happening. The idea of innovation, this is not something that is going to come about by one or two people sitting in a room full of whiteboards. The ideas, the opportunities, and converting those ideas and opportunities into a reality, that is going to come from every member of the team. Some of the best ideas are going to come from people at all levels throughout the organization. This is a team sport, this is a team effort. This is not about any one individual. This is about us all working together in pursuit of a common goal.

Bill Berkley: You need everyone on your team to be working on it, looking at it, examining it, and be committed to embracing change, to embracing innovative ways of doing things to do better, and not to be afraid of failure just because you tried something new. If you try something new and it doesn't work, you set it aside and you move ahead.

Rob Berkley: Our view is that innovation, again, is not about one person with one idea, but this is about everyone pulling together to really grapple with, "How do we make this a better business? How do we bring more value to customers?" Ultimately, that is something that we need everyone engaged in at all levels of the organization.

Innovation is not just about the one brilliant idea. Innovation is a constant effort of questioning the status quo, and, in every action and activity that we're engaged in, "How do we do it better? How do we reinvent ourselves? How do we bring more value to customers?" That, undoubtedly, has to be something that is happening at all levels of the organization. If we want to have the future that we would all like to have, then we all as a team need to engage in this effort.

How Do You Innovate?

Bill Berkley: I think you have to make an environment that's receptive to other people's ideas. You have to make an environment that accepts the fact that failure is inevitable when you try new things. You have to make an environment where it's much better to try something that's thoughtful and have it fail than be afraid to try things. If you don't try things, you can't bring about change, you can't be on that leading edge, you can't do the best job for your customers, you can't possibly optimize risk-adjusted return.

From our point of view, it's the whole thing. You get there as a team because the team has to embrace each person's contribution and make them feel like, "I value what you do, and if it doesn't work out, it's okay. Let's look for the next thing."

Rob Berkley: There are no failed initiatives, there are no failed experiments. They may be unexpected outcomes, they may be not at all what we had anticipated, but what we are very focused on is trying to create an environment where people are encouraged to experiment, they're encouraged to question, they're encouraged to try and find new and different ways to do what we have been doing all along.

I think the idea of innovation through people, or that tagline or title has really come about as a recognition that this progress, this opportunity is not going to be driven by anything other than the collaboration of the team, working, yes, as individuals but as a team to try and move the business forward. Innovation does not come through computers. Innovation comes through people with new ideas and doing something with those ideas.

Bill Berkley: It's even more than that. It's that people need to be accepting of those ideas. As Rob pointed out, they can't say, "This failed." They have to say, "Okay, what did we learn?" because every time you try something new, you learn something, and then you build on it.

You may try something else new that's a little different that succeeds, and that wouldn't have happened if you didn't try something else that didn't succeed. It's really all about people benefiting from what each other's trials and efforts are, so it's really a team effort. That innovation comes about over a period of time with process, lots of the pieces of innovation are small, and every now and then it's, "Eureka! I found it." It's a wonderful thing, and it makes a big change.

Rob Berkley: This is a call to participation, not just a call to action but a call to participation throughout the organization. Regardless of your role, regardless of your position, we need your engagement, we need your support, we need your participation in order to help move this forward. The best ideas are often found in cubicles and not corner offices. It's a key ingredient in what our future will be.

Bill Berkley: Ten or twelve years ago, we put in our annual report that, "Everything Counts, Everyone Matters®." That was really something that's not far from this idea, and that is that every single person in our company can contribute to this process. Everyone has an idea, because they know their job, they know their particular place in our universe better than anyone else. They can contribute. They can make a difference. The reason it's so important for everyone to contribute is because they have that expertise and that knowledge. For us to really succeed, we need all those people to have innovative ideas that let us reach that star.

Everyone has a place to contribute. Everyone has your own place, your idea. I think that starting from a blank sheet is really the optimization of innovation, is you start with a blank sheet and say, "Okay, if knowing what we know today and knowing what the world is today, how would we create an insurance company to do the very best for our customers, for our shareholders, for our employees for the society we operate in? What would it look like? What are the things that would make it extraordinary? How could we give the very best returns and, at the same time, give the best value to our customers?" Maybe you would think of things in a different light altogether.

Rob Berkley: We are so encumbered by our day-to-day life and the process, and how we operate every day. What we're looking to do in this effort around innovation is to almost unencumber ourselves, and, as suggested, stare at the blank sheet of paper, and if you were going to start from scratch, what would you build?

Reflection Time

The above talk by the chairman and the CEO is pretty amazing. They clearly and compellingly put forth *why* WRBC believes that a new way of working—innovation— should become part of the mission of every employee. Think about that. They are inviting every- body to learn how to innovate.

I asked you to visualize hearing this message as an employee of WRBC. I want to focus for a minute on innovation from a behavioral perspective because it is one of the types of thinking that the digital age increasingly will require humans to do.

How did it feel hearing their words?

Do you understand why they want you to be an innovator?

Are they empowering you to try to innovate? How many times did they say that they needed all employees to innovate?

Did they address your fear of doing innovation experiments that may fail?

How did they address that fear?

What role does teamwork play in their definition of innovation?

In May 2018, WRBC's senior leadership began as a team designing the system that would support an innovation culture. That system responded to the following three questions about innovation: Why innovation? What is innovation? How do you innovate? Answering those questions required new mindsets, behaviors, and processes.

We started with the senior leadership team, about 16 people, in a two-day workshop. They made meaning of the questions together in small teams and created a short list of Berkley Innovation Behaviors doing the same process that you recently did—defining observable sub-behaviors that evidence the desired behavior and sub-behaviors that evidence a lack of the desired behavior. Then that list of observable sub-behaviors was iterated by a team over a month.

On my recommendation, they adopted a *growth mindset* and NewSmart mindset and agreed to the principles of *psychological safety, self-determination theory,* and an *idea meritocracy.*

Their work produced seven key innovation behaviors.

Berkley Innovation Behaviors:

1. **Managing Self**

2. **Reflective Listening**

3. **Courage**

4. **Evidence-Based Decision-Making**

5. **Effective Collaboration**

6. **Challenging the Status Quo**

7. **Resilience**

A note to employees announcing the seven Berkley Innovation Behaviors described them as "the foundation for the new ways of thinking and working together that will lead to better outcomes. Practiced with

daily rigor and discipline, they will help us infuse our culture with a new spirit of curiosity, collaboration, and positive action."

In August 2018, the company held three-day workshops for approximately six subsidiaries at a time. Each operating-unit president came with a diverse team of four or five colleagues to participate in various experiential, making-meaning workshops. The workshops focused on the needed mindsets and behaviors and on how to use innovation processes. The following is a copy of the letter from senior leadership that served as the workshop invitation.

Please read this letter as if you were an employee of WRBC. Please underline the points that resonate with you.

Dear Colleagues:

As many of you are already aware, over the past year we have launched a comprehensive company-wide effort to incorporate a strategy of innovation into our culture and our operations. We would like to share with you our reasons for embarking upon such a wide-reaching initiative, and ask you for your participation in these efforts. We are pleased to share with you the enclosed video expressing those thoughts.

Our world is continually changing. As consumers, we are aware that technology is changing the way we conduct our daily lives, whether it is how we order groceries, buy tickets, watch movies, or conduct our banking. What may not be as readily apparent is that our industry is in the early stages of the same type of disruption. We are historically a traditional, transaction-based business that until now has succeeded, or failed, in a significant way on the basis of operational excellence. But we are now in an era where performing as we once did—albeit at a very high level of quality—will no longer be enough. We must learn to perform the day-to-day functional aspects of running our businesses while generating the creative thinking that leads to innovations both big and small. And we must institutionalize the processes, mindsets, and behaviors that will allow us to sustain this momentum. Innovation must become an ongoing, sustainable part of our culture.

We are not changing who we are—we are enriching our culture with a new element. Our core values, with a constant focus on Accountability; People-Oriented Strategy; Responsible Financial Practices; Risk-Adjusted Returns; and Transparency, remain steadfast. What we hope to do now is enhance our existing strengths with a new drive for innovation, building on the competitive advantages of our decentralized model and our greatest asset—you, our people.

This will be an ongoing process that will require new ways of thinking and doing from each and every one of us, from running our daily operations to meeting customer needs and to anticipating the "next big thing" on the horizon. It will require new behaviors, built on collegiality and collaboration in a psychologically safe environment. And it must be a commitment by all to a new, and better, way of growing our business as we strive for even better outcomes through risk-adjusted return. But most of all, it will require the participation and the contributions of those at every level of the organization—the very best ideas are more often born not to those in the corner offices, but to people who are close to the task, the customer, and the communities in which they live and serve. This has been the cornerstone of our competitive advantage since our inception.

This is an exciting time. Change is always a daunting prospect, but with it also comes unlimited opportunity—an opportunity for all of us to improve how we work and how we live. This is our investment not just in our business but in each of you. Our model, with its autonomous, decentralized structure, is ideally positioned to allow for each individual to think outside the normal structures and barriers and contribute the unique solutions that will make us better as employees, as operating units, and as an enterprise that strives to make a difference.

Over the coming weeks, you will be hearing more from your team leaders and colleagues about the ways in which you can add your voice and the significant value you bring to our enterprise to this initiative. This is above all a team effort—and it will succeed only to the extent that every member of our W. R. Berkley family lends their ideas, their energy, and their commitment.

We invite you to join us as we build the company of the future.

Bill Berkley and Rob Berkley

Reflection Time

What did you hear Bill and Rob saying to you, and
what journey were they inviting you to join?

What phrases or sentences really connected with you?

How much of what they said could apply to you and your work life?

What are your three key takeaways?

WRBC Behaviors

Here again are the seven Berkley Innovation Behaviors that senior leadership identified as crucial to creating a culture of innovation along with observable sub-behaviors that can be used to assess whether the main behavior is being achieved. The following is WRBC's actual work product that they use in all their companies. It reflects a very good behavioral approach to Hyper-Learning.

For each desired behavior, two sets of measurements are required:

■ What observable actions evidence that the behavior is present?

■ What observable actions evidence that the behavior is not present?

MANAGING SELF	
What observable actions evidence that the behavior is present?	**What observable action evidences that the behavior is not present?**
■ Open-mindedness	■ Closed minded—always right
■ Does not reflexively defend, deny or deflect	■ Emotionally defensive
■ Good at not knowing	■ Arrogant
■ Non-judgmental—non-opinionated—data driven	■ Quick to judge—Quick to conclude
■ I am not my ideas—a quiet ego	■ Poor listener
■ Fully present with a calm demeanor	■ Negative body language
■ Willing to change one's position	■ Multi-tasks
■ Seeks out opportunities to learn	■ Not data driven
■ "Yes, *and*"	■ Opinionated
■ A critical thinker	■ "Yes, *but*"
■ Manages one's emotions	■ Does not emotionally connect with others
■ Emotionally connects with others	
■ Be NewSmart	

REFLECTIVE LISTENING	
What observable actions evidence that the behavior is present?	**What observable actions evidence that the behavior is not present?**
▧ Makes eye contact	▧ Does not make eye contact
▧ Positive open body language	▧ Negative body language
▧ Is fully present—does not multitask	▧ Multi-tasking
▧ Does not interrupt	▧ Interrupts
▧ Asks clarifying questions before telling/advocating/disagreeing to seek understanding what the other person is saying	▧ Responds without asking questions or reframing
▧ Reframes to make sure he/she understands	▧ Attacks the speaker
▧ Reflects before advocating/thinks before speaking	▧ Rushes to conclusion—shuts down others
▧ Critiques the idea not the person	▧ It is all about me—looking good—winning the debate
▧ Listens to learn not to confirm: open minded	▧ Raises voice—fails to manage one's emotions
▧ Seeks the best result not being right	
▧ Ask questions to understand	
▧ Seeks to learn not confirm	

COURAGE	
What observable actions evidence that the behavior is present?	**What observable actions evidence that the behavior is not present?**
▪ Takes risk / willing to experiment / willing to fail	▪ Unwilling to take risks—unwilling to try new things
▪ Admits when wrong—good at not knowing	▪ Guarded and closed lipped
▪ Seeks out disconfirming views	▪ Avoids difficult conversations
▪ Willing to navigate ambiguity	▪ Not open—non-transparent regarding beliefs
▪ Volunteers for new projects	▪ Does not stress-test thinking with others
▪ Openly shares view/opinion	▪ Does not frequently seek feedback
▪ Challenges the Status Quo	▪ Rarely speaks up to higher ups
▪ Willing to have difficult conversations	▪ Afraid of making mistakes, looking bad or disagreeing with higher ups
▪ Challenges the views/opinions of higher-ups	
▪ Asks for help	
▪ Asks for feedback	
▪ Willing to be vulnerable	
▪ Transparent about one's thinking and reasons/why	
▪ Embrace difficult conversations	
▪ Be authentic, be transparent	

EVIDENCE-BASED DECISION MAKING	
What observable actions evidence that the behavior is present?	**What observable action evidences that the behavior is not present?**
■ Verbalizes the use of Critical thinking questions/processes	■ Did not rigorously use Critical Thinking questions/processes
■ Unpacks one's assumptions	■ Good at knowing
■ Stress-tests one's beliefs with others	■ Ego is invested in being right
■ Seeks out disconfirming data	■ Defensive thinking
■ Evaluates the quantity and quality of data	■ Closed minded
■ Uses the Pre-Mortem thinking tool	■ Has not stress-tested views with others
■ Will change views when presented with better data	■ Did not seriously evaluate data
■ Give me the data—not your opinion	■ Poor listener
■ I am not my ideas—ego is minimized	
■ My mental models are not reality—openness to seeking data	
■ Quiet ego	
■ Open-mindedness	
■ Reflective Listening	
■ Stress tests one's beliefs	

EFFECTIVE COLLABORATION	
What observable actions evidence that the behavior is present?	**What observable action evidences that the behavior is not present?**
■ Leader affirmatively establishes Psychological Safety at beginning of the meeting	■ Leader does not establish Psychological Safety
■ Leader establishes that collaboration is not a competition	■ Some people are not "fully present"
■ Leader defines the purpose of the meeting upfront	■ The highest-ranking people dominate the discussion
■ Everyone is fully present—fully attentive; good eye contact; good body language; emotionally connected to each other with no multi-tasking by anyone	■ Some extraverts dominate the conversation
	■ The conversation is not a genuine open discussion—the answer is predetermined
■ Leader and others enable the "collision of ideas"	■ The real goal is consent & compliance not Effective Collaboration
■ People recognize and positively reinforce "Challenging the Status Quo"	■ People get personal in their critique
■ People recognize and positively reinforce "Courage"	■ Some people are close-minded
■ People are open-minded—seeking the best result	■ Some people do not Reflectively Listen
■ Everyone writes down their ideas/views first before anyone speaks	■ The Leader does not use the Effective Collaboration processes.
■ Leader of the meeting speaks his/her views last	■ People whose views should be heard are not in attendance
■ Leader makes sure everyone speaks	■ The meeting size is too big to allow for Effective Collaboration
■ "Yes, *and*" not "Yes, *but*"	■ Everyone does not speak
■ Younger members and introverts asked to speak first.	■ Certain people aggressively advocate their views and push to a conclusion quickly

EFFECTIVE COLLABORATION	
What observable actions evidence that the behavior is present?	**What observable action evidences that the behavior is not present?**
■ Encourage all views—leader requires everyone to speak ■ High emotional recognition ('thank you for sharing. Great points.' etc.) for younger members and introverts ■ No personal attacks ■ Respectful, active listening ■ Build upon ideas—not just attacks ideas ■ Leader uses After-Action Review Process at end of meeting ■ Leader seeks individual input at end of the meeting—"How well did you and we collaborate?" ■ Enable Psychology Safety ■ Collaborate—don't compete ■ Best idea wins—an Idea Meritocracy	■ Some people violate the rules of "quiet ego"; "don't attack the person"; "Yes, *and*" instead of "Yes, *but*"

CHALLENGE THE STATUS QUO

What observable actions evidence that the behavior is present?	What observable action evidences that the behavior is not present?
■ Frequently asks "why", "what if?" "why not"	■ Go along—get along; play the corporate game
■ Speak up	■ It is not broken mentality—why try something new?
■ Disagrees with higher-ups with curiosity and data	■ We tried that years ago and it did not work—so that is a bad idea
■ Willingness to be the contrarian	
■ Seeks to explore and discover—not to maintain the status quo	■ Will that make my superior mad or unhappy?
	■ Rarely speaks up or disagrees
■ Seeks out disconfirming information	■ Rarely seeks out disconfirming information
■ Fights complacency	■ Avoids difficult conversations
■ Uses the Pre-Mortem Thinking Tool—What if we are wrong?	■ Not comfortable trying new things
■ Initiates difficult conversations	■ Fixed mindset
■ Avid learner, reader and seeks out the new opinions/ ways of doing things	
■ Looks outside the company/ industry for new ideas	

RESILIENCE	
What observable actions evidence that the behavior is present?	**What observable action evidences that the behavior is not present?**
■ Leaders role model and talk about and enable the NewSmart Mindset ■ Mistakes and experiments that produce surprises—results different than expected—are treated as learning opportunities ■ Use After-Action Reviews to quickly learn from mistakes and surprises and move on ■ Have the courage to try again ■ Invest your ego in being a continual good learner ■ Help others be resilient ■ Acknowledge and emotionally reward resilience ■ Quickly show your confidence in others by quickly giving them a new project ■ Reward Courage and Resilience emotionally ■ Use After-Action Review learning process after every mistake/ surprise.	■ Leaders "punish" mistakes or failures—privately or publicly ■ Leaders do not share their failures and mistakes ■ Leaders do not enable the "courage to try, explore, experiment" ■ Leaders do not help their people bounce back ■ Leaders do not role model the NewSmart Mindset ■ A person does not quickly bounce back ■ A person is emotionally distraught for days after a mistake/surprise result ■ People are ignored or ostracized after mistakes/surprises ■ The Courage to try again is not recognized and positively reinforced"

Reflection Time

What did you learn from the WRBC story?

Did Bill and Rob's story about **the *why*** resonate with you?

Earlier, I asked you to imagine you worked at WRBC. Let's continue with that point of view. Assume you are a new employee of WRBC and that you have been asked to read over the WRBC behaviors and discuss your ability to behave this way with your team leader.

Your team leader will ask you three questions:

1. Do you understand why these behaviors will help you succeed at WRBC?

2. Which behaviors do you need to improve?

3. Are you willing to adopt these WRBC behaviors and hold yourself accountable?

I am very grateful to Bill Berkley and Rob Berkley for sharing their approach and their Innovation Behaviors with you. They are a powerful learning tool.

I am sure you realize by now that their Innovation Behaviors are the same behaviors at which a Hyper-Learner needs to excel.

Now I invite you to do the following workshop as the capstone for this chapter. This will help you finalize your list of desired Hyper-Learning Behaviors and will help you focus on which desired behaviors you should prioritize for improvement.

WORKSHOP: HYPER-LEARNING BEHAVIORS DIAGNOSTIC

I invite you to take the following Hyper-Learning Behaviors Diagnostic to help you focus on creating your personal Hyper-Learning Behaviors Development Plan. Please answer the questions honestly. I have used most of this content with over 3,000 senior executives. When people are honest, there are very few grades of 4 or 5 (or for negatively stated questions, grades of 1 or 2) because most of us have not been trained in learning behaviors. The most common score is a 3.

Use this diagnostic to create your Hyper-Learning Behaviors Development Plan, including the behaviors you need to improve and your strategy for doing so. This plan together with your Daily Intentions and your Hyper-Learning Mindset are your Hyper-Learning *enablers*.

Hyper-Learning Behaviors Diagnostic

© Edward D. Hess

Scale of 1–5:   1 = Very rarely   2 = Rarely   3 = Sometimes 4 = Often   5 = Most of the time

1. A Quiet Ego

_____ My work colleagues would describe me as having humility.

_____ My spouse or significant other would describe me as having humility.

_____ I have been told I am arrogant.

_____ Work colleagues would say I know my weaknesses.

_____ If someone disagrees with me, I quickly defend myself.

_____ I often say, "I don't know."

_____ When I act badly at work, I apologize to that person in public if the act occurred in public.

_____ I take ownership publicly of my mistakes.

_____ I am open about my weaknesses and ask people at work for help.

_____ Colleagues would say I am compassionate.

_____ Colleagues tell me I am empathetic.

_____ If someone disagrees with my thoughts, I often react negatively.

_____ In a conversation I want the other person to leave thinking I am smart.

_____ I frequently put myself emotionally into another person's shoes.

_____ I believe leaders must be strong and not show weakness.

_____ I actively try every day to "quiet my ego."

_____ I am aware when I am becoming very "me" oriented.

> Scale of 1–5:   1 = Very rarely   2 = Rarely   3 = Sometimes
> 4 = Often   5 = Most of the time

_____ I want people to know that I am very smart or even smarter than they are.

_____ I evaluate daily my humility and whether I was arrogant or "all about me."

_____ I believe "I am not my ideas."

_____ I understand that it is "not all about me."

_____ I think mostly about myself—not about others.

_____ I engage in meditation practice regularly.

_____ I express gratitude to people very frequently.

_____ I keep a gratitude journal.

_____ I define my self-worth by being better than other people.

_____ My ego is invested in winning.

_____ My ego feels good when I earn more money than my friends earn.

_____ I need to be better than other people in order to feel good about myself.

_____ I am always comparing myself to other people.

_____ I frequently write thank-you notes to people.

2. A Quiet Mind

_____ My mind wanders when I am in meetings.

_____ When someone else is talking, my mind is coming up with my response.

_____ I can sit in a meeting and be totally focused with a completely quiet mind (inner silence) when others are speaking.

Scale of 1–5:   1 = Very rarely   2 = Rarely   3 = Sometimes
4 = Often   5 = Most of the time

_____ My mind frequently talks to me.

_____ My mind frequently critiques me.

_____ My mind likes to judge other people.

_____ When I am listening to someone, my mind is totally silent.

_____ When another person is talking, I often multitask.

_____ When I think I know what someone is going to say, I interrupt them to get to the point.

_____ When I have lots of meetings, I tend to think about my past meeting in the beginning of my new meeting.

_____ I know how to achieve inner silence.

_____ I can achieve inner silence at will.

3. A Quiet Body

_____ I am very sensitive to signals from my body.

_____ I can feel myself getting angry or upset through my heart rate.

_____ I am sensitive to my body temperature.

_____ I am sensitive to feeling stress in my body.

_____ I am aware of how fast I am breathing.

_____ I actively manage my breathing to reduce stress.

_____ I do deep breathing exercises daily.

_____ I generate positive emotions when I am feeling negative.

_____ I know how to mitigate negative emotions.

_____ I minimize the time and effect of my negative emotions.

_____ I regularly greet others with a genuine smile.

> Scale of 1–5: 1 = Very rarely 2 = Rarely 3 = Sometimes
> 4 = Often 5 = Most of the time

____ When I am feeling anxious, I take steps to relieve my anxiety.

____ I never raise my voice at anyone.

____ I am conscious of my body language when I am around others.

____ I exercise regularly.

____ I know how many hours of sleep are optimal for me.

____ I very frequently sleep my needed hours.

____ I am pretty rigorous about eating healthy food.

____ I am very disciplined regarding my alcohol consumption.

____ I get an annual physical every year to monitor my health.

4. A Positive Emotional State

____ I am aware of my emotions.

____ I label my emotions.

____ I try to manage my emotions.

____ I can easily generate positive emotions.

____ I can minimize the impact of negative emotions when I want to.

____ I get myself in a positive emotional state before talking with someone.

____ I project positivity through my genuine facial expressions.

____ I smile regularly at people as I pass them in the hall.

____ I always smile at people when I am introduced to them.

____ When I join a meeting, I acknowledge others with a genuine smile.

> Scale of 1–5:   1 = Very rarely   2 = Rarely   3 = Sometimes
> 4 = Often   5 = Most of the time

____ I often generate positive emotions at work by thinking about my loved ones.

____ When I connect with people warmly, they often connect back with me warmly.

____ I check in on my emotions (how I am feeling) during my day.

5. A Hyper-Learning Mindset

____ I feel good when I come across as smarter than other people.

____ My views about the world are real.

____ If my views are challenged, I try to understand the other person's views first.

____ I avoid making mistakes—mistakes are bad.

____ The older we get, the less we need to learn.

____ My IQ sets a limit on how much I can learn.

____ I frequently tell colleagues I do not know.

____ I am known for asking questions.

____ I am known for knowing the right answers.

____ Asking questions is a sign of not being smart.

____ I am happiest when everything is like it was yesterday.

____ My stories about how the world works are true.

____ I feel most comfortable when I am in control.

____ I share my fears, concerns, and vulnerabilities with several friends.

____ If a bad thing happens to me, I automatically react quickly.

> Scale of 1–5: 1 = Very rarely 2 = Rarely 3 = Sometimes
> 4 = Often 5 = Most of the time

____ My emotions automatically drive how I behave.

____ I believe I have choices as to how to act.

____ I rarely act on autopilot.

____ I believe that everything is always changing.

____ Learning is mostly done by the end of schooling.

____ I use daily learning processes.

____ I have a *growth mindset* every day.

____ I define myself by how much or what I know.

6. Connecting, Relating, and Collaborating

____ I know my emotional intelligence weaknesses and have a plan to improve them.

____ I relate personally to people before getting to business.

____ I try to demonstrate to people that I care about them.

____ I try to understand where people are coming from.

____ I try to be an emotionally positive person.

____ I try to be totally honest with people.

____ I evaluate daily the quality of my emotional connections.

____ I am sensitive to the messages I send through my body language.

____ I stop and make sure before I enter each meeting that I am emotionally and mentally prepared to be present—to be fully attentive in that meeting.

____ I view collaboration as a competition to see who is right.

Scale of 1–5:   1 = Very rarely   2 = Rarely   3 = Sometimes 4 = Often   5 = Most of the time

_____ My goal in collaborating is to avoid looking dumb.

_____ My goal in collaboration is to not lose face.

_____ I stop regularly to engage with people during the day.

_____ I do check-ins with my direct reports and ask about them as people.

_____ I ask people at the end of a meeting whether they are in a "good place."

_____ When collaborating, I try to inquire as much as I advocate.

_____ In collaborating, I act as if *what is accurate* is more important than *who is right*.

_____ In collaborating, I focus on *what* is wrong, not *who* is wrong.

_____ In collaborating, I am mindful of who is not engaged.

_____ In collaborating, I seek to engage the quiet ones.

_____ In collaborating, I am mindful of the elephant in the room.

_____ In collaborating, I often will raise the hard issue or talk about the elephant in the room.

_____ In collaborating, if I don't know I say so.

_____ In collaborating, I am mindful of my body reactions and body language.

_____ I am aware when I react defensively.

_____ I usually tell people what to do or how to do it.

_____ I go out of my way to show gratitude to people.

_____ Every day I ask people how are they doing, and I show them that I care about their answers.

> Scale of 1–5:   1 = Very rarely   2 = Rarely   3 = Sometimes
> 4 = Often   5 = Most of the time

7. Reflective Listening

_____ I am a nonjudgmental listener.

_____ I am a nondefensive listener.

_____ When I listen, I focus on whether the speaker agrees with me.

_____ I often get bored listening to others, so my mind wanders.

_____ I interrupt people when I know the answer.

_____ I wait until a person asks for advice before I volunteer advice.

_____ I often paraphrase back what I think the speaker is saying and ask if I am hearing them correctly.

_____ If I don't understand, I often ask the speaker to say it a different way.

_____ I apologize when I interrupt someone speaking to me.

_____ I begin formulating my answer/response in my head while someone is talking.

_____ I often respond by telling the speaker that I had a similar experience.

_____ I often tell people I know how they feel.

_____ While listening, I am aware of my body reactions.

_____ I finish people's sentences out loud or in my head.

_____ As I listen, I try to make eye contact with the speaker.

_____ As I listen, I am aware of my emotions.

_____ Before engaging in an important conversation, I ask myself if I am ready to be open-minded.

_____ Before engaging in an important conversation, I calm my emotions.

> Scale of 1–5:   1 = Very rarely   2 = Rarely   3 = Sometimes
> 4 = Often   5 = Most of the time

_____ I usually don't answer quickly; I reflect.

_____ While listening, I am sensitive to the speaker's emotions, tone, and body language.

_____ In difficult conversations, before responding I thank the speaker for having the courage to talk.

_____ I often assume I know what the speaker will say next.

_____ I often ask questions intended to confirm my view.

_____ I often ask questions that will lead the speaker toward my view.

_____ When listening, I pause to try on the person's idea or belief to see how it feels.

_____ I listen to learn, not to confirm.

8. How-to-Learn Skills

_____ I am not my ideas.

_____ I accept the science of adult learning: I naturally seek to confirm and defend my views.

_____ I understand the limitations of my mental models.

_____ I am open-minded.

_____ I am fair-minded.

_____ I am mindful—really present in the moment with my full attention.

_____ I use data to make my decisions.

_____ *What is right* is more important to me than *who is right*.

_____ I confront the brutal facts, even if they make me look bad.

Scale of 1–5:   1 = Very rarely   2 = Rarely   3 = Sometimes
4 = Often   5 = Most of the time

_____ I approach having difficult conversations; I do not avoid them.

_____ I exhibit intellectual humility in my interactions with everyone.

_____ I have learned to decouple my ego from my views.

_____ I actively manage my thinking daily.

_____ I actively manage my ego daily.

_____ I actively manage my emotions daily, especially my defensiveness.

_____ I use good thinking processes daily.

_____ I use good collaborating processes daily.

_____ I grade myself daily and keep a learning journal.

_____ I have a checklist of my need-to-improve areas.

_____ I share my need-to-improve areas with teammates and ask them to help me improve.

_____ I do not fear mistakes or deny my weaknesses.

_____ I model learning resiliency—bouncing back quickly from mistakes and failures.

_____ I critique ideas, not people.

_____ I give all my associates the permission to speak freely.

_____ I reward candor.

_____ I am honest and transparent about my weaknesses and mistakes.

_____ I hold myself to the same high standards as I hold others.

_____ I actively seek constructive feedback from others about my behavior.

Scale of 1–5:   1 = Very rarely   2 = Rarely   3 = Sometimes
4 = Often   5 = Most of the time

____ I unpack my assumptions underlying my thoughts daily.

____ I seek to stress-test some thoughts/beliefs daily.

____ I evaluate the results of my decisions and lessons learned.

____ I use mental rehearsal daily to play things out in my mind.

____ I use mental replay daily to reflect on my actions/decisions in order to learn.

____ I ask my direct reports monthly to give me candid feedback on my performance.

____ I tell myself daily that I have to think deeper about an issue.

____ I use the pre-mortem thinking tool.

____ I model an idea meritocracy daily with my teams.

____ I enable daily psychological safety with my teams.

9. Building Trust

____ I am direct, courteous, and honest with others.

____ I keep my word and my commitments.

____ I am authentic with others.

____ I engender trust by taking the first step to be vulnerable.

____ I focus on others when conversing with them.

____ I truly try to get to know others deeply so I can understand them.

____ I do not gossip about others.

____ I keep in confidence things that are said to me in confidence.

> Scale of 1–5:　1 = Very rarely　2 = Rarely　3 = Sometimes
> 4 = Often　5 = Most of the time

_____ I keep in confidence things said to me by others when they are being courageously vulnerable.

_____ I thank people for having the courage to challenge my ideas.

10. What Did I Learn from My Diagnostic?

When you are done, reflect on your scores. Do not average your scores under each behavior. Focus on where you got the most scores of 1 or 2 (or for negatively stated questions, 4 or 5). What does that tell you? If you were honest, answers provide good information pointing you in the direction of improvement.

WHAT'S NEXT?

How do you change behaviors? Improve behaviors?

I won't go into theories of behavior change in too much depth here (chapter 8 of my previous book, *Humility Is the New Smart*, discusses them in detail), but here is a short primer for you.

1. For successful people like you to change your behavior, you first need to change your story about how you define yourself. You are being asked to become a Hyper-Learner. That likely requires behaviors different from the behaviors that have brought you success so far. If you want to remain successful, you need new behaviors—a New Way of Being that enables Hyper-Learning. You need to create a new story by asking yourself, what would happen if I adopted the needed Hyper-Learning Behaviors? How will these behaviors benefit me?

2. Hopefully, the Daily Intentions and Hyper-Learning Mindset principles you identified in chapters 1 and 2, respectively, will help

you change your behaviors. Their purpose is to help you create and operationalize your new story. You should go back and review your Daily Intentions and your Hyper-Learning Mindset principles and make changes based on your learnings from this chapter. You should do that throughout this book as you continue to learn.

3. The third key part is that your personal story has to deal with your FEAR. What concerns you about the need to become a Hyper-Learner? What concerns you about trying to achieve Inner Peace? Does it seem too hard? Does it seem like it takes too much time? Are you fearful of not being able to do this? Are you fearful of being transparent and honest with others about what you need to improve? What is holding you back?

4. You will be able to change your behaviors when you become convinced that the upside of changing outweighs the downside of not changing. Think about that. What is the downside? Well, if the scientists and thought leaders are correct, the downside is huge. At least I think so. Why do I believe it is huge? Think about what could happen if you can't excel at doing the skills that smart technology can't do. I am not trying to scare you. I am trying to invite you to think deeply about the content in this book, assess your situation, and make the best judgment you can using critical thinking processes.

5. After you have created your new story, take the following steps to change your behavior:

    (a) Start with a foundational behavior—one that enables other behaviors. Pick one or two sub-behaviors with respect to which you scored the lowest. Reflect upon why you behave the way you do. What benefit does it give you? What negative effect could it be creating? Why should you change that behavior? How do you specifically propose to change? What will you do behaviorally?

(b) Find an accountability partner or partners from trusted team-mates at work and, ideally, also at home. Tell your partner that you want him or her to observe you and appropriately "call you out" when you behave in the nondesired way.

(c) Measure yourself daily. Use visualization techniques to see yourself behaving differently before each meeting. My experience is that you will change when you become fully committed to changing.

6. Have a behavioral checklist that you review before each meeting. Take two minutes before each meeting and take deep breaths to calm down and be fully present. Then say relevant mantras such as: "I am not my ideas." "Listen to learn, not to confirm." "Collaboration is not a competition." "Ask questions before telling."

7. After meetings, mentally replay your performance. If you behaved inappropriately, think about how you felt then. What triggered your behavior? Is that an early warning sign? How can you improve?

8. If you are having difficulty, talk it out with a trusted other and seek the advice of an expert, someone who is good at the desired behavior. Ask that person how he or she learned to behave the desired way. Get advice. Change is hard but doable. And you will never run out of behaviors to change or improve. It is a JOURNEY—part of the journey to your Best Self. Make the journey fun. Celebrate your successes and do not get down when the journey gets hard. Mental visualization and deep reflection are very helpful.

ONWARD!

CHAPTER 4

The Susan Sweeney Personal Transformation Story

In chapters 1 through 3, we focused on the journey to Best Self—achieving Inner Peace by having a Quiet Ego, a Quiet Mind, a Quiet Body, and a Positive Emotional State, and we discussed the need for cultivating a Hyper-Learner Mindset and excelling at Hyper-Learner Behaviors.

In this and the next chapter, you have the opportunity to learn from two senior executives that I have come to know well and with whom I have been on an amazing journey. Each of their stories is different because they are different people. Each person shares how he or she has pursued a New Way of Being and a New Way of Working.

While you read these personal stories, look for approaches that feel right for you. Notice what each person worked on. Try to understand each person's *why*, *what*, and *how*.

Please take notes as you read. Focus on mindsets, behaviors, and practices (processes). What do you want to consider doing?

There are so many wonderful things to learn from Susan's experience in this story. I have read it four times, and I love rereading it because of the granularity of sharing. Please keep a list of your own learnings.

Susan Sweeney is president of an EnPro Industries subsidiary. Her background is in engineering and general management. Before joining EnPro, she was an area executive manager for two different areas for General Motors. She has an MBA and a doctorate of education in organizational leadership and innovation.

Here is Susan's story in her own words.

My Practices

- Set aside time to reflect
- Daily meditation
- Practice gratitude
- Seek out learning opportunities
- Discuss with others
- Take notes
- Teach
- Replace "but" with "and"
- Question the stories I am telling myself

When I thought about how I have changed over the last five or six years, the fact that I am the president of GGB and have been in this position for six years says it all. My entire work career was a pattern where I changed jobs (and usually geographical locations where I lived) every two or three years. When Steve Macadam first asked me to take this position [as president], I was terrified. I think I discovered a new level of anxiety that I didn't know existed. On one hand, I felt I had the capacity, yet there was no guidebook on how to lead a global, very complex organization, and I was the first woman in the role leading a very traditional and male group. I had twice moved from being a peer within a team to being "the boss," and not all the team members were thrilled with this change.

Another significant dynamic was that I was also going to be the first woman on the EnPro Executive Council (EEC). It seemed like a lot. And admittedly, most of the pressure I was imagining and putting on myself was coming from within. At the same time, I was working on attaining my doctorate for organizational leadership, learning, and innovation. I am a lifelong learner and something clicked that brought my leadership drive and passion for learning crashing together in a way that was additive. Combining the learning and practice was a good way for me to enter into this new space of leadership—a space where my previous practices and successes weren't going to be enough in this new role.

Practicing Vulnerability

Historically, I had built a lot of walls around myself as a protective means and kept work and family very separate. I have had a career of "being first"—the first woman in multiple leadership roles in a large automotive manufacturing organization, the first woman plant manager and VP of global operations, the first female division president. Although difficult as these "firsts" were, they were also a normal part of my work experience. I think it is hard to understand this point if your cultural or life lens isn't challenged and you are comfortable taking on roles where the previous person looked like you.

For most of my career, I didn't feel that I could bring my "full self" as an integrated person to work and thus spent a fair amount of my energy protecting myself from those around me. Don't get me wrong, I did work with some terrific people and have made some great friends at work. The feeling that I had throughout most of my career was that I had to be careful and people were waiting for me to fail. I was also driven by a very deep feeling that I was not enough. Although I logged a lot of "successes" and made a lot of good decisions, I barely acknowledged these as I pressed on for the next challenge and win.

I didn't share personal aspects of my life or family at work as I didn't want to be open or vulnerable to those I worked with—mostly because I found myself in a "defensive" position (at least in my mind) most of the time. I realize some of these feelings were warranted from not feeling psychologically safe (and at times physically safe) in the environments in which I worked. In retrospect, the majority of these emotions resulted from the story that I was telling myself. I have learned this through the deep work on myself, my mindsets and behaviors that have been guided through the opportunities presented from EnPro and the opportunity to "practice" at GGB and EnPro. My realization has been that the way I was trying to protect myself with "walls" and dividing personal from professional so strongly wasn't entirely healthy.

I have learned that putting myself out there more and being authentic and vulnerable is hard and where the real opportunity to grow occurs. It isn't comfortable. I share with people all the time that getting uncomfortable is an important part of the learning and growth process, so I have to make sure that I do this myself and share with others when I am doing it in real time. Pushing myself to my learning edge is my responsibility as a person and a leader.

Being able to be me—all the time—is my current situation. It makes me a whole lot happier and is probably why I am still in the same job after six years. I should add that the work is incredibly engaging. I am able to exert my independence through my working situation. I am able to work with people in a very different way than I have ever experienced, and my input is valued. This has come about by developing a strong trust in those I work with and being accepted as I am—flaws and all. The atmosphere of safety is one that I value and am working hard to expand into all the spaces in which I work. I think I am making a positive impact on those around me and in the world, which is one of my key life objectives.

My style is very direct, and I progressed throughout my career by working extremely hard and figuring out how to get things done. As an effective problem solver, my historical "modus operandi" showed a shocking lack of awareness. Someone would come to me with a problem or issue and I would get on the phone and begin working on the solution before the person in front of me finished explaining the problem. I told myself that I was helping the person. In truth, I was showing a lack of respect and poor listening skills. I told myself that this is what leaders did—solve problems. In truth, it was poor behavior that wasn't a good leadership trait, and I realized I had to fundamentally change what I thought made me a good leader. Much like the Bible story of fishing versus teaching someone to fish, I needed to start teaching and give space for others to learn to catch their own fish.

I have really transitioned from leading with "command and control" to a more humble, servant leadership approach. Command and control and establishing a healthy fear was an effective way to manage the large manufacturing plants I worked in. Command and control tactics were taught and used similar to traditional military to run the large manufacturing sites I had worked in much of my career. Without consciously realizing it, the behaviors that functioned for me at work spread to other areas of my life.

While I was in the original Transformational Leadership Change workshop with Steve M., my husband texted me a photo of the inside of our dishwasher with the caption "all good here and under control." While this image might not resonate with everyone, it was the best "tipping point" I could have received to lighten up. You see, I have always thought there was a right way to load the dishwasher and a not so right way. This translated into me usually reloading the dishwasher—and giving a great excuse to my kids and husband not to help with the dishes. The photo was sent at just the right time and I started laughing— and shared the story with the 24 other TLC participants that I had a lot of work to do to stop taking myself so seriously. This translated into a great discussion with my kids and husband when I returned home about how I was going to stop criticizing about the dishwasher. Actually, I swore not to interfere with any loading or unloading of the machine and assigned it to the kids to manage. I have pretty much stuck to my promise. It was a good reminder of how I needed to be less serious and have more fun. I share this story when asked about key learning moments and how I have changed my behaviors. I no longer see the command and control style as being effective in my life.

Sharing Stories

Several years ago, one of my direct reports, the plant manager of one of our sites in France, had the courage to tell me that I needed to slow down, explain my thinking, and help the team understand my thought process. He was kind enough to add that the group trusted me and wanted to follow me—they just couldn't understand or keep up with my thought processes. He stated that making my thoughts and mental models more explicit would help the group understand the "why" behind my decisions. At the same time, I was receiving feedback that I should share my stories more with my team. I fundamentally didn't like talking about myself and somehow this seemed like bragging or self-promotion. The way I was raised was that you worked hard and recognition would come—no need to tell everyone about the good work I was doing. It was obvious, wasn't it? The interesting thing to me is how many people that I have met who have a similar perspective and get really upset that no one recognizes all the great work they are doing (even when they haven't shared information about their work). I realized that it is important to talk about what I was doing and why I thought it was important or linked to a larger picture.

I have learned that stories are a fundamental way that people connect and build trust, and sharing a story in an authentic way can help my connection to another human being. Sharing a story can help a person or group learn from me as a leader. It is also a practical way to make sure your leader and peers are aware of the work you are doing. Because I work in a global environment where everyone on the team is located in different locations—and often different time zones—sharing updates and stories to help others learn is really important. There have been many instances where a group in one country solves a problem and we later learn that two or three other teams are working on the same issue. Not only is it a waste of resources and time to have so many people work on a single issue, we likely could have solved the issue more quickly just by connecting interested people from different locations.

I actually did some work with a coach on "my compass" and guiding values. She encouraged me to write down some of my stories so that I would have them readily available to share with others in a way that would make me comfortable and help those on the receiving end benefit. It helped me to think about this sharing as not really being about me. GGB and EnPro encourage coaches and seeking outside expertise to help learn and grow. This was certainly a pivot point for me and helped me to accept that I needed to start sharing my stories. Stories can be a teachable moment and the story helps with understanding. I reframed my point of view from thinking that telling a story was an invasion of my privacy to a belief that sharing was a way to help others learn and grow. I still set the boundaries of what I share, I have just substantially lowered the height of the wall.

Reflection and Thinking Deeply
I have also come to realize that my tendency to plan and fill all my time was restricting me from deeper thinking and contemplation. Creating space to just "be" and think about my work and the world is really important. It took me quite a while not to feel guilty when I just sat outside and looked at the trees. At first, I thought I should be "doing something" and if someone were to come upon me, wouldn't they think that I wasn't working?

My definition of work has lightened up over the last few years and is less about the hours logged at a particular location and more about creating space and improving the quality of my thinking and work and thus actually accomplishing more. Although I still work very hard and continue to have a high capacity to "get things done," I also now know that it is important to deeply think, and read, and talk to people outside of my direct line of responsibility to see what might materialize.

I make a point to regularly lead discussions at work, in the community, and at local universities to test ideas and see where there is interest in the way we are working and how we are creating a different kind of company. I make myself available to those in the organization who want to talk—about themselves, concerns, the business, a broad range of topics. I mentor a lot of people inside and outside the company and believe sharing and challenging is part of my role. I truly enjoy seeing people taking on personal growth challenges and working through the tough stuff.

I started a practice a few years ago where I started reaching out to those folks in the business who didn't seem to have a "seat at the table" to make sure they received recognition and knew they were valued. It was a simple practice that has really helped me and the organization in a different way. It also is a way for individuals who may not feel heard or even potentially marginalized to have a voice and to understand that they are valued. I followed up last year adding a monthly call that is set up with different groups of people across the company with no agenda—I simply make myself available to answer questions and engage in whatever topic the group wants to discuss. Each month is focused on a different country and group. I am often amazed at the questions and get a great pulse of what is of concern across the company. I also feel it is important that people feel they have access to the leader, and this is a simple way to demonstrate this belief and put it into action.

Centering and Meditation

I have long had a practice of using a "cool down" period of taking a walk and removing myself from high tension and stressful situations after getting upset or angry. At EnPro, I discovered the practice of centering and practicing mindfulness before engaging in work—not simply as a response after being pinched. This has been a game changer for me.

I struggled when I first began practicing centering and meditation. My initial forays into the practice were a mess and I constantly found my thoughts wondering off . . . wondering if I was "doing this correctly" and wondering what the "outcome" was supposed to be. It was awkward. It helped that we were practicing centering with guided practices at all of our group meetings within the EEC and EnPro meetings. Following was much easier for me in the beginning than leading a centering practice and helped to build the muscle and confidence in the practice. I also did a fair amount of research to understand the neuroscience better and found the scientific explanations helpful when sharing with my team and others in the organization.

GGB is composed of many left-brain engineers and scientists due to the nature of our work. This made it important to meet the team where they were in the explanation and practice of meditation. At one point in the beginning of this practice, I invited the union chairman into an office to share what we were doing since I saw that this practice was going to likely be expanded throughout the organization in one form or another. For me, the practice of meditation has been the ability to stop the "self-talk" or obsessive replaying of conversations or situations that had previously taken up a lot of my mental energy. I now refer to this as the "gerbil wheel" in my head as it reminds me of that structure my gerbil used to run on when I was a kid.

I now realize that the mental chatter is actually a way that our brains work to protect us and help us form stories to protect our egos and help us feel safe. This constant mental chatter rarely serves me well, however, so consciously stopping it and using the practice of meditation to quiet the gerbil wheel is something that I have learned to do. I often share this description of how meditation has helped me as it seems to connect with others and resonate. I don't pretend to be a meditation guru and push myself now to lead this process when in meetings with colleagues. I am now significantly more comfortable in the practice of centering and meditation and have multiple apps on my phone to facilitate this practice on a daily basis. My staff are now very comfortable calling for a "centering break" when a discussion gets super tough. Rarely does anyone object and often participants express gratitude for the extra centering time. This might seem weird to an outsider, but it is a very normal practice in our team and I am convinced that it helps us tackle the tough issues more effectively.

Team Learning

I have integrated many different practices into meetings I lead—particularly staff meetings. I started a few years ago to integrate learning and new experiences into our interactions in order to push the group, both as individuals and as a cohesive team. As I often say, learning means being uncomfortable, so I intentionally push this edge (in a safe way) with my staff team. My intent is to build the business acumen of each individual and the team as a whole so that we work at a higher level and more effectively. I also want to build a group that serves the organization—a staff that is seen as a strong unit and supportive of the organization in a way that is different from most hierarchical organizational structures. It is in alignment with The EnPro Way.

My intent is to have everyone in the team understand the complex business that we lead in a more integrated way and be able to make more informed and quality decisions because each person understands not only their functional area but the financials, the talent, the markets, and the integrated whole. This is a very different approach for the group and I think they are loving it. Before, we operated in a very functionally siloed structure with little understanding of the company's financials or how each group affected each other. Today's team is very different, and their financial and business acumen continues to grow.

My direct reports understand that it is their responsibility to express their ideas and thoughts—particularly when they differ from mine. This is important for me and the business as I have strong opinions and have a tendency to become attached to my ideas. Having my team challenge my mental models, assumptions, and perspective is healthy. It is also often uncomfortable. It often leads to a better idea or more thoughtfully engineered plan. Inviting multiple perspectives and points of view on a situation takes more time, can be challenging, and is always worth the effort. It is a change I have made that I continue to foster. It is not consensus leadership. I am not waiting until everyone agrees on a course of action. It is a conscious effort to make sure that I have had multiple viewpoints from different lenses.

My closest thought partners are quality thinkers who don't push a personal agenda and are willing to challenge my ideas. It has helped recently as I have integrated Ed Hess's concept of "make my idea better" and separating the idea from the person. I now regularly use the phrase: "Help me make this idea better—I am not attached to the idea." Setting the stage and using this language helps level the hierarchy in any room and promote idea meritocracy. It also helps us arrive at a better spot.

Feeling Loved and Safe

A few years ago, I realized the staff team was struggling communicating with their teams and I brought in Cris Gladly to facilitate a session on how to communicate with emotional intelligence and awareness. Her basic message was that people need to feel loved and safe in order to process whatever you are telling them. She integrated work from Gary Chapman's *The 5 Love Languages* and learned how individuals perceive gifts and recognition differently—think about someone who values verbal recognition receiving a physical gift—if the intent and how it is received don't match, your message of appreciation is lost. It was also the first time that the group had openly used the word "love" in the discussion of the business and our team. I think it broke the ice and opened an opportunity for the team to look at our work leading the organization in a different way. I can always tell when a learning point has landed when the group continues to use the new language and integrates it into the communal speech used by the team. This is one that has lasted—make sure someone feels loved and safe before sharing tough messages. AND, it is likely that you will have to share information multiple times. Just because you feel that you have communicated well doesn't mean that someone has heard you.

Since communicating is always a challenge, we tackled this issue again this year in a different way by bringing in a person to teach us improv. The workshop was interactive both physically and verbally and a lot of fun. One exercise was having a person say a single word with the next person adding a single word. The obvious question was "When will we be finished?" The not-so-obvious response from the instructor was "You will know." As we went around the room constructing sentences, it took twists and turns and always came together with an obvious conclusion. It was a fun way to learn, and we still use this process to close our meetings as a "check-out."

Meeting Environment

The locations of staff meetings (we meet anywhere from four to six times each year in person and at least monthly on a video call) are also given a lot of consideration. We decided a few years ago to nix the traditional non-windowed conference room as it provided absolutely no inspiration and seemed to quickly drain our collective energy. We now meet in locations where we can take advantage of being outside, insist on rooms with windows, and usually insist that there are no tables so that we can put our chairs in a circle and not hide behind typical office furniture. There are a lot of little known, beautiful, and inexpensive locations where a team can meet and have inspired meetings. We move our locations around geographically to be mindful of teammates who are coming from different parts of the world.

Everyone gets an equal chance to be jet-lagged. We often integrate physical activity or training in the morning before we start. Often there are options—yoga, running, walking, etc.—and a different person in the team leads each day. I share the responsibility and accountability of the meeting with the staff team and no longer set up the details or agenda. I used to be quite controlling on this and have learned that as the group has built their business acumen and worked hard on themselves, they need more opportunities to lead, and setting up key staff meetings and other global meetings for the organization is another opportunity to lead. I now simply review the intent of the meeting and let it flow. It is a huge change and works so much better for everyone.

Meeting Practices

We follow the centering/meditation practice to start every meeting, followed by a check-in, review of agenda, identifying note taker, timekeeper, etc. We expect participants to use "I" statements, make mental models explicit, speak up and contribute, and put thoughts into the room with the general session (not sidebar conversations). In the beginning, I often felt like the single person checking for behaviors and participation. That is no longer the case, and I have gone from talking all the time to active listening (almost) all the time. It is a good change for me and for the group.

Practicing Gratitude

As a good problem solver, I was very comfortable identifying problems and pointing out what was wrong on a daily basis. This was a habit that must have served me well at one point but was not serving me well as I took on new responsibilities. I started to use the meditation practice I had in place to practice gratitude. Staying grounded in gratitude helped me view the world differently. I made a point of expressing appreciation for people and the work they were doing. I made a point of expressing gratitude daily and often. It sounds like a small thing.

However, I started to realize that as I shifted from pointing out the problems to acknowledging the great work people were doing, it started to change my attitude and the response I received from others. I continue to practice daily gratitude. Changing my perspective and lens on how I view the world is powerful.

It reinforces the need for me to continue to look in the mirror when I feel compelled to blame others. What did I do to cause an issue or reaction? What approach could I have taken that might have resulted in a different outcome? Have I recognized a particular person or situation where someone is really going above and beyond? It doesn't take a lot of effort, but it does take a purposeful commitment to practice gratitude daily. Simple, yet powerful practice.

Using the Word LOVE at Work

At some point a few years ago, we started using the word "love" at work. It started awkwardly. I still remember one colleague stating that they were entirely uncomfortable using the word at work. I think we even joked through a few "I love you, man" type interactions at a few of our executive sessions. What I have noticed, and what we talk about directly now, is how appropriate the word "love" (platonic love) is in the work setting and how it needs to be nurtured to come out more.

I now regularly say to my direct reports, "You know that I love you and here is the message I need to give you." This seemed to be more accepted after our workshop on communication and making sure that people were feeling safe and loved before giving feedback. I think it works because my team knows that I want the best for them and do care deeply for each of them.

Inquiry versus Advocacy and Listening

When my boys were in middle school and junior high, I signed up to coach "Odyssey of the Mind." This meant that I would work with a group of five to seven kids who may or may not know each other (or like each other) and help them over the course of six months to form a functional team capable of competing in a problem-solving competition that involved both spontaneous problem solving and solving a more complex, long-term creative problem following guidelines established by the hosting organization. The most critical function of the coach was to help this group effectively form into a team without using any form of advocacy or giving of answers. Effectively, as the coach, I could ask questions but not provide answers.

By far, this was one of my more difficult parenting challenges, and I chose to coach a total of seven teams over five years. That is a lot of quality time with my teenage kids. I share this because I used what I learned at work. I realized that I was advocating too often in my work environment and not providing enough space for failure (and learning) for my direct reports and teams. My past view of this would have been justified as helping my team. The reality was that I was providing the answers promoting my single point of view of how to resolve any given issue. I have learned that the best way to lead and build good leadership acumen is to ask real, genuine probing questions that likely require some reflection (i.e., there is no immediate "right" answer).

In a world that is becoming increasingly complex, gaining multiple inputs, insights, or lenses on any given situation is helpful. There is never one single "right" answer, and I try to ask questions and encourage equal participation from whoever is attending a particular meeting. I encountered frustration from my direct reports when I first started this practice as they wanted me to "get to the point and define the direction" we were going to go on a particular issue. While I have never had any problem putting forth my opinion, I now wait and ask others what they think. It forces people to put forth their opinions and builds the muscle for each person to articulate their point of view—regardless of my point of view. It also builds individual accountability for the idea put forth. Having a different idea is encouraged. I have often said that I don't need a bunch of "yes" people as I know my own opinions and thoughts. I need colleagues that have thoughtful and/or insightful views that are different than mine and that force me to review my mental model and point of view. Frankly, the challenge isn't always fun or convenient, but it almost always forces me (and the team) to come up with the best possible response to any situation.

While I rely on using inquiry as a standard go-to practice, I do rely on thought partnering when wrestling with tough issues or problems. If asked, I will share my best thoughts on a situation all the while openly admitting that I don't necessarily have the answer. I do have a fierce independent streak and tend to challenge peers and others even when not asked.

I believe I progressed through the majority of my career because I am persuasive with a bias toward action. This served me well until I realized that I was limiting the organization with my knowledge and that I had to really work on recognizing my mental models, suspending judgment, and questioning the stories that I was telling myself that made me confident that I was right.

Questioning the Stories I Am Telling Myself

I often share the story of my early experience working in Baltimore with a team of engineers who were working to improve the customer warranty issues on a mature vehicle platform. I sat next to an engineer who never seemed to answer my questions or respond when I spoke to him. I started telling myself all kinds of stories as to why he didn't answer me. Most of those stories weren't pretty. One day, I decided to ask him to lunch so I could confront him as to why he always ignored me. My intention was to share how disrespected I felt by his lack of response. He accepted my invitation and we set a date. On the agreed-upon day, as we were being seated, he leaned over and said to me, "You may want to sit on my left side. I am deaf in this ear and won't be able to hear you if you sit on that side." I was a bit taken aback. I certainly felt stupid. So much for those stories! I had no knowledge of his physical condition and had spent considerable time making up reasons why he didn't "hear" me. It turned out that he and I became quite good friends and have still stayed in touch twenty years later. I like to think of this situation when I start to tell my-self a story and identify the real facts of the situation.

Replacing "But" with "And"

My most recent practice (learned from Ed!) is replacing the word "but" with "and." It is amazing how many times I have found myself starting to use the word "but" and catching myself. Not only does this practice reinforce my mindful and deep listening practice, it forces me to be purposeful in my chosen words. Acknowledging what someone has said, giving value to it and saying "yes, AND" has proven to be quite powerful. It is additive. It helps build a bond and connection versus a competition or a situation where one idea is viewed as better than the other.

Reflection Time

What do you think? A good story?

1. Please make a list of Susan's discussion topics (from her topic headings).

2. For each topic, please reflect on what you learned with the following questions:

(a) Do you have the same issues Susan had?

(b) Why did she want to change?

(c) How did Susan change?

(d) Is this something you want to change?

(e) How will you do that?

3. What Quiet Ego practices does Susan use?

4. What Quiet Mind practices does Susan use?

5. What Quiet Body practices does Susan use?

6. What Positive Emotional State practices does Susan use?

7. What are your top three takeaways?

8. What did you think about her discussion about love (platonic) in the workplace?

This book discusses love in the workplace, and when I use the term *love* in this book, I mean *platonic* love—a deep, mutual, and warm form of caring about the well-being of others and a deep acceptance and appreciation of others as unique human beings.

With love and gratitude, thank you, Susan.

CHAPTER 5

The Marvin Riley Personal Transformation Story

Marvin Riley is the CEO of EnPro Industries. Before joining EnPro, Marvin was an executive with General Motors, working within the General Motors Vehicle Manufacturing Group where he held multiple positions of increasing responsibility from 1997 to 2007.

Marvin completed the Advanced Management Program (AMP) at the Harvard Business School and has an MBA degree from Johns Hopkins University and a BS in electrical engineering from Howard University. He has served on the board of directors of TimkenSteel since August 2018.

Marvin and I first connected in the late fall of 2014 when I received a call from him wanting to talk about my *Learn or Die* book. Marvin has a fascinating American Dream story, as you will read. But what is so interesting to me and I believe will be to you is Marvin's candor and vulnerability in sharing his story of how "that" Marvin became the "new" Marvin.

As you read his story, please reflect on WHY Marvin undertook his transformation journey, WHAT about himself he wanted to change, and HOW he went about it.

Here is Marvin's story in his own words. I hope you enjoy it as much as I do. Please read slowly and "make meaning" of his story. If you do that, I know it will connect with you in your own personal way.

My Beginning

I remember the damp cold air and never feeling warm. I remember the constant desperation attempts to pay the water bill or the electricity light bill. I remember never having money to go on field trips and being left behind. I remember playing tackle football on the grass field with the concrete sidewalk running through the field. I remember being burglarized by the neighbors in the apartment downstairs. I remember drugs being sold about three houses down from mine. I remember always checking behind me when I was walking home. I remember the chilling seriousness of my mother's voice and the dry callousness of my father's hands. I remember everything was loud: the music, the voices, the cars, and the sirens. These memories are so much more than memories. These memories are building blocks for who I grew to become.

This environment shaped me and, in many ways, this environment is and was me. My mental models were and are still influenced every single day by this foundation.

It's not safe

Life is hard

Trust no one

Be tough and be ready

Hustle to get yours

Watch your back

It's survival of the fittest

These phrases are what I told myself each and every day. Unfortunately, this didn't fade when I grew out of my youth, it has been the multidecade fuel to prove that I was good enough, smart enough, and worthy. I wanted to achieve my way out of everything that surrounded me. Manage the distractions coming from every direction and achieve. I remember when I broke the high school rushing record in football, I didn't even tell my parents. I literally didn't care as it was just another achievement. I just wanted to get to the next game so I could keep on grinding.

I was fiercely independent and on my own mission to change my condition. I decided that nothing was going to stop me from achieving and all I had to do was continue to work hard, trust no one, and put achievement-based points on the board. This was also the period in my life where I decided that I had to find my own way, I had to do it all by myself.

Things really changed for me when my best friend and college roommate was shot multiple times by an active shooter at a house party we both attended. My roommate didn't die although another student did and others were severely injured. It was a harsh reminder that life was hard and could be snatched from me in an instant. This incident permanently changed me and it also destroyed my calibration. My ladder of inference was now hijacked by extreme distrust and equating difficult situations with potential loss of life. This made me very intense and very impatient. It also made me see everything through the lens of fear.

My Ego Loved Winning

Upon graduation from undergrad, I moved away to work where I had no previous attachments and I never wanted to stop working. I focused heavily on being productive and learning everything that I could about everything. This work ethic was rewarded by the company and I was promoted several times. I was also rewarded because I was intense and impatient. My surroundings just fed my ego and affirmed all of my bad habits.

I was promoted to the point where I was leading people and my intensity was always on display. I had no problem confronting you if your department was falling behind. I also had no problem doing this in front of other people. It was about hitting the numbers and literally nothing else. I would even insert myself to solve a problem or physically do something to keep our production going to hit the numbers. Over time I became more fun to be around; however, you never wanted to be on the other side of me if you missed your numbers. It was not going to end well regardless of why. It was winner take all, and my ego loved winning.

My parents never raised me this way, and deep inside I always felt like something was incongruent. As my parents weren't college educated, I never really looked to them for advice once I left home for college. I decided that I had to figure everything out on my own. I also felt like my approach was working because I was being promoted and recognized for my behavior. I wasn't smart enough to know that the deep values about human connection exhibited by my parents transcended any school-based education. I have many memories of times where I showed absolutely no empathy. My default mode for myself and everyone was to suck it up and work harder.

My Pivotal Moment
It wasn't until the time of the financial crisis that I realized that I needed to change. I knew deep inside that my intensity and lack of empathy was misguided. After laying off many people in multiple factories across multiple countries, I realized something important. I realized that the people who were closest to me had also lost touch with their feelings and also lacked empathy.

My realization happened on a beautiful summer day in Paris when I was walking up the Champs-Elysées toward the Arc de Triomphe. I stood at the circle of the Arc de Triomphe and just watched the cars as they entered and exited the circle around the monument. It looked a little like my life, which could easily be described as organized chaos. I then noticed something very important. More cars were being allowed to enter the circle from certain streets than others. This was in many ways a mirror of my life. I realized then and there that I only allowed tough minded, sport loving, technical people into my circle. If you loved engineering, you were in, and if you loved marketing, you were out. If you loved football, you were in, but if you loved painting, you were out. This was the perfect place to put me right up against my edge because the French didn't watch American football and they love art.

This moment was a pivotal moment in my life. I realized that I had surrounded myself with people who confirmed what I already believed, cared more about tangible things than the people who produced those things, and were completely "me" focused. I basically realized that I surrounded myself with mirror images of myself, and I didn't really like myself anymore.

This time away from my own echo chamber allowed me to reflect and examine my worldview.

This self-examination and self-awareness didn't happen in Paris by accident.

During this time frame I had recently completed a 360-feedback process and two transformational leadership programs and I began to experiment with meditation. Without making a conscious choice, I had subconsciously set myself on a course of deep introspection and deep personal transformation. I began to journal, and I began to intentionally seek out people who were different from me in every way.

I realized that these individuals were so full and so much more in touch with reality than me. I realized that there was something deep inside of me that was really hurting. I began listening to the same music that my parents would play in my house as a child. Spirit-filled reggae music with positive lyrics like that of Bob Marley. I remember constantly repeating Marley's lyrics: "Emancipate yourself from mental slavery, none but ourselves can free our minds."

Freeing Myself

I began to read everything I could find on human development and human transformation. I began seeking out people who cared about a common humanity and wanted to be a force for deep love and deep care in the world. I wanted to work in a new way and I wanted to live in a new way.

During one of my staff meetings I read every word that was said to me in my 360 feedback out loud to everyone. It was hard, it was emotional, and I could hardly hold back the tears. I committed to everyone there that I would change and that I wanted their support to hold me accountable.

I sought mentorship from my CEO at the time, as he had done extensive work in this area. Luckily, he saw something in me and agreed to support my development. It started with raw unfiltered feedback that I needed to hear. He introduced me to many people who were experts in the field, and he took his personal time to teach me about self-awareness.

I then began to practice by using work as the raw material to develop myself. When I saw someone in a meeting make a face, I checked in to see what they were thinking. If they disagreed with me, I put a little space between hearing their point of view and my reflective defensiveness, which was my immediate go-to in the beginning. I began wanting everyone to experience the new me, and I wanted everyone who worked for me to treat their employees differently.

I wanted to scale this new way of relating to people, but I lacked the social technology to scale what I was doing. My CEO was leading a transformation that was about the individual, and we both saw a gap in the ability to scale the work beyond the individual level.

After a multiday solo experience in nature, I came back with an open awareness but also more conviction to find a way to scale the transformation work that was changing me from the inside out. During my time in nature I realized that people simply work better and show up differently when the leader sets the field with positivity and psychological safety. I didn't have the language for it then, but I knew it at a tacit level.

One morning while watching CNBC, I heard Ray Dalio talking about an idea meritocracy and I heard about a book called *Learn or Die*. This book sounded like something similar to the work we had been doing, but it was different. It seemed to have the essential elements of how to build practices into our daily work. This book, he said, also had the details of what an idea meritocracy was all about.

I downloaded the *Learn or Die* book and drove to get my car hand-washed. As this process normally takes an hour, I walked over to Starbucks to grab a coffee. A few hours later my phone was ringing repeatedly as if there was an emergency. I completely forgot about my car while reading *Learn or Die* and was completely engulfed in reading and journaling about how I would implement an idea meritocracy in my business unit.

Creating the Perfect Workplace

I wanted everyone to be in a psychologically safe work environment. I wanted to fill the workday with positivity, and I wanted everyone to feel competent in what they were doing. I really wanted everyone to connect, relate, and collaborate, but most importantly I wanted everyone to adopt the phrase "I am not my idea." I needed to adopt this more than anyone as I didn't want anyone to just adopt my bad ideas because I was the boss, and I wanted everyone to feel comfortable to challenge everyone's critical thinking so we can always get to the best idea.

Since reading that book, I have been on a mission to create the perfect workplace.

I want everyone to practice behaviors that evidence being open-minded, mindful, actively listening, courageous, curious, and collaborative.

I want everyone to feel psychologically safe to be exactly who they are in the world.

I believe everyone comes into this world already perfect and should feel that way at work.

I have been maintaining my daily meditation practice because I also notice that I'm the single biggest impediment to achieving this work environment. During my developmental journey I learned that the leader caps the developmental level of the organization, and as Leo Tolstoy says, "Everyone thinks of changing the world, but no one thinks of changing himself."

One Marvin

During my process of building a better workplace, I have also been building a more integrated life. My life outside of work has really evolved to me being more and more of the same person inside and outside of the workplace. I view this as an important and critical step in the journey. Fully releasing my desired and dreaded images by bringing my life together as one evolving unit. I'm more vulnerable at home now when before I felt like I needed to always be stern and firm.

Quite frankly, my vulnerability has given me more freedom to be who I wanted to be all along. I consider myself to be a work in process; however, I am acknowledging my need to be a better listener and more empathic.

I have developed daily standardized work to hold myself accountable to practicing what I say I want to become. I have found transformation is hard and requires tremendous rigor and discipline. Some of my daily and weekly standardized work includes:

- Exercise (aerobic and anaerobic)
- Daily meditation
- Journaling
- Intentional practice of inquiry versus advocacy
- Expressing gratitude
- Active constructive response
- Behavioral self-assessment: open-mindedness, curiosity, listening, humility, mindfulness, collaboration, courageousness, empathy
- Daily reading (nonfiction and fiction to improve perspective taking)

My standardized work will not work for everyone, but it is how I hold myself accountable. This is maintained primarily on a checklist that I review and update to see how I'm doing. My plan going forward is to build my own database in order to improve the quality of my thinking and being.

Love and Purpose

My changes allow access to people from the side streets who previously weren't allowed to enter. They feel welcome to enter my life and they feel welcome to enrich my life. I smile when someone challenges my thinking and holds me accountable for who I'm working to become. This has been very hard for me but very rewarding. The most rewarding has been me realizing what my parents were trying to teach me all along. All that matters is love. Lead with love and be a beacon for love and kindness in all situations.

As I think about my purpose and my work in this world, I try to anchor on my noble goal. My noble goal is to provide access to higher education and development for underprivileged individuals. My life has been a journey of greater education and development and I want this for everyone. No one should be denied the ability to live into the highest and truest expression of themselves because of their circumstance or from being denied access to greater knowledge.

I hope my story can be helpful to someone who wants more out of life and wants more for everyone around them each and every day. I also hope my daily and weekly practices will provide insight into the rigor and discipline I've used even if the practices themselves may not be ideal for everyone.

Go take on the world. It's waiting for new leaders every day.

Reflection Time

1. What do you think?

2. What resonated with you?

3. Why did Marvin change?

4. What did he want to change about himself?

5. How did he go about doing that?

6. I believe Marvin's story contains some fundamental principles about how to achieve Inner Peace.

Do you agree or disagree? Why?

7. What are those fundamental principles?

8. How is Marvin working on having a Quiet Ego? Quiet Mind?

9. What role do daily practices play in Marvin's life?

10. Why are practices important?

11. I believe Marvin is a Hyper-Learner. What evidences that in his story?

12. What does he do to continually learn?

I am deeply grateful to Marvin for sharing his story with you.

Marvin, thank you.

With love and a big HUG.

Do you remember that Marvin stated that his goal was to build the perfect workplace? A workplace where every individual has the opportunity to bring his or her Best Self to work and to develop his or her abilities to do meaningful, purposeful work?

We now are going to move to part 2 of the book, which is about a New Way of Working and Humanizing the Workplace. Together we are going to explore the meaning of a "perfect workplace."

My guess is that many of you are thinking, "I am not a CEO like Marvin. I can't change my workplace." Yes, *and*. . . .

Many of you are probably leaders of teams or organizational groups or units or functional areas or leaders of geographies or products or services or subsidiaries. Why can't you change how your group or team works?

And many of you are members of teams and have influence. Why not try to influence your team leader to adopt new ways of working that will enhance team performance?

PART 2

Hyper-Learning Requires a New Way of Working

CHAPTER **6**

Humanizing the Workplace

Part 1 of this book defined *what* a Hyper-Learner is, explained *why* you should become one, and provided the knowledge and skills for *how* to do it. The answer to how to become a Hyper-Learner for most of us is a New Way of Being—a journey to our Best Selves that includes cultivating Inner Peace, developing a Hyper-Learning Mindset, and actively engaging in Hyper-Learning Behaviors. So far, you've created your Daily Intentions, identified the principles of a Hyper-Learning Mindset for yourself, and begun the process of identifying and assessing the Hyper-Learning Behaviors you need to adopt.

Part 2 now focuses on the environment where you do your work. Using the same *why, what*, and *how* approach, this chapter describes the **New Way of Working** that enables organizations and their people to be Hyper-Learners. Chapters 7 and 8 take a deeper dive into three key concepts fundamental to that New Way of Working: **Caring, Trusting Teams**; **High-Quality, Making-Meaning Conversations**; and **collective flow**. Chapter 9 provides an in-depth overview of the journey of EnPro Industries to a New Way of Working.

Understanding the type of work environment that will enable the highest levels of human cognitive, emotional, and behavioral performance as the digital age progresses is important because, if you work on a team or are a team leader, you can influence the culture and environment of how that team operates or functions. You can have a team culture that differs from the corporate culture. And if you have the opportunity to influence the corporate culture, even better. **Remember, it is all about how people behave with each other.**

It all comes down to what you can control or influence. You can control you. If you lead a team, you can influence the team by creating rules of engagement (of how you want to behave and work together). If you lead a functional area or a business unit or a geographical unit, you can likewise step up and use the key concepts in this book.

THE WHY

Why do we need a New Way of Working?

We need it because the dominant way of working in most organizations today will not enable Hyper-Learning. In fact, it will inhibit Hyper-Learning. That dominant way is based in large part on achieving compliance through fear, with the leadership model being *command* and *control* (i.e., directing others).

As the digital age advances, human beings must perform at their highest cognitive, emotional, and behavioral levels. Individuals must come to work with a state of mind and body reflecting Inner Peace, ready to fully engage in the higher-order cognitive, social, and emotional tasks that smart technology won't be able to do well.

Hyper-Learning requires a work environment that embraces the science of adult learning (that we are suboptimal learners) and a work environment that mitigates the two big individual inhibitors of learning: ego and fear.

Hyper-Learning requires a work environment that is team-oriented and highly collaborative, not an individualistic, survival-of-the-fittest, competitive environment.

You can't effectively coerce or command individuals to do the tasks that smart technology won't be able to do well.

To fully enable humans to Hyper-Learn requires a New Way of Working that fundamentally challenges the cultures, policies, and procedures of traditional workplaces.

TABLE 6.1	
Old Way of Working	**New Way of Working**
Command and control leadership	Humanistic leadership
Individuals compete and win	Teams win
Fear	Psychological safety
Individuals play cards close to the chest	Transparency and candor
"Yes, *but*"	"Yes, *and*"
Highest-ranking person dictates	An idea meritocracy
Listening to confirm	Listening to learn
Advocating/telling	Asking questions
Always knowing	Being good at not knowing
IQ	IQ, EI, SI
Internal competition	Collaboration
Big ME	Big WE (the team)
Money dominates	Meaning and purpose
Hierarchy	Distributed power
Soulless	Soulful
Sameness (clones), homogeneity	Diversity
Human machines	Human uniqueness
	Trust
Financial measurements	Financial and behavioral measurements

TABLE 6.1 (CONTINUED)	
Old Way of Working	**New Way of Working**
Competition	Compassion
Survival of the fittest	Helping others be successful
Defensiveness	Trust and vulnerability
Seek power	Seek to empower
Linear thinking	Creative, innovative, and emergent thinking
CYA	Speaking up
Leave your Best Self at home	Bring your Best Self to work

Reflection Time

I invite you to carefully review the old way of working and new way of working lists in table 6.1 and circle which of the two descriptors in each row best defines or applies to your current workplace. Which characteristic dominates?

What do those results say to you?

Is your work environment people-centric?

If not, how would you describe it?

Are there areas where you can change how *you* behave and invite others to join you in behaving that way?

Are there areas where you would feel comfortable talking about change with the person you report to?

THE HOW

Humanizing the Workplace will require organizations to operate as **idea meritocracies** and embrace the psychological principles of **positivity, self-determination**, and **psychological safety**.

The digital age will continue to place higher and higher expectations on leaders, requiring them to excel at the desired Hyper-Learning Mindsets and Behaviors and to serve as role models of the types of thinking, emotional engagement, and collaboration—the team play—that is needed. I believe that **leadership must become enable-ship**, and that the chief executive officer of the future must become the **chief *enabling* officer** with primary responsibility for facilitating the levels of human performance needed for continual Hyper-Learning, innovation, and multi-stakeholder value creation.

It is time for the old ways of working to die.

The old ways of working involve internal competition, power plays, internal political gamesmanship, hierarchies, silos, ego, fiefdoms, a short-term focus primarily on quarterly earnings, cultures that promote survival-of-the-fittest mentalities, and attitudes exemplified by phrases like go along to get along, the boss knows best, keep your head down, don't make waves, just do as you're told, don't challenge the status quo or a higher-up, and keep the boss happy.

These old ways generate anxiety, anger, frustration, fear, and worry. They are not conducive to human creativity, innovation, agility, adaptability, value creation, or strategic differentiation.

The old ways are not conducive to human growth and development.

The old ways are not conducive to Hyper-Learning.

The old ways of working will not work in the advancing digital age.

The old ways inhibit the highest levels of human performance. By emphasizing survival-of the-fittest mentalities and hyper-internal competition, they reinforce crass individualism and zero-sum thinking, which inhibits the development of diverse, cross-functional, Caring, Trusting Teams, which are needed for Hyper-Learning and innovation.

The old ways must be replaced by a humanistic, enabling system that liberates people to think and emotionally engage at their highest levels and to have the courage to innovate, create, and thrive in an idea meritocracy.

This new kind of system must support team environments that enable people to behave with each other in ways that lead to the highest levels of collective human performance that result in High-Quality, Making-Meaning Conversations and *collective flow*.

That is how businesses will create value as the digital age progresses.

That is how people will find more meaning in their work.

That is how high employee engagement will happen.

Humanizing the Workplace is a pathway to your being, belonging, and becoming!

Work becomes a way that you can express your human uniqueness to the world.

Humanizing the Workplace is much more than being people-centric. People-centricity is necessary but not sufficient.

Humanizing the Workplace requires people to connect, relate, and engage with each other in ways that enable the uniqueness of each individual to contribute to the common purpose and meaningful mission.

Humanizing the Workplace means that you can bring your Best Self to work because you are cared about and respected as a unique human being and that is evidenced by how people behave.

Humanizing the Workplace means that the desired values and behaviors are woven into the daily way of working—the daily fabric of the organization—through practices that are used by all people every day.

In chapter 9 you will see an example of how this can be done.

Reflection Time

Reflect on your work environment.

How would you describe it?

Do you feel safe being you at work?

Do you trust your manager or boss?

Does your boss care about you as a unique human being?

Do you feel valued as a unique human being by your colleagues?

Please go back to table 6.1 and revisit your circles. What needs to change in order for you to bring your Best Self to work?

Does your work environment enable you to continually reinvent yourself as will be needed in the digital age?

Assume the person to whom you report came by and asked to talk with you. He or she said, "I want you to bring your Best Self to work, the same Best Self that you are with your friends and loved ones."

What would that mean to you?

What new behaviors would you bring to your work?

What current behaviors at work would you drop?

Gary Hamel says, "To put it bluntly, the most important task for any manager today is to create a work environment that *inspires* exceptional contribution and that *merits* an outpouring of passion, imagination and initiative."[92]

Does your employer care about your uniqueness as an individual human being?

Is your work designed to play to your strengths?

Do you have a personal development plan that your manager has committed to make happen?

Can you speak freely and honestly with your boss or higher-ups without the fear of negative consequences?

Can you be yourself at work? Is your Best Self at home different from the self you bring to work?

How many work friends can you be totally transparent and authentic with?

Can you be the "real" you at work?

Is your work meaningful and purposeful?

Reflection Time

What did your answers tell you about your work environment?

Can you be all you can be in your current work environment?
Keep this in perspective: according to a Gallup poll,
85 percent of employees would likely answer, "No!"

Leaders are starting to understand how the highest levels of human performance occur. **Such performance originates with small teams of people who care about each other, feel psychologically safe with each other, trust each other, and believe in the purpose of their work.**

The unique cognitive and emotional capabilities of human beings are what will differentiate organizations as the digital age advances.

Those qualities are evident in work environments that enable Hyper-Learning and are not coercive or stifling.

FOUR KEY CONCEPTS

The New Way of Working that will enable Hyper-Learning will require organizational leaders to cultivate an **idea meritocracy** and embrace three key psychological principles: **positivity**, **psychological safety**, and **self-determination.**[93]

Idea Meritocracy

This is the model that both Google and Bridgewater Associates use.

In an idea meritocracy, the best data-driven idea or judgment wins irrespective of rank, compensation, or power. What determines any course of action is the best idea or judgment, not whose idea or judgment it is.

Is your place of work an idea meritocracy? Or does positional rank or power win most of the time?

Positivity

Leading research by cognitive, social, and positive psychologists, including Barbara Fredrickson and Alice Isen, has produced strong evidence that positive emotions enable and enhance cognitive processing, innovative thinking, and creativity and lead to better judgments and decision making. On the flip side, research has shown that negative emotions—especially fear and anxiety—have the opposite effect. Fear and anxiety in the workplace can take many forms, including fear of looking bad, speaking up, making mistakes, losing your job, or not being liked.

The work environment must be designed to reduce fears, insecurities, and other negative emotions. This concurs with eight major research studies that found that consistently high-performing businesses have high employee engagement and that such engagement occurs in people-centric cultures.[94]

You already learned in part 1 how positive emotions enable Hyper-Learning and how negative emotions inhibit Hyper-Learning.

Is your place of work a positive emotional environment? Or is fear fairly widespread?

Self-Determination

Initially developed by psychologists Edward L. Deci and Richard Ryan, self-determination theory (SDT) is one of the most well-known theories of human motivation. The theory is that intrinsic motivation—the tendency to seek out new and challenging situations and expand cognitive and behavioral capacities for their own sake as opposed to fulfilling social obligations or gaining some extrinsic reward—is supported when three innate human needs are met:

- *Autonomy.* The experience of volition and initiative. An example of this would be having input into how you do your job and feeling valued as a unique human being, not just a means to a corporate end.

- *Relatedness.* A sense of mutual respect and reliance with others. One example might be having a best friend at work.

■ *Competence.* Succeeding at optimally challenging tasks and being able to attain desired outcomes, such as having the opportunity to grow and develop.

According to SDT, if employees feel that they have autonomy, relatedness, and effectiveness at work, they're more likely to be highly engaged and thus more likely to perform at high levels.

WORKSHOP: SDT ASSESSMENT

SDT is so important. Here is a diagnostic I use with my client companies. I designed it for managers to assess whether they're meeting the self-determination needs of the people who report to them. If you are a manager, I invite you to answer the questions separately for each person you manage and to create a plan to better meet each individual's self-determination needs.

If you do not have direct reports, I invite you to assess how your manager or managers might fare under the diagnostic.

SDT Manager Assessment for Each of Your Direct Reports

© Edward D. Hess 2019

For each question answer True (T) or False (F).

Autonomy

____ I frequently give my direct reports the opportunity for input into how their jobs are done.

____ I tell them their opinions count and adopt them if they are better than what we are doing.

____ I always have time to listen to them when they have issues.

____ I have frequently done things that show I care about them as individuals, not just as my direct reports.

____ I have frequent one-on-one check-in meetings and ask each of them how I can help them.

____ I ask each of them what I'm doing that he or she wants me to do more of. I ask what I'm doing that she or he wants me to do less of.

____ I ask them what I am not doing for the group that they think I should be doing.

____ I ask them what they think our team's number one problem is and how they would remedy it.

____ I ask them, what is the best thing about working here?

Relatedness

____ I know who is the best work friend of each direct report.

____ At least once a month, I take each direct report out to lunch and talk about my life and their lives so I know them and they know me personally.

_____ I create opportunities during work time for people to build personal relationships with other team members.

Competence

_____ I know the professional goals of each direct report.

_____ I have worked out a personal development plan with each of them.

_____ I have ensured that each direct report has received training each of the last two years.

_____ If it would help them, I have assisted direct reports in getting promotions outside my group.

_____ I encourage my direct reports' development by giving frequent feedback to each of them at least weekly.

This is what I mean when I use the term *humanizing business*: knowing the people you work with well—their strengths, weaknesses, and goals and who they really are; knowing about their lives outside of work and their hopes and dreams; and knowing what they believe to be their human uniqueness—what they bring to work and can use to contribute to the purpose of the organization.

Psychological Safety

Feeling psychologically safe is feeling safe from retribution, which could be social ostracism, being passed over for good assignments, having bonuses or raises reduced, or even being transferred out of the team or fired on trumped-up charges. Studies show that without psychological safety, people will not fully embrace the hard parts of thinking and innovating: giving and receiving constructive feedback; challenging the status quo; asking and being asked the hard questions; being non-defensive, open-minded, and intellectually courageous; and having the courage to try new things and fail. Amy Edmondson, a professor at Harvard Business School who has conducted some of the best research on psychological safety, has found that it's an essential element of organizational learning.

Psychologically safe environments have cultures of candor and are characterized by the permission to speak freely and make learning mistakes (within financial risk parameters). They are cultures that offer all employees a voice by devaluing elitism, hierarchy, and rank (other than with respect to compensation). Google's research shows that psychological safety is the strongest determinant of high-performance teams.[95]

It's not enough to give permission to speak freely. Speaking freely should be acknowledged and emotionally rewarded publicly. Leaders and managers must publicly seek challenges to their views and beliefs. In this type of environment, leaders have to be human too. Overbearing, all-knowing, elitist leaders will be severely challenged under the New Way of Working.

The importance of psychological safety for Hyper-Learning is echoed in the words of renowned humanistic psychologist Abraham Maslow, who stated that a person "reaches out to the environment in wonder and interest, and expresses whatever skills he has, to the extent that he is not crippled by fear, to the extent that he feels safe enough to dare."[96]

These four concepts—idea meritocracy, positivity, self-determination, and psychological safety—help an organization become more humanistic, people-centric, and human-development-centric.

Do you remember Marvin Riley's goal of creating the perfect workplace? I believe that workplace must be humanistic and based on people-centricity, human development, and the four principles above.

LEADING OR ENABLING?

The New Way of Working requires a humanistic, people-centric, human-development-focused leadership model.

The dominant leadership model in many organizations today is a relic of the Industrial Revolution. It's based on hierarchy and favors all-knowing leaders who command, control, and direct others. That type of leadership will become obsolete as the digital age advances because one cannot effectively command, control, or direct others to cognitively and emotionally perform at their highest levels. You can't command or control someone to think critically, innovate, or emotionally engage with others. You cannot effectively command, control, or direct someone to be a Hyper-Learner.

Leaders must become **enablers** of organizational and human excellence. Enablers create the right environment for Hyper-Learning, model the desired mindsets and behaviors, and take responsibility for the culture. Leaders must themselves become passionate Hyper-Learners and create Caring, Trusting Teams (the subject of the next chapter). **No one gets a pass under the New Way of Working.** Managers must become

enablers too, by becoming coaches tasked with the development of people and the removal of institutional obstacles to Hyper-Learning.

The Four Es

Leaders become **enablers** by modeling the Four Es: **Engage, Embrace, Excel**, and **Enable**.[97]

ENGAGE with the world as a lifelong learner with a Quiet Ego.
Lifelong learning requires that you constantly stress-test your mental models and be wary of insularity, complacency, and overconfidence. Lifelong learning requires Hyper-Learning.

EMBRACE uncertainty, ambiguity, and complexity like a courageous scientist.
The pace of technological change will likely accelerate, and the magnitude of the change will at various points become exponential. Traditional approaches to making strategy and managing organizations in such an environment increasingly will become obsolete. The comfort of "knowing" will be fleeting. Yearning for stability and predictability will in many cases be futile. Being self-focused will in many cases be a reason to "short your stock."

EXCEL at managing self and *otherness*.
Leaders of the future must be leaders with high emotional intelligence who embrace and enable otherness: a focus on connecting and relating to and emotionally engaging with other stakeholders in the pursuit of a purposeful organizational mission.

To excel at otherness requires managing *yourself*, which means managing your thinking, emotions, and behaviors and intentionally taming your ego and fears on a daily basis. Excelling at managing *yourself* has two parts: (1) increasing the quantity and the quality of the behaviors necessary to optimize thinking, collaborating, and learning and (2) minimizing the behaviors that limit or impede that result.

ENABLE **the highest levels of human development and performance.** As the digital age advances, integrating the highest levels of human performance with the best technology will be a strategic imperative. In fact, the strategic differentiator in many industries will be the human component because, for example, artificial intelligence will be readily available to all businesses at a low cost via cloud services. In those cases, the organizations with the best human thinkers, listeners, collaborators, and learners—in other words, Hyper-Learners—will have a competitive advantage. Developing teams of Hyper-Learners requires a leadership and talent model that is based on human development, and that means that the *human resource* function must be transformed into a *human development* function.

Chapter 9 offers an organizational story from EnPro Industries about enabling human development.

THE YEARNING FOR MEANING

One morning in October 2019, while I was working on this chapter, I received a message from a former executive education student whom I taught in a servant leadership course. He is a very successful, high-level executive and researcher with an MD and a PhD. He is also a caring person, and we have stayed in touch over the years. That morning he was seeking advice because he was considering leaving his company. The work environment there was not humanistic, and senior leaders did not value or enable meaningful work relationships.

He came to realize that no one at his company really knew each other, that everyone was consumed with getting tasks done, and that there were few true work friendships. People were nice to each other, he said, but they didn't really care about each other and didn't help each other be successful. He said he had no emotional connections with others, that his boss was not open to using work time to build those connections, and that there was little interpersonal joy—just a get-it-done mentality.

Everyone was very well paid, so that was not the issue. The issue was the lack of emotional connections and meaningful work relationships. While he loved his work, he said that many days he felt like walking out and never coming back.

That is sad.

But it is not uncommon. It speaks to the importance of emotional connections with others and the human need to find meaning to answer the existential question: Why do I exist?

My friend Ray Dalio says the best things in life include meaningful work and meaningful relationships.[98]

I am moving toward believing it is all about having meaningful relationships—at work and away from work. The most meaningful work generally requires meaningful relationships. If I am correct, the workplace has to move in the direction of becoming a much more humanistic environment that enables human emotional connection. Having best real friends at work will be key and that means being your Best Self at work.

Satya Nadella, the CEO of Microsoft, felt strongly that Microsoft needed to rediscover its soul by embracing empathy and aligning human purpose and organizational purpose. In his book *Hit Refresh*, Nadella says that one of the first things he did with his leadership team was to have a consultant facilitate a conversation in which the senior leaders could be completely open and transparent with each other in sharing their personal passions and philosophies with complete candor. Very similar to my friend's story above, Nadella said he felt like people did not really know each other, and he explains in the book how hard it was for his group to be that vulnerable.[99] That is the type of openness, vulnerability, and sharing of one's humanity required to begin humanizing work.

I am a big fan of John O'Donohue's work. In his book *Anam Cara*, O'Donohue wrote extensively about the need for work to be an arena where human potential is allowed to emerge and flourish. Work can be how people find their meaning and express their unique contribution to humankind.

That type of work environment produces joy, not dread or just going through the motions or just wishing the end of the workday would come faster.

Joy cannot occur in an environment dominated by compliance and power over others because such an environment leads to fear and submission.

Joy can only happen in an environment that values you as a unique human being and in which you are encouraged to play to your strengths and further develop yourself.

Human uniqueness gives birth to creativity, innovation, and emergent thinking, none of which smart machines can do well and all of which are areas where humans will be able to create value as the digital age advances.

That is the game going forward for all of us—to bring our Best Selves (our hearts or souls) to work every day in the pursuit of meaningful work that creates value for others.

My guess is that right now you might be thinking, Hess is getting really touchy feely.

Maybe I am. But it comes from what I am experiencing in my world of working with people in corporations, government agencies, schools, and universities. **People are yearning for *more* from their work.** They want more meaning and richness and to experience more joy. **They want higher-quality emotional connections with others.** And it's not just coming from younger generations.

Most workplaces must be humanized: it is only then that we human beings can fully bring forth without fear our creativity and imagination, the power of our subconscious minds, and our hearts and souls.

Reflection Time

Recall a time at work when you felt joy throughout your whole body, when you beamed with a big smile that lasted a while.

What were you doing?

With whom?

Why do you think you felt so joyous?

How often does that kind of all-encompassing joy happen to you at work?

Are there certain ways of working for you that are more likely to produce that big kind of joy?

What can you do at work to make it happen more often?

Are there certain people at work with whom you are more likely to experience that kind of joy because of how they behave and engage with you?

Do they feel joy working with you?

How can you work together more?

Is your workplace a psychologically safe place?

Does your workplace meet your self-determination needs?

Is your workplace an emotionally positive workplace?

Does your workplace operate as an idea meritocracy?

What can you do to make your workplace more humane?

CHAPTER 7

Creating Caring, Trusting Teams

Chapter 6 introduced the principles of a New Way of Working. In this chapter, we explore what that New Way of Working looks like in practice. We are not going to focus on efficiency, processes, system thinking, infusing technology into the business, or utilization of social media to connect better with customers.

Instead, we are going to focus on care, trust, and collective intelligence because they will be the secret sauce of personal and organizational success as the digital age advances.

Earlier you learned that according to the science of adult learning, no one—not me and not you—can achieve Hyper-Learning alone. We need others to help us get beyond our cognitive biases and our innate tendency to favor confirmation, affirmation, efficiency, and cohesiveness in how we think, perceive, and experience emotions. We need others to help us become our Best Selves in order to be Hyper-Learners. Remember Dr. Bourne's statement to me: **"All learning comes from conversations with yourself (deep reflection) or with others."**

You also learned that the value humans can add in the digital age increasingly will come from areas where smart technology will continue to be deficient: higher-order critical, creative, imaginative, and innovative thinking and high emotional engagement with others. Those activities can only be accomplished with others—either in small work teams and/or in daily interactions with colleagues, customers, or other stakeholders.

Team structures will come to dominate the digital age, and only a special kind will make the most effective team performance more likely.

That structure is a Caring, Trusting Team. It comprises a small group of people who truly care about each other as unique human beings and who are invested in each other's successes and happiness.

That mutual *caring* enables two integral and interdependent factors necessary for the highest levels of human collaboration: trust and feeling safe.

This chapter is about how to excel in small work teams and explains why team excellence requires the right **diversity** of people on the team (backgrounds and capabilities), agreement by those people on a **common purpose, common values, and rules of engagement**, and most importantly (arguably), **high-quality emotional connections** among those people.

THE IMPORTANCE OF DIVERSITY

You have learned that we humans are very biased toward confirming our mental models about what we think we know. My mental models are different from yours. People's mental models are influenced by their gender, where they were raised, how they were raised, the type of education they've had, their life experiences, and their work experiences. Clearly more diversity enables a team to "see more" and generate different views or perspectives concerning a particular project or activity. Diversity of background, training, and education is very helpful. Later in this chapter you will learn from research on collective intelligence that **gender diversity** is particularly important to team high-performance.

COMMON PURPOSE

This is achieved when each team member has "bought into" the purpose of the team and the importance and relevancy of its objective. That comes about by having meaningful team conversations. There needs to be a common *why* that has been openly and freely discussed and agreed upon by all team members. High-performance teams have a specific purpose that every team member believes in and is committed to achieving.

COMMON VALUES

Here I am talking about common values such as integrity, truthfulness, respect, and human dignity. We often take values for granted, but in a multicultural world, having a conversation about values is so critical because the same words might mean different things to different people. Definitions may differ among people because of generational, cultural, or experiential differences. As a result, teams need to **make meaning** of the values they want members to abide by.

RULES OF ENGAGEMENT

Teams need to create rules of engagement that define how team members agree to behave toward each other and identify behaviors that are encouraged and those that are unacceptable. There can be many reasons why a behavior is unacceptable or inappropriate. For example, the behavior might be personally dehumanizing or offensive or it might impede exploration or debate. The behavior might encourage competition rather than collaboration or minimize or intimidate participation by others.

Common good behaviors that teams should explicitly encourage include:

- Candor

- Open-mindedness

- Permission to speak freely

- Psychological safety

- Critiquing of ideas, not people

- Listening to learn, not to confirm

- Collaboration over competition

- Saying "Yes, *and*" as opposed to "Yes, *but*"

- Not rushing to judge but engaging in exploration and discovery

- Valuing and ensuring the equitable participation of all team members

- Mitigating against domination of conversations by only a few people or the highest-ranking people

Some companies I have worked with have codified their rules of engagement, posting them in every meeting room. Their teams grade themselves after each meeting and note areas of needed improvement. All of that data is logged and continually reviewed to improve the quality of team collaboration.

HIGH-QUALITY HUMAN CONNECTIONS: TEAM EXCELLENCE IS EMOTIONALLY BASED

High-performance collaboration and team effectiveness require high-quality emotional connections among team members. Professor Jane E. Dutton's work in the area of high-quality connections is foundational. I highly recommend her book *Energize Your Workplace: How to Create and Sustain High-Quality Connections at Work*. High-quality connections between people are based upon mutual positive regard and mutual trust. High-quality connections engender positive emotions that enable learning and well-being. For example, people who trust each other will be more candid with each other and feel safe in exploring their views with each other, all of which can lead to better learning. Professor Dutton offers "five strategies for creating respectful engagement: being present, being genuine, communicating affirmation, effective listening, and supportive communication."[100]

Now let's look at the science of how high-quality positive connections happen.

The Calm-and-Connect Response

In her book *Love 2.0: Creating Happiness and Health in Moments of Connection*, positive psychologist Barbara Fredrickson explains how the neuropeptide oxytocin plays a key role in social bonding and attachment. Oxytocin is sometimes called the bonding hormone, cuddle hormone, love hormone, or trust hormone, and it's associated with the *calm-and-connect* response—a distinct state of the body and brain in direct contrast to the *fight-or-flight* response, which is associated with high stress and arousal.

The calm-and-connect response is what sets you up physiologically to trust and bond with others, and the presence of oxytocin affects connecting behaviors (such as facial expressions, smiling, and making eye contact) and heightens your awareness of others' behavior and the physical cues and body language that indicate whether or not they are willing to connect with you. **The fundamental question is, how do teams cultivate environments that facilitate calm-and-connect rather than fight-or-flight responses?**

When a new team is formed, it's common for some team members to be unfamiliar with each other. Think about when you've had that experience. What were you thinking about in that first team meeting? My hypothesis is that some of you had self-talk like this: "Hmm. Who is that person? What is his agenda? Is she a nice person or is she full of herself? I think my friend said she was very competitive. I heard he is very smart and lets you know that. How am I going to fit in? Maybe I should be quiet until I figure out everyone's personal agenda. Wonder why this team leader was chosen?"

That is why before you actually start working on a new team project, the team leader should engage members in making-meaning conversations that allow them to learn about each other before going through the process of creating a common purpose, common values, and rules of engagement.

Trust and Psychological Safety

Trust is foundational. Without trust you cannot reach the higher levels of human connection and team performance necessary for Hyper-Learning. One of the leading researchers of trust is Paul J. Zak, who described how to build a culture of trust in *Trust Factor: The Science of Creating High-Performance Companies*. Zak says, **"Trust requires viewing those with whom one works as whole and complete human beings, not as pieces of human capital."**[101]

Google has studied what makes certain teams effective in the search for the "secret sauce" of high performance. The most important factor it discovered was **psychological safety**, and the company learned that the safer team members felt, the better.[102] I suggest that the precondition for feeling psychologically safe with others is trusting that other team members will do you no harm. What do you think?

When I have discussions about trust with business leaders, what do you think is their reaction? Well, of course, no one is against trust. Most people I have worked with assume they are trusted. The first reaction of many leaders is to assume they have already garnered trust in their organizations. The second reaction is a concern about time. It takes time to build trust, and time is a precious commodity when you are running a lean efficiency machine. Many leaders are not willing to free up the time necessary for their people to build truly trusting relationships. However, every company that I know of that has invested in trust, giving people time during the work day to build trusting relationships, has found the ROI far exceeds their expectations.

I believe trust serves as a strategic advantage for organizations in the digital age.

Reflection Time

Please reflect on these questions and write down your answers in your Learning Journal before going on to the next topic.

Name two people at work you really trust.

Why do you trust them?

What have they done that makes you feel you can trust them?

What behaviors give you the feeling that you can trust them?

Now let's reverse it. Name two different people at work whom you believe trust *you.*

Why do you believe they trust you?

What have you done to earn their trust?

What behaviors evidence your trust?

How would you build trust with a work colleague you don't know well?

Please try this: "I trust someone when I feel _____."

What do you need to feel or know before you can truly trust someone?

Positivity Resonance

As I mentioned in chapter 2, Barbara Fredrickson has found that positive emotions enhance our abilities to learn, be creative, positively connect with others, and grow as people. Positive emotions free us to be more open to the world and more able to embrace life and opportunity. Positive emotions draw us out of our self-focus. Negative emotions exacerbate our self-focus.

Positive emotions are associated with the release of oxytocin, which I previously mentioned is associated with a calm-and-connect response within the brain and body. According to Fredrickson, oxytocin can "jump the gap between people such that someone else's oxytocin flow can trigger one's own. A biochemical synchrony can then emerge that supports mutual engagement, care, and responsiveness."[103]

When you combine this synchrony with shared positive emotions and mutual care, you get what she calls *positivity resonance* or *Love 2.0*, which is not about romantic love or sex, but what she defines as a "micro-moment of warmth and connection that you share with another living being."[104]

Let's slooow down and think about the phrase *a micro-moment of warmth.*

What is a micro-moment?

Have you ever felt warmth with a work colleague?

What did it feel like? Did you feel relaxed? Did it feel good or bad? Did you respond more expressively or did you respond by playing it close to the vest or cautiously?

Micro-moments of warmth and connection are the building blocks of caring, trusting relationships. They are integral to the calm-and-connect response, which can lead to mutual caring and interest in helping co-workers be successful in ways that are meaningful. Internal competition goes away. You feel safe with that other person. You do not have to be worried about motives or hidden agendas. You can be totally focused on being your Best Self at work because your colleagues, or at least some of them, want you to succeed because you want them to succeed. Reaching that stage is heavily influenced by the cultivation of positive emotions and the syncing up with others emotionally and biochemically.

Isn't it fascinating that our bodies and emotions can link up with another just like two railroad cars can link together? Being in sync can mean lots more than just agreeing on the right answer to a work issue.

Teams that facilitate these kinds of physiological and emotional human connections have built the foundation for what the next chapter discusses: having High-Quality, Making-Meaning Conversations and attaining the highest state of collaboration that is reflected in what I call *collective flow*.

Connecting with People

How about you make tomorrow a Smile Day?

Try to put yourself in a positive emotional state, and whenever you walk by someone at work, slow down and give her or him a big smile. Then say something positive like "Have a nice day" and see what happens. If you genuinely mean it, you should feel good doing that every time.

So how did it feel? Did you experience a warm feeling?

And how did other people respond? Did they smile back?

What did they say?

Why not adopt that behavior every day if it feels good?

Now, think about how you engage at the beginning of a meeting or while you are with others waiting for the meeting to begin. Do you smile at people and say something positive? What effect would it have if you did?

If you were leading a meeting, how could you start the meeting in a way that helps people be in a positive emotional state?

Here is what I do at the beginning of every class I teach and every workshop I do with clients: First I ask everyone, "Are you really here?" Then I ask them, "Why did I ask that question?"

Next, I ask, "Are you in a positive mood?" Then I ask them, "Why are positive emotions important?"

Finally, I ask them to turn to the person sitting on their right side and smile at him or her. Genuine smiles begin the emotional connection process just like making eye contact does. Combine them and you are off to a good start.

Another way to begin the connection process is to ask people questions that indicate you care about them as individuals. That usually means asking specific questions about a person's family or hobbies or last trip or outing. Detailed questions demonstrate that you care enough about someone to remember important things in that person's life.

In chapter 9, you'll learn about the process that EnPro Industries uses to begin each meeting. That process is designed to enable a calm-and-connect response, presence, and caring.

Caring

John Bogle is a legendary entrepreneur and founder of Vanguard Mutual Funds, which today has over $5 trillion of assets under management for over 30 million investors. Bogle and I crossed paths one time and his kindness and generosity of spirit was front and center. He built his organization on several rules and **Rule #1** according to his book *Enough: True Measures of Money, Business, and Life* was:

> **"Make Caring the Soul of the Organization—Caring is a mutual affair, involving: (1) Mutual respect from the highest to the humblest among us: Each of you deserves to be—and will be—treated with courtesy, candor, friendliness, and respect for the honorable work you perform and (2) Opportunities for career growth, participation and innovation."**[105]

Reflection Time

What does the word *caring* mean to you?

What does the "soul of the organization" mean to you?

If you felt that I cared about you, what would
I have done to make you feel that way?

A person who truly cared about you would
behave in what ways?

Name a person at work whom you believe cares about you.

Why do you believe he or she cares about you?

How does he or she evidence caring about
you? What does he or she do?

Now let's switch gears. Think about a person at work
whom you believe does not care about you.

Why do you feel that way? What behaviors make
you feel that he or she does not care about you?

Please reflect and write down your answers in
your Learning Journal before going on.

Now what did you learn? What behaviors that
enable caring do you want to adopt? What behaviors that inhibit caring do you need to stop doing?

What am I trying to do with this learning approach?

I am trying to make meaning with you even though
I can't see you or be with you physically.

I am trying to have conversations like we would have if we were together. Why? Because learning primarily comes from having conversations.

If you were to ask me those same reflection questions, here's how I would answer (I am *not* saying my answers are the right answer; I am only sharing).

I would feel that the person cares about me if the person:

- Tries to understand me as a unique human being in a nonjudgmental way and tries to understand what I'm saying and feeling by truly listening and asking questions or asking for clarification or paraphrasing back to me what I said to make sure she or he understands

- Shows he or she is fully present when we talk and makes eye contact with me and smiles at me a lot

- Is someone with whom I feel comfortable and relaxed

- Asks me how they can help me and offers advice when I request it

- Wants me to be happy and successful and helps me perform well

- Cares enough about me to disagree and challenge me in a positive way (he or she "has my back")

- Abides by the Golden Rule and is someone with whom I feel safe and comfortable being myself around—safe enough to share my hopes, fears, concerns, hurts, and insecurities

- Is someone with whom I can be transparent and authentic and who returns that authenticity and transparency by likewise being vulnerable

Collective Intelligence

Another key collaboration principle is collective intelligence. Some of the best work in the area of collective intelligence has been done at Carnegie Mellon University and at MIT. Here is a synthesis of the key research findings that I believe are relevant to the New Way of Working.

Collective intelligence is defined as a group's ability to perform well on a wide variety of different tasks, and it extends beyond the cognitive abilities of the group's members. Having a group of very skilled people is not enough. We've already discussed the need for a diverse group of people—people with different experiences, backgrounds, cultures, and thinking styles.

The research on collective intelligence suggests that diversity of gender is particularly crucial. In fact, research suggests that the greater proportion of women you have on a team the higher the group's collective intelligence.[106]

The reason is that collective intelligence is based on how people collaborate—how they relate to and behave with others.

Specifically, a group's level of collective intelligence is correlated with (1) the social sensitivity of team members, (2) conversational turn-taking, and (3) the proportion of women in the group.

Social sensitivity involves perception of social cues, reading others' emotions, and empathy. Research shows that on average women are more socially sensitive than men.

In team activities, men are found in general to be more autocratic and transactional and to exhibit socially dominant behaviors while women are found to be generally more interpersonal and democratic and to smile more.[107]

Let's take a moment to reflect on the research that shows how men and women in general approach collaboration differently. If you, like me, are a man, what do you think it says about how we are at collaborating?

I believe it says we are SUBOPTIMAL!

I believe it means that we need to learn to change our behavior.

WHY *CARING, TRUSTING* TEAMS?

Based on your reflections and doing the above exercises, why do you think the New Way of Working needed for Hyper-Learning requires Caring, Trusting Teams?

I find it very interesting that according to Carl Rogers, one of the founders of humanistic psychology, effective counseling requires the same type of environment that I submit is needed for excellent collaboration in the workplace. Rogers said that to have an effective, growth-producing counseling relationship, the following was necessary:

■ Transparent honesty between the parties

■ Genuine caring for the client

■ Empathetic understanding of the client

■ Mindful presence and listening

■ Mutual trust[108]

Reflection Time

Why would the same type of caring and trust that Rogers said was needed for an effective counseling environment be needed in a collaborative work environment? Please write your answer in your Learning Journal.

Did you consider that in both environments:

• Dealing with reality is important?

• Trust is necessary for people to improve?

• Trust is necessary for people to be open to constructive feedback?

- Trust negates fear?

- Trust enables psychological safety?

- Trust is created by caring about a person as a unique human being?

- Caring is evidenced by truly listening to the other person?

Please allow me to give my answer to the question I just asked you:

"Collaboration means different things to different people, just like one's concept of a team is heavily influenced by one's experience. Not every team experience is a good one, and in my experience many teams fall way short of being excellent. Well, the digital age increasingly will demand higher standards because the quality of collaboration and the effectiveness of teams will make the difference between mediocrity and excellence. And that comes down to how people engage with and emotionally connect to each other—how they relate. The quality of conversations is going to be key. That is why in the next chapter I stress the need for High-Quality, Making-Meaning Conversations, not just regular conversations. High-Quality, Making-Meaning Conversations require caring and trust among team members."

Everybody I meet tells me they are good collaborators. I am beginning to believe that just showing up at a meeting that goes okay is good enough for many people.

Unfortunately, that kind of collaboration will not be enough as the digital age advances and the New Way of Working requires environments characterized by an idea meritocracy and lots of innovation and exploration into doing business differently. As you'll learn in the next chapter, those conversations require people to challenge others' thinking or engage in emergent thinking, which requires people to trust the spontaneous and imaginative processing of their subconscious minds and put forth "wild" ideas. For the reasons I've outlined, those activities require a high level of participation from Caring, Trusting Teams.

Caring, Trusting Teams are built upon emotionally positive human connections.

Historically in the business world, logic, linearity, and operational excellence have been the dominant themes.

Bringing your Best Self to work (Inner Peace) and building work relationships based on emotionally positive connections with others and syncing up with others biochemically will be quite a change, but it will be a change for the better—it will humanize the workplace and allow people to become much more than breathing robots.

WORKSHOP: BUILDING THE TOWER OF CARE AND TRUST

You know by now that I am big on behaviors. In this chapter, you've learned about the power of Caring, Trusting Teams in the workplace, and the underlying importance of genuine human connections to building mutual care and trust. Please reflect on the following Tower of Care and Trust, which presents the building blocks of care and trust starting from the bottom of figure 1.

What does this Tower of Care and Trust say to you? Reflect and please write down your answer in your Learning Journal.

What would you do to begin building the Tower of Care and Trust with a colleague?

Figure 1: Tower of Care and Trust

Here is what the Tower of Care and Trust says to me:

"Building trust and care takes time, and I earn that by how I behave. It all starts with connecting to someone through eye contact, smiles, and exuding positive emotions and positive body language followed by exploratory talk.

"Once I've made a connection, I have to try to relate to that person in a manner that opens up the conversation. I might ask, 'How is your day going?' If I'd engaged in small talk with the person before, I might further ask about the person's family and say, 'I hope they are doing well.' If the person seemed rushed or busy, I might make the conversation short but leave the person with a positive thought, such as 'I hope you have a great day!' or 'We should do coffee or lunch soon,' and then follow up later that day to schedule coffee or lunch.

"To make a genuine connection, eventually one of us will have to take a big step and be totally vulnerable with the other. The highest-ranking of us has to be vulnerable first. Being vulnerable sends a message that I trust the other person enough to share something I wouldn't share with everyone. An example of vulnerability would be asking the other person for help or advice with a difficulty.

"With vulnerability comes more emotional engagement. That engagement can't be judgmental or hierarchal. It has to be human-to-human, and each of us must exhibit positive regard for the other through our behavior and words. The next stage is feeling safe with each other, and at some point, we have to ask each other, 'Do you feel psychologically safe with me?' If one says, 'No,' then the other has to ask, 'What can I do to help you feel safe with me?' When each of us feels safe, we are in trust mode and we can continue to build trust with every interaction. If after building trust, I do something that makes the other person start to question that trust, I have to invest in earning it back. Not surprisingly, rebuilding trust takes a lot of effort and time. Trust is hard to earn and easy to lose."

Okay, let's move on. I hope this exercise helped you think about how to build trust.

Reflection Time

What is the best team you have ever been a member of?

What made that team the best?

What team and individual behaviors contributed to it being the best?

How did that team differ from other teams?

How did it feel being part of that team?

What takeaways do you have about how to enable greatness in a team?

Please make some notes in your Learning Journal. You will need this information in a few minutes.

Now, what is the worst team you've ever served on?

What made that team the worst?

What team and individual behaviors contributed to it being the worst?

How did that team differ from other teams?

How did it feel being part of that team?

What takeaways do you have about how not to be like that team?

Please make some notes in your Learning Journal.

WORKSHOP: YOUR PERSONAL CARING, TRUSTING TEAM BEHAVIORS CHECKLIST

Let's assume you want to be a more caring team member and you want to behave in ways that make it more likely that team members will trust you. What are seven **behaviors** you could engage in more frequently to make other team members more likely to perceive you as a trustworthy person who cares about them individually?

Sometimes people find it easier to first identify behaviors that would evidence not caring about the other person and then invert those behaviors.

I suggest you take some time with this. Consider doing a couple of drafts over the next week in your Learning Journal and then creating a checklist on your phone that you can review *before* each team meeting and use to grade yourself *after* each team meeting.

My hypothesis is that if you choose relevant behaviors and start engaging in them more frequently, your interaction with your team members will become more meaningful and fruitful. And you may make a few new friends.

WORKSHOP: TEAM RULES FOR COLLABORATIVE ENGAGEMENT

Make believe that you have been asked as a member of a team to list the **seven most important Team Rules for Collaborative Engagement** considering the learnings of this chapter. How will your team members strive to behave in your meeting?

Write down your list in your Learning Journal. (For assistance with this exercise, consider reviewing the Hyper-Learning Behaviors in chapter 3 because rules of engagement are all about behaviors.)

～

I hope you found this chapter meaningful and helpful. One key learning for me has been that I need to SLOW DOWN to be more *caring* and take the time to build more *trust*. This requires spending time at the beginning of every meeting allowing people to connect, being more fully present, and cultivating positivity toward the meeting and the people participating. Once people buy in to the story in these chapters and create their Team Rules for Collaborative Engagement, it does not take a lot of time to reach the desired starting environment.

It does take time to build that capability.

Having High-Quality, Making-Meaning Conversations

Let's set the stage for this very important chapter. This chapter is the ultimate. It's what we have been working toward since the prologue, and it assumes a number of things:

- That you've made the decision to stay relevant in the digital age by becoming a Hyper-Learner and adopting a New Way of Being (your Best Self)

- That you understand that to become your Best Self in order to Hyper-Learn you must develop Inner Peace, adopt a Hyper-Learning Mindset, and embrace Hyper-Learning Behaviors, and that you've completed the relevant workshops (i.e., you've created your Daily Intentions, identified the principles of your Hyper-Learning Mindset, and determined the Hyper-Learning Behaviors you need to add or improve)

- That you understand the importance of Caring, Trusting Teams and the New Way of Working necessary for Hyper-Learning; you have begun the process of behaving in ways that embody a New Way of Being and a New Way of Working; and you have created your personal Caring, Trusting Team Behaviors Checklist and your Team Rules for Collaborative Engagement.

This chapter is about having High-Quality, Making-Meaning Conversations—a special kind of conversation that, as you will learn in this chapter, facilitates Hyper-Learning by making possible "wow" thinking, emergent thinking, sense-making, and collective flow.

To enable such a conversation requires people to leave their egos and fears at the door, tolerate uncertainty, and not only trust others but trust themselves—more liberated, peaceful versions of themselves that are more receptive to and comfortable with exploring novelty, differences, and even the unknown.

It is a self that can overcome the ingrained human tendencies toward seeking confirmation of past learning, maintaining cohesiveness of one's mental models, and reflexively defending one's views.

Reflection Time

What is a conversation? How do you define it?

Please write down your definition of a
conversation in your Learning Journal.

THE COMMON PURPOSE OF CONVERSATIONS

I believe there is a fundamental, common purpose to having conversations. We human beings evolved and became the dominant species (so far as we know) because we became social animals. We learned to cooperate and work together to survive by hunting and gathering food safely.

It is through conversations that we continue to meet our innate needs for social connection and belonging to a group or team.

We all want to be heard and understood by others.

Being heard and understood by others is how our uniqueness—our humanity—is validated.

Being heard and understood by others is how we validate what we believe.

Being heard and understood by others is how we build trust with others.

Being heard and understood by others is how we learn.

Being heard and understood by others makes us feel good, liked, approved of, and part of something bigger than ourselves.

So how can you be heard and understood by others? You have conversations.

Now it gets more complex. I engage with you to be heard and understood. And you choose to either engage with me or not. If you do engage with me, in most cases you'll want to be heard and understood, too. That special kind of nonsuperficial, mutual conversation is what I call a **High-Quality, Making-Meaning Conversation**.

A High-Quality, Making-Meaning Conversation is a mutual conversation where each person is striving to be understood by the other *and* where each person is striving to understand the other.

A High-Quality, Making-Meaning Conversation is not two people having their own monologues. It is not a debate. It is not a contrived conversation designed to get a preordained result. It is not a going-through-the-motions conversation, nor is it a conversation where the answer or the result is always a compromise or the meeting of others halfway. It is not a conversation to determine a winner. It is not a competition. It is a conversation that ends in mutual understanding.

An example of a High-Quality, Making-Meaning Conversation in the workplace might be a respectful, discovery-type conversation in the pursuit of critical thinking that unpacks underlying beliefs, assumptions, facts, lack of facts, and differences, all in the spirit of an idea meritocracy.

Another example might be an exploratory conversation in the pursuit of creativity, imagination, innovation, sense-making, or emergent thinking, or it might be a conversation involving a progress update, feedback, or mentoring. It might be a conversation involving a project or it might be a conversation for purposes of building a caring, trusting relationship.

What is common regardless of the type or purpose of the High-Quality, Making-Meaning Conversation is that the participants seek to be understood and to understand each other in a caring, trusting, noncompetitive manner that is respectful of everyone's human dignity, and that they accept that according to the science of adult learning, they are suboptimal thinkers who need the help of others to think at their highest levels.

I believe we can learn a lot about how to have High-Quality, Making-Meaning Conversations from early Native American leadership practices I've studied. Typically, early Native Americans would meet by sitting in a circle, usually around a fire. They **took turns stating their beliefs or positions without interruption**, and no questions were allowed until everyone in the circle had stated their positions with the chief speaking last. Only after a lot of conversation—talking and talking until they really talked—were they ready to make meaning together. After that, the chief announced the course of action or decision, after which some historians have said, he would look over his shoulder at his wife to see if she nodded approval of his declaration.

WORKSHOP: PRECONDITIONS FOR HIGH-QUALITY, MAKING-MEANING CONVERSATIONS

I've approached this chapter as trying to have a High-Quality, Making-Meaning Conversation with you about what it is like to have a High-Quality, Making-Meaning Conversation. The purpose is to help you excel at creating and participating in more of this type of conversation.

With that in mind, in your Learning Journal please create a list of pre-conditions you believe are necessary for two people to have a High-Quality, Making-Meaning Conversation. In other words, what factors enable a High Quality, Making-Meaning Conversation?

This will take you some time to think about. You are creating a list of *preconditions.*

Consider how the content in earlier chapters might influence your answer.

Recall that chapters 1 through 3 described the building blocks of the New Way of Being necessary for Hyper-Learning (Inner Peace and a Hyper-Learning Mindset and Behaviors). How do those building blocks affect how you engage in conversations with others?

Chapter 6 described the New Way of Working, and chapter 7 described Caring, Trusting Teams. How do they relate to having High-Quality, Making-Meaning Conversations?

Please take a break here. You have a lot to think about.

Have a High-Quality, Making-Meaning Conversation with yourself about how all of the content fits together keeping in mind that it ultimately comes down to how you behave.

Then please write out your answer.

∼

Here are my thoughts regarding the above *preconditions* exercise. (Please read this only **after** you have done the previous workshop. That is the best way to learn.)

"I've imagined you've invited me to have a High-Quality, Making-Meaning Conversation as part of a new small team. I know I need to bring my Best Self to the meeting. I need to come to the meeting with Inner Peace because that will enable me to behave in ways conducive to learning and exploration. So, my goal would be to walk in with a Quiet Ego, a Quiet Mind, a Quiet Body, and a Positive Emotional State.

"I hope that you as team leader would engage the new team in creating a common purpose and agreeing upon common values in order to begin to understand each other as people. I hope you would explain to the group that this is the beginning of building a Caring, Trusting Team, which is our desired result.

"I hope that you would also engage us in creating our rules of engagement for behaving with each other and that you would engage us in confirming that our team embraces an idea meritocracy and seeks to have a psychologically safe environment, including having permission to speak freely with respect for each team member's human dignity. I hope that we would agree that one of our team's values is 'do no harm' and that we would talk about how to mitigate the two big learning inhibitors, ego and fear.

"I would suggest that the team also agree to embrace the concept of impermanence—that everything is always changing and that what we think we know may no longer be true."

What did I miss in my answer?
What did I have that you did not have?
Do any of the differences warrant additions to your answer?
Oh, my goodness, I did miss something. I missed discussing how we as team members connect emotionally and begin to demonstrate that we care about each other, which begins the trust-building process that we discussed in the previous chapter.

Yes, High-Quality, Making-Meaning Conversations require caring about and trusting each other.

WORKSHOP: HIGH-QUALITY, MAKING-MEANING CONVERSATIONS IN THE WORKPLACE

When would High-Quality, Making-Meaning Conversations be important in the workplace?

Please reflect and write down your answers in your Learning Journal.

What do you think?

Are they necessary to build authentic relationships and Caring, Trusting Teams?

Are they necessary for decision-making in an environment that supports an idea meritocracy?

Are they necessary when discovery, insight, creativity, innovation, and imagination are required?

Are they necessary for giving feedback to people?

Are they necessary when receiving feedback?

Are they necessary when you are being asked to do a task or undertake a project?

Maybe it would be easier to list when conversations involving making meaning are *not* necessary. What do you think?

∼

I have learned over the years that people tend to believe that everyone else defines or interprets words and phrases the same as they do.

I have also learned, through High Quality, Making-Meaning Conversations, that the world I have constructed in my mind and my beliefs, definitions, and stories of how the world works are likely to be materially different in many ways than yours. The truth is that each of our mental models and even our definitions of certain words and concepts are highly influenced by both nature and nurture.

In his book *The Secret of Our Success*, Joseph Henrich explains it this way: "**Underlying these failures is the assumption that we, as humans, all perceive the world similarly, want the same things, pursue those things based on our beliefs (the 'facts' about the world), and process new information and experience in the same way. We already know all these assumptions are wrong.**"[109]

That is a powerful statement. The same word can mean different things to different people. My view of how the world operates is only my view. It is not your view. I need to understand your view and you need to understand my view in order for us to have a High-Quality, Making-Meaning Conversation.

ENABLERS OF HIGH-QUALITY, MAKING-MEANING CONVERSATIONS

Human Dignity and Respect

High-Quality, Making-Meaning Conversations can be hard. They require all parties to respect each other and uphold each other's dignity. What I have learned over the decades is that it's hard for people to let go of their beliefs and adopt new beliefs that are better supported by data and experience. It is hard for people to admit when they are wrong or made a mistake. And I have learned that everyone is fearful of not being liked, not being respected, and in today's world, losing their jobs. The only differences are the degrees to which people are fearful and how people manage their fears. Recognizing these universal truths goes a long way in making meaning with others.

Another aspect of respecting others is recognizing that people do vary quite a lot in what they find emotionally hurtful. Some people are very sensitive to the slightest perceived insult even if it is unintentional. It's better to err on the side of respecting the dignity of each person. It doesn't matter that you do not think your words or behavior are hurtful. Never critique the person; critique the idea and do so in a manner that increases the probability that the other person actually hears you. If you have a different view, ask questions first to make sure you understand the other person's viewpoint. Then say something positive—start out with what you agree with. Then offer your differing views in a calm, nonpersonal manner setting forth your data.

Respect for others is mission critical. In his book *Dialogue*, William Isaacs defines respect this way: **"Respect is, in this sense, looking for what is highest and best in a person and treating them as a mystery that you can never fully comprehend."**[110]

Reflection Time

Let's reflect upon Isaacs's statement. What does it mean to you that I am a "mystery that you can never fully comprehend"?

If you believed that, how would that affect your behavior toward me?

How would you react when I say something about you that is not really you?

Would you be defensive? Angry at me? More understanding of my ignorance?

May I share? I will forever remember this conversation. My wife is a special person. She is very smart. She has an ABD in microbiology, a law degree, and a PhD in health policy, and she studied developmental psychology as a graduate student. This particular discussion turned into a debate, and although it's rare, I was winning this one. (But who's counting? Unfortunately, I was.) I emphasized how wrong she was and kept trying to get her to admit it. Finally, she looked at me with pleading eyes and said, "Give me a break. I am just a small-town girl from Iowa trying to do good." I had overstepped. I had not respected her personal boundaries. That was and is wrong. I was floored and felt awful and hugged her and asked for forgiveness.

There is a mutuality of human dignity and respect that must be observed in seeking understanding. In a true High-Quality, Making-Meaning Conversation we are asking each other to be vulnerable, to share our innermost thoughts, and if appropriate, to reach down into ourselves and allow our imagination and creativity to emerge.

Making meaning is not a competitive or judgmental process. It is a discovery and an exploratory learning process. Understanding each other's views or positions and the foundation beneath them is a precondition to evaluating what each person thinks or believes (if that is even appropriate in context). You can't truly evaluate or critique others' views until you truly understand what they are saying and what they believe and feel.

I remember advice on leadership that I received from a mentor. He said, "Ed, always leave everyone in a good place emotionally. Do no harm. Be very sensitive to how people are receiving your message."

At the end of every meeting I convene I have found it very helpful to ask the attendees, "Is everyone in a good place? Is there anyone not in a good place?" And if necessary, we discuss what we can do to get everyone in a good place.

Asking Questions

The best High-Quality, Making-Meaning Conversations happen when people ask questions and when they *reflectively listen*.

Some of the best work on asking questions has been done by Emeritus Professor Edgar Schein of MIT. In his book *Humble Inquiry*, Schein says, "We must become better at asking and do less telling in a culture that overvalues telling."[111] Telling is not asking. Telling sends the message that I know more than you. Telling is a power play. Telling has no place in High-Quality, Making-Meaning Conversations.

You may be asking yourself, how do I explain my positions if I can't "tell" people? Good question. There is a difference between telling and *sharing*. There are differences in tone, word usage, overall approach, and in many cases, emotions. Sharing is devoid of ego and certainty of knowing. Sharing is not competitive. Sharing is not an attempt to dominate. Sharing is not winning or losing.

When you share, you should make explicit that you are sharing and not expressing certainty. When you disagree with someone, you should first explain the points on which you agree. Then you can share your questions, concerns, or disagreements. Sharing the positive first helps tamp down defensiveness.

When you share, it helps to explicitly state that you may be wrong, but here is what you believe. This takes us back to chapter 2 and the NewSmart principles: I am not my ideas, my mental models are not reality, and I will treat my thoughts and beliefs (not values) as hypotheses to be constantly tested and modified upon discovering they are not correct.

I have found it is helpful when I disagree or have concerns to say, "Here is my hypothesis," not "Here is what I believe."

So, questioning is required in High-Quality, Making-Meaning Conversations and *how* you ask the questions is important.

Asking Additional Questions

I have learned that asking **"What do you mean?"** is one of the most important learning and understanding tools that exists.

Other useful questions or statements depending on the purpose of the work conversation are:

- I do not understand "X." Can you please say that a different way or help me understand what you mean with some examples?

- The three Ws: Why? What if? Why not?

- What are our differences?

- What are we missing?

- What assumptions are we making? Have we unpacked them to see what underlies them?

- Have we looked for disconfirming information?

- If we did this, for what reasons might it not work?

- What must be true for this idea or answer to be a good one?

- How can we reframe this discussion or problem?

- "Yes, *and*" as opposed to "Yes, *but*"

- What do you think? Why do you think that?

- What are you feeling?

- Is everybody okay?

- Anyone have a different way of looking at this?

- Are there variances, surprises, or outliers in the data? What could they mean?

- How could we build upon this idea?

- How could we connect these different views?

- Who might have had this challenge or problem already? Have we looked there for learnings?

- Have we visualized the outcome if we do this?

- How do we test this out without taking big risks?

- Do we have enough credible data?

- How can we minimize the big downsides to zero?

Reflection Time

What questions would you add to that list?

High-Quality, Making-Meaning Conversations are often exploratory, discovery conversations. They can lead to redefining or reframing the issue, exposing the elephant in the room that people have tried to avoid, or coming up with a completely different approach. They are a crucial part of evaluating, decision-making, project planning, and designing experiments.

As the digital age advances, our assumptions and past learnings will become less and less viable, and we will have to overcome our confirmation and cohesiveness biases and accept that our external environment and other people are constantly changing and are often not what we initially perceived them to be. That means making-meaning will become an even more necessary skill and process.

Reflective Listening

Carl Rogers provided some important advice when he said, "I have found it of enormous value when I can permit myself to understand another person. . . . Our first reaction to most of the statements which we hear from other people is an immediate evaluation, or judgment, rather than an understanding of it."[112]

Let's pause to review human thinking and *being* tendencies:

- **We all are wired to be speedy thinkers who seek confirmation, affirmation, cohesiveness, and homeostasis.**

- **Our egos often are tied up with what we think we know and that leads to defensiveness, denial, and deflection in the face of contradictory information.**

■ We listen to confirm, not to learn.

■ We often approach collaboration as a competition, not as a way to learn.

■ We are poor listeners because we tend to let our minds wander or begin making up our response while the other person is still talking. We tend to interrupt people before they have finished sharing their views.

■ We are, in a sense, prisoners of our past experiences, and we can be cognitively blind.

All of those proclivities can inhibit High-Quality, Making-Meaning Conversations and are why a key behavior most of us need to practice and get better at in order to make meaning with others is *reflective listening.*

William Isaacs said:

"To listen is to develop an inner silence."[113]

I love that sentence. That should be of no surprise. Correct?
    What does "inner silence" mean to you?
    Are you in a state of inner silence when you listen?
    If you are in a state of inner silence, what are you *not* doing?

Reflection Time

Please think about *how* you listen. What goes
on in your mind?

In your Learning Journal, please make a list of
all the things your mind likes to do.

৵

If you are like most people, your mind likes to wander. It likes to judge and critique in real time what is being stated. It likes to create your rebuttal or response while the other person is still talking. It likes to multitask with your devices.

Now, be honest, how can you truly understand what other people are saying if you do those things while they are talking?

Would William Isaacs say you had inner silence?

Oh, I get it. You figure out quickly what the other person means and is saying and then your mind becomes a chatterbox.

How do you figure it out so quickly?

Oh, my goodness. Are you making the same assumption that Joseph Henrich described above? I paste it here for your review:

"Underlying these failures is the assumption that we, as humans, all perceive the world similarly, want the same things, pursue those things based on our beliefs (the 'facts' about the world), and process new information and experience in the same way. We already know all these assumptions are wrong."

Reflective listening resonates with me strongly. Why?

Because I used to be an awful, pathetic listener. I did everything wrong. I would make up my answers while another person was talking, and when I felt I had enough information to assert my position, I would interrupt him or her to "tell" my thoughts. That was my usual way of listening at work and at home. It is embarrassing to admit it, but it is true. I was a speedy (and lucky) guesser of other people's meaning most of the time. But I was a crappy listener, and I showed no respect for people. I was not a reflective listener. I was an assertive arrogant interrupter.

To be a reflective listener, you need a Quiet Ego, a Quiet Mind, a Quiet Body, and a Positive Emotional State. Reflective listening requires emotionally connecting with the speaker in ways we discussed in the last chapter on Caring, Trusting Teams.

Below is a list of other key enablers and corresponding inhibitors of High-Quality, Making-Meaning Conversations.

In connection with this list, I invite you to review your work product from chapter 3—the list of behaviors and observable sub-behaviors that you determined would evidence the desired main behavior and the observable sub-behaviors that you determined would evidence the lack of the desired main behavior.

Enablers	Inhibitors
Quiet Ego	Self-focus or arrogance
Quiet Mind	"Talky" mind
Quiet Body	Stressed body
Being fully present	Mind-wandering or multitasking
Open mind	Closed mind
Reflective listening	Judgmental listening
Respect and exploration of differences	Avoidance of differences
Courage	Fear
Authenticity	Disingenuousness
Pausing to reflect	Being reflexive
"Yes, *and*"	"Yes, *but*"
Curiosity	Indifference
Caring	Not caring
Trust	Lack of trust
Not rushing to judgment	Rushing to judgment
Empathy	Self-absorption

Enablers	Inhibitors
■ **Being good at *not* knowing**	■ **Being bad at *not* knowing**
■ **Exploration**	■ **Rigidity**
■ **Asking questions**	■ **Telling**
■ **Seeking understanding**	■ **Seeking confirmation**
■ **Collaboration**	■ **Competition**

THE ULTIMATE GOAL (THE "MAGIC")

The pinnacle of High-Quality, Making-Meaning Conversations—our ultimate goal—is attaining the highest levels of Hyper-Learning (which are cognitive, social, and emotional). You've learned that in the new digital age workplace, Hyper-Learning is a team activity, because for humans to think in ways that technology can't, they need to work together. That is why we spent two chapters focused on teams. So, let's assume we are all members of a small team. How will we know if we're excelling at Hyper-Learning?

Collective Flow

Have you ever been so engrossed in a project or activity, so consumed by the enjoyable challenge of it, that you lost sense of the passage of time? Did you feel like you and the activity had become one—that you *were* the activity? Some people call this being in the zone or being in the groove. Psychologists call it a state of *flow* and have found that it's associated with positive emotions and peak performance.

Visualize a time when you were in a state of flow. Were you at work or engaged in sports or doing a hobby?

What did it feel like? How would you describe it?

Were you all-in and oblivious to anything else?

Did you lose a sense of time?

Was it joyous? Was it exhilarating?

How would you rate your performance?

Would you like to have many more of those experiences?

Now think about recent teams you've been a member of. Did any of those team experiences reflect a state of flow? By that I mean was there a time when every team member experienced being in the zone during a team activity?

When team members experience a joint, interdependent state of flow together, that is what I mean by collective flow. I argue that when teams experience collective flow, they are performing at their best and are primed for Hyper-Learning.

Now let's try to figure out the factors that may make collective flow more likely.

What do you think are the foundational prerequisites? Or under what circumstances does a team have the possibility of achieving a state of collective flow?

Reflection Time

What must happen for you, me, Tom, Jane, and Susan (our hypothetical five-member team) to reach a state of collective flow? **Please make up your list of collective flow factors or prerequisites and write them down in your Learning Journal before moving on.**

Now some questions for your consideration:

Do each of us need to come to the meeting in a state of Inner Peace as defined in chapter 1?

Do we need to be a Caring, Trusting Team as defined in chapter 7?

Do we each need to have improved key Hyper-Learning Behaviors, especially reflective listening?

Do we need to have agreed upon and committed
to team rules of engagement?

Do we need to have agreed upon common values
and a common purpose for the meeting?

Do we each need to have established positive
emotional connections with each other like
we talked about in chapter 7?

Do we need to have agreed that each person has
permission to speak freely and that we are going to be
an idea meritocracy with psychological safety?

My experience is that a state of collective flow can occur only after a team has worked together for a length of time and has the following characteristics:

- Caring, trusting relationships among members

- Team members who behave in ways evidencing their journeys to Inner Peace

- The ability to make meaning together in ways discussed in this chapter

- Team commitment to rules of engagement

- Team commitment to an idea meritocracy and psychological safety

- Team behaviors that cultivate courage, curiosity, transparency, authenticity, mutual respect, and High-Quality, Making-Meaning Conversations

Can a team consistently achieve a state of collective flow? My personal experience is yes.

Why have I introduced you to collective flow? Because it is an attainable aspiration, and when a team is in a state of collective flow and has in effect become one, it has the possibility of engaging in another goal of High-Quality, Making-Meaning Conversations: emergent thinking.

I believe that collective flow is the gateway to the highest levels of creative and innovative thinking, emotional engagement, and higher-order critical thinking.

Collective flow is how the "magic" of you is optimized and shared with the world.

Emergent Thinking

I have been fascinated by emergent thinking for quite some time.

My first exposure to emergent thinking was reading a 1999 interview with W. Brian Arthur. Professor Arthur is a luminary—an economist who started the Economic Complexity Theory Group at the Santa Fe Institute.

Emergent thinking has roots in Eastern philosophy in that it requires a mindset of impermanence—a fundamental understanding that everything is changing all the time and that to perceive those changes we have to be fully invested in observing the world without preconceived notions or judgments. We need to just *be*—observing, sensing, or listening intensely to what is going on to absorb it and let it enter our minds and bodies with no conscious action on our parts. We need to soak in the world and appreciate what is *emerging* in a world that is constantly changing. That is what we are trying to sense and tap into by just observing.

Emergent thinking requires heightened awareness of and attention on the outside world as if we ourselves do not exist. And it requires empathetically observing of others. In my opinion, it is like being in a state of flow with what you are observing. Emergent thinking is looking for the unfolding of emerging patterns.

Step one of being able to perceive the world this way is a state of Inner Peace.

In Arthur's words: **"You're acting out of an inner feel, making sense as you go. You're not even thinking. You're at one with the situation. . . . You act from your inner self."**[114]

Step two is pausing and not immediately starting to think about what you have just perceived. Let it alone. Let it be. If you let it incubate in your body, something will emerge without you having to do anything consciously. Thoughts will pop into your mind. **Immersion *by* you sets up emergence *from* you.**

Step three is to take some kind of proactive action to test your idea.

Last year, I was in a meeting with two of the guest storytellers in this book—Marvin and Susan—and another senior leader of EnPro. The three of us have a history of being able to achieve collective flow. And in this particular meeting, something emerged out of me, and I immediately said, "I have no idea where that came from." It was not anything that I had thought of before. It emerged after a period of deeply listening to them with inner silence. And it led us to an entirely unplanned conversation that was helpful regarding something they were discussing. It was magical—it just emerged.

Emergent thinking is the focus of an institute at MIT called the Presencing Institute, which was co-founded by Otto Scharmer, a senior lecturer at the MIT Sloan School of Management, and influenced by Brian Arthur's work.

WORKSHOP: HYPER-LEARNING TEAMS

Imagine that you have been asked to join an important new work team charged with recommending a process to empower every employee to be an innovator. The team is cross-functional, made up of people with diverse backgrounds who have not worked together before. There are five team members—three men and two women of varying tenure at the company. All are very experienced high performers. The company has been more of a traditional operational excellence company with a traditional leadership model driven by hierarchy.

You have been chosen to be the team leader. You are going to hold a one-day introductory meeting with your team off-site. Your goal is to spend the day making meaning together.

Based on what you have learned, please design your approach to the day.

Where would you start?

How will you progress?

How will you engage the people to optimize their learning?

What would you like to accomplish by the end of the day?

This workshop is an invitation to make meaning of this chapter and the previous chapter on Caring, Trusting Teams, incorporating your learnings from the book so far.

Have fun!

CHAPTER 9

EnPro Industries: Enabling the Full Release of Human Possibility

This chapter is a deep dive into how an organization can transform itself into a much more humanistic people-centric organization. That transformation requires the leaders to transform themselves by modeling the new desired mindsets and behaviors and creating and using daily practices designed to enable those behaviors. Then it requires scaling those mindsets, behaviors, and practices throughout the organization.

The EnPro story is pretty amazing. EnPro is a global, engineering-based manufacturing company with both union and non-union employees. None of those factors inhibited its transformation. I am deeply grateful to EnPro's senior leaders for sharing their personal stories and the company's organizational story in this book.

ABOUT THE COMPANY

EnPro Industries is a public company headquartered in Charlotte, North Carolina, and the diversified manufacturer of proprietary, engineered products involving sealing technologies, bearings, reciprocating compressors, and diesel and dual-fuel engines.

It operates 30 primary manufacturing facilities in North and South America, Europe, and Asia; employs approximately 6,000 people worldwide; and sells its products to more than 50,000 customers in over 100 countries across the globe. The company's revenue is about $1.5 billion.

Among EnPro's subsidiaries are the Garlock Group, which is the number-one manufacturer of industrial gaskets in the United States; the Technetics Group, which is the number-one worldwide manufacturer of metal seals for nuclear applications and number-one worldwide for semiconductor PVD chamber solutions; and Stemco, which is the number-one U.S. manufacturer of wheel-end seals for heavy-duty trucks and trailers. EnPro's client list includes big companies such as Boeing, SpaceX, Shell, Volkswagen, John Deere, PACCAR, and Airbus.

The company was spun out of Goodrich Company in 2002 to isolate a potential asbestos liability. The liability was resolved in 2018.

In chapter 6, we discussed the need to humanize the workplace. As you continue reading this chapter, please think deeply about how EnPro is humanizing its workplace.

The following information on EnPro's values and cultural principles comes from the company's website under the Culture tab (https://www.enproindustries.com/culture).

These values and cultural principles are not standard in corporate life.

Please take your time and read them.

Does your organization have values and principles like these? Should it?

ENPRO'S VALUES

"Our Values

"**Safety:** Our most important obligation to each other and our families. We require all employees to pledge annually to uphold this as our top priority. We place a relentless focus on creating a safe and healthy work environment.

"**Excellence**: An expectation to continuously strive for world class performance in our individual behavior and business performance as measured against the highest standard we know or can imagine.

"**Respect:** This is the cornerstone of how we behave toward others and is built on the belief in the inherent good intentions and orientation toward growth in fellow human beings. We believe all people are fully worthy of growth and development."

Reflection Time

Did you notice the dual focus on excellence
in EnPro's stated values?

Does your organization have a dual focus on
excellence in terms of both business performance and individual behavior?

Please reread EnPro's value of **respect** again slowly.
Would you have defined respect like that?

Does EnPro's description of respect remind
you of Carol Dweck's *growth mindset*?

What does EnPro's value of respect mean in
your own words?

ENPRO'S CULTURAL PRINCIPLES

"Commitment to Our People

"People drive EnPro's success. Our colleagues—the most valuable part of EnPro—are empowered to develop themselves as they build capability into our businesses via creativity and initiative. We are committed to helping them develop. This commitment enables us to attract and retain a diverse workforce of top-tier talent, positioning us for continued growth.

"In a time of rapidly changing markets, where the pace of change is ever accelerating, EnPro chooses to aggressively respond by investing in human development—confident that these investments will produce the flourishing of our people and financial returns. We have invested in development workshops that have directly impacted more than 6,000 colleagues at all levels. These workshops involve learning through doing, which in turn spurs learning by experimenting, accelerating how quickly our people and teams gain knowledge."

"Dual Bottom Line

"Our purpose is to enable the full release of human possibility.

"As a Dual Bottom Line company, human development carries equal importance to financial performance.

"There is no trade-off between the two and we measure both. People who are focused on developing themselves pursue excellence, and when excellence is pursued, financial results are superior.

"Our human development philosophy is evident in our daily behavior and supported by an education system built on everyone teaching and learning from others. We recognize people learn and change from the inside of themselves on their terms, consistent with their beliefs."

Reflection Time

Please go back and reread each sentence of EnPro's
Dual Bottom Line cultural principle.

Please stop after each sentence and reflect
on what the words mean to you.

What does "enable the full release of human potential"
mean to you? How would you describe it in a sentence?

What does the second sentence of the **Dual Bottom
Line** cultural principle mean to you?

Have you worked for companies that stated something similar?

Was it true?

What does the last sentence mean to you? How does it
compare with the model of learning in this book?

Let's continue with EnPro's cultural principles:

"Working Your Way

"We believe the people closest to the job should have the most
input into how it is performed. Our employees have the freedom to define—and redefine—how and what they do. This
philosophy has led to success and the creation of long-term
gains.

"Diversity and Workforce Equality

"EnPro values diversity and is committed to providing equal
opportunity for all employees. Discrimination based on gen-

der, race, disability, ethnicity, nationality, religion, sexual orientation, protected veteran status, or gender identity will not be tolerated. At EnPro, we encourage mutual respect among all employees.

"We are committed to fair living wages for all employees, and our wages and benefits are competitive within our industry and local labor market. Our working hours contribute to a healthy work-life balance. The right to pursue your life's vision and purpose using EnPro's work as a vehicle applies equally to everyone.

"Continually Learning

"At EnPro, "learning & development" is not just another corporate catch phrase. Instead, it is an engrained element of our culture and a foundation on which we build our business and enlarge our capabilities. EnPro offers an educational assistance program, industry courses, a learning library, as well as many leadership development programs. It is our philosophy to hire and retain highly motivated employees and provide them with a vehicle that will enable them to continue to grow."

Reflection Time

Based on its values and cultural principles, if you had to describe EnPro as a company in five words or fewer how would you describe it? What is its "heart"?

Please reread "Working Your Way."

Which of the three psychological principles discussed in chapter 6 does "Working Your Way" help meet?

WORKSHOP: ENPRO CEO SPEECH

This exercise involves a speech that Marvin Riley recorded and shared with all EnPro employees in the summer of 2019, soon after EnPro's board of directors appointed him CEO.

Please take a moment and visualize yourself as an employee of En-Pro who's been asked to watch the recording with your team today. Visualize going into a conference room where there are coffee and soft drinks. You sit down and smile at your colleagues, and then Marvin Riley, the new CEO, comes on the screen and starts speaking. Visualize yourself leaning in to focus on the new CEO's talk because you are naturally concerned about how he may change the way things are done at the company.

> "Hello, I'm Marvin Riley, the new CEO of EnPro. I wanted to take a moment to speak directly to you, as I've been asked a number of questions about my vision and what changes I plan to make now that I'm CEO.
>
> Before I do that, I'd like to first start by saying thank you to Steve Macadam, who was our CEO for the past 11 years. I deeply care about Steve and will forever be grateful to Steve for what he has done for me.
>
> He's made me a better leader, a better father, and a better human being. Steve took on asbestos and won. Steve committed himself to building a culture and should declare victory, as he won there as well. This culture allowed me to flourish and release my full potential. The imprint that Steve has made on EnPro will last forever. Now let's talk directly about my vision, especially as it relates to the Dual Bottom Line.
>
> Someone asked me if I plan to keep the Dual Bottom Line culture. For a moment, I was a bit stunned. I found it to be a strange question. However, after some reflection, I realized that my understanding of the Dual Bottom Line is very different than the person who asked me the question. For me, the Dual Bottom Line lives in the heart and soul of the company and can never be removed. It's

my responsibility to spread the Dual Bottom Line way of working and to ensure everyone has a common understanding of what it means to enable the full release of human possibility.

Steve and I believe that each human being comes into this world with a perfect soul, fully worthy of dignity and greatness, bearing their own unique set of aptitudes and capabilities forged to pursue a certain destiny. The pursuit of that destiny is uniquely a lifelong journey for each individual, and I'm committed to providing an environment that enables this to unfold for everyone.

You know, I'd like to tell you a story about [employee name omitted] who is currently leading the continuous improvement effort at GPT. She joined GGB almost 10 years ago when she was 21 years old and quite inexperienced. She was working at GGB during the day and pursuing her bachelor's degree at night. The servant leaders at GGB cared so much about her that they even allowed her to study at work sometimes.

All she did was promise to do her best, and that she did. She then left GGB and came to the U.S. to pursue personal growth and a desire to improve her English. She left everything and everyone she knew on that mission. She became a production coordinator, then became a logistics manager, completed her supply chain and project management certification, and was recently promoted to projects and continuous improvement management.

I'm sharing this story with you because my vision is to ensure that [employee]'s story of hope, development, growth, and opportunity is accessible to everyone. Releasing possibility requires grit, determination, yet reflection and courage, but most of all, our support.

As I go about my day at EnPro, I'll be focused on creating psychological safety, supporting the self-determination needs of all employees, and creating value for our shareholders.

No one should ever come to work at EnPro and not feel safe to be exactly who they are. Diversity and inclusion are a buzzword in most companies, but here, it's your absolute right. Everyone must feel safe, every day.

Now let's talk about self-determination, because that means having autonomy, connection, and competence. I'll be working every day to ensure that everyone feels freedom to do their job, they feel cared for by their manager and their peers, and they also are getting support with the skills they need to be excellent at what they do.

This also means supporting everyone when they make mistakes. I view failure as the best opportunity to learn, and we should never waste a good mistake.

Now let's talk a little bit about value creation. At EnPro, we must play to win. We must strive for excellence in everything that we do. We must focus on our earnings and focus our cash flow, because every penny we spend at EnPro has been provided from our shareholders.

We have an obligation to spend that money as if it's our own. That notion can easily be forgotten, but this is a Dual Bottom Line culture. As I travel to your locations, I'll be in search of excellence. I want to see how you're serving the customer better today than you were serving them yesterday. I want to see excellence in sales, manufacturing, engineering, human resources strategy, basically everywhere.

I'll be in search of your best ideas. We must share our ideas and collaborate in order to win. The best idea must always win, regardless of title or hierarchy, even when it comes to me, because I love my ideas, but guess what? They're not always good ideas. You have permission to tell me when I'm sharing one of my classic bad ideas.

Okay, I want to do something else. I want to talk about our practices, because our practices shape EnPro.

Speaking in "I" statements, centering, journaling, letting go of the ego, sitting in a circle, giving and receiving feedback, that is who EnPro is. Winning is about getting better every day, playing to our strengths while working with rigor and discipline.

Every day I wake up wanting to express more empathy and more humility. I'm owning up to my mistakes. I'm admitting when I'm wrong. I'm working hard to not take myself too seriously.

I'm asking more questions rather than advocating my opinion, and I'm doing so because this is the next frontier of my own growth and development. Even though I'm the CEO of EnPro, it doesn't mean that I get to stop developing myself.

I'm looking forward to this journey with you, going to the edge with you. We learn at our edge, we grow at our edge, we must reshape EnPro from the edge. The edge always redefines the core. Thank you. Now, let's go win together.

Reflection Time

What was the first thing Marvin did?

What fundamental point that is emphasized in this book is Marvin validating or confirming?

What did he talk about next?

Why do you think he emphasized EnPro's **Dual Bottom Line** cultural principle upfront in his talk?

What does this paragraph mean to you?

"Steve and I believe that each human being comes into this world with a perfect soul, fully worthy of dignity and greatness, bearing their own unique set of aptitudes and capabilities forged to pursue a certain destiny. The pursuit of that destiny is uniquely a lifelong journey for each individual, and I'm committed to providing an environment that enables this to unfold for everyone."

Do you believe that about yourself? Is work how you pursue your journey of uniqueness?

What did Marvin say about psychological safety? If
you do not remember, please reread that part.

What did Marvin say about searching for the best ideas?
If you do not remember, please reread that part.

What did Marvin say about self-determination needs?
If you do not remember, please reread that part.

Toward the end, Marvin talks about his personal
development plan. What are the five things he
mentions he is personally working on?

Have you heard a very senior leader share
his personal development plan?

Why would a leader do that?

If your leader did that, what would you think?

Make believe that you and I sat next to each other in the
meeting listening to Marvin's talk and that after he was finished
I asked you, "What did you think?" How would you respond?

I suggest you take a break now and let the first part of the EnPro story
incubate in your mind and heart. Then come back to explore EnPro's behaviors and practices. Thank you for your engagement.

ENPRO'S BEHAVIORS

EnPro emphasizes and teaches employees six key company behaviors. En-
Pro introduces these behaviors through workshops led by senior leaders. The workshops include videos and short three- to nine-minute

exercises in which employees engage with other team members to make meaning of the behaviors and talk about how to behave.

Before introducing the behaviors, the company always begins with this slide (figure 2):

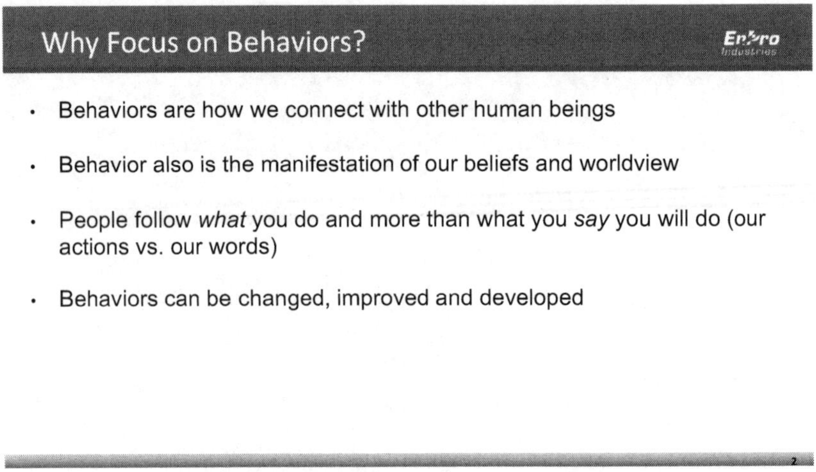

Why Focus on Behaviors?   *EnPro*
Industries

- Behaviors are how we connect with other human beings

- Behavior also is the manifestation of our beliefs and worldview

- People follow *what* you do and more than what you *say* you will do (our actions vs. our words)

- Behaviors can be changed, improved and developed

Figure 2: Why Focus on Behaviors?

Why does EnPro introduce its behaviors with this slide?

How would you answer the question posed: Why focus on behaviors?

What would you add to the answer EnPro gives on the slide?

Now here are the company's slides introducing five of the behaviors (figures 3–7). The sixth behavior, *collaboration*, is discussed later in a different format (figure 8). Notice the company's concise definitions of the behaviors and explanations for *why* each behavior is important and *how* each can be observed.

Review these behaviors with a critical mind—please make meaning of what the company is doing by trying on each idea to see how it feels to you. I am asking you to do more than just read.

Does the behavior connect with you? How would you amend the slides? This is a learning experience. EnPro has built a good system, but it is not perfect.

Evaluate "How It Can Be Observed" for each behavior. Make notes in your Learning Journal.

Open Minded

The ability to accept new information with the curiosity to examine things from all angles.

WHY	How It Can Be Observed
• Increased creativity & enhanced innovation – essential to learning	• Centers regularly
• Less swayed by singular events	• Listens to understand, doesn't fall victim to distractions
• Better connect, collaborate and understand others	• Recognizes own mental models
• Understand others better	• Ask questions before offering suggestions
• A requirement to accessing source	• Willing to try new things

Figure 3: Open Minded

How would you define being *open-minded*?

Please write it down.

What observable sub-behaviors would you add or amend?

Deeply Listen

A way of hearing in which we are fully present with what is happening in the moment without trying to control it or judge it.

WHY	How It Can Be Observed
• You will likely learn something new	• Takes in _all_ cues when receiving communications before reacting
• Increased empathy and deepen relationships	• Makes regular eye contact
• Increased self-awareness	• Able to read body language of others & reacts appropriately to it
• Improve communication with colleagues	• Asks questions to understand

Figure 4: Deeply Listen

How would you define what it means to *deeply listen*?

Please write it down.

What do you think of the company's list of observable sub-behaviors that would evidence deeply listening?

Can the list be improved? How?

Curious

 The impulse to seek new information and experiences, and to explore new possibilities.

WHY	How It Can Be Observed
• It's the engine that drives learning	• Asks open-ended questions & receives honest answers without judgment
• Change requires adaptation; adaptation requires learning	• Seeks out new information and regularly reads books
• A requirement in today's fast changing world	• Isn't afraid to ask questions

Figure 5: Curious

Manage Self - Mindful

The ability to pay attention, on purpose, in the present moment without judgement

WHY	How It Can Be Observed
• It's the gateway to development	• Meditates regularly
• Decreased stress & anxiety	• Pauses before responses on "hot topics"
• Empowers us to begin from our own intentions, thinking, & actions	• Understands the full impact of his/her actions including future consequences
• Integrates essential core 9 functions of the prefrontal cortex tending to well-being and better executive functioning of the brain	• Does not show defensiveness or blame others

Figure 6: Manage Self - Mindful

How would *you* define being *curious*? Please write it down.

What observable sub-behaviors would you add or amend?

How would *you* define what it means to *manage self* and be *mindful*? Please write it down.

What observable sub-behaviors would you add or amend?

Courageous

 Courage is the ability to do what frightens us despite the fear we feel in the moment.

WHY	How It Can Be Observed
• Provides opportunity to live your fully authentic life	• Can speak to and lives out his/her own values
• Creates sense of purpose	• Enjoys uncertainty, demonstrates vulnerability regularly
• Serve others better through more influence for positive impact	• Speaks up on the hard things
	• Others feel comfortable giving feedback (assessments) regularly to you

Figure 7: Courageous

How would you define being *courageous*? Please write it down.

What observable sub-behaviors would you add or amend?

COLLABORATION AT ENPRO

EnPro treats collaboration as (in my words) an overarching or higher-level behavior or process that requires utilization of the five other EnPro Behaviors to be effective. This multilevel approach to key behaviors, which is similar to WRBC's approach described in chapter 3, is evident in the company's Resource Guide: Collaborative (figure 8). After reviewing that document, ask yourself if EnPro's approach to collaboration would help you become a Hyper-Learner.

Resource Guide: Collaborative

What is Collaboration?

Collaboration is a process through which a group of people constructively explore their ideas to search for a solution that extends one's own limited vision.

Benefits of Collaboration

→ Encourages people to share knowledge and resources. We can use it to pool our negotiating power, to coordinate strategies, or to create new products

→ Creates opportunities for cross-skilling and networking, and can even improve employee engagement levels

→ Enables the organization to be more cost effective, innovative and competitive

Collaborate effectively by practicing the observable behaviors below

Open Minded	Deeply Listen
The ability to accept new information with the curiosity to examine things from all angles	A way of hearing in which we are fully present with what is happening in the moment without trying to control it or judge it
• Centers regularly • Listens to understand, doesn't fall victim to distractions • Recognizes own mental models • Ask questions before offering suggestions • Willing to try new things	• Takes in all cues when receiving communications before reacting • Makes regular eye contact • Able to read body language of others & reacts appropriately to it • Asks questions to understand

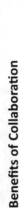
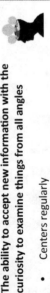

Curious	Manage Self (Mindful)
The impulse to seek new information and experiences, and to explore new possibilities 	The ability to pay attention, on purpose, in the present moment without judgement 
<ul><li>Asks open-ended questions & receives honest answers without judgment</li><li>Seeks out new information and regularly reads books</li><li>Isn't afraid to ask questions</li></ul>	<ul><li>Meditates regularly</li><li>Pauses before responses on "hot topics"</li><li>Understands the full impact of his/her actions including future consequences</li><li>Does not show defensiveness or blame others</li></ul>
Courageous	**Create Psychological Safety**
The ability to do what frightens us despite the fear we feel in the moment	The experience in a group of feeling free to speak up with ideas, questions or concerns - safe to take interpersonal risks 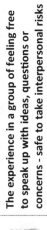
<ul><li>Can speak to and lives out his/her own values</li><li>Enjoys uncertainty, demonstrates vulnerability regularly</li><li>Speaks up on the hard things</li><li>Others feel comfortable giving feedback regularly to them</li></ul>	**Four Steps:**<ul><li>Step 1- Framing the Need for Voice</li><li>Step 2- Invite Participation by Situational Humility</li><li>Step 3- Demonstrate Curiosity and Practice Inquiry</li><li>Step 4- Respond Productively</li></ul>

Access to all recorded sessions, resource materials & are available now!

EnPro Online Learning Library
@https://cocreating.enproindustries.com

EnPro Learning

Figure 8: Resource Guide: Collaborative

ENPRO'S PRACTICES AND MEETING MANAGEMENT WORKSHEET

To support the company's desired behaviors and ways of working, EnPro has also created a list of 25 practices that every employee is encouraged to embrace on a daily basis. I have included a paraphrased version of the list in figure 9. In documentation shared with employees, the company further defines and elaborates on each practice, explaining:

1. What it (the practice) means

2. Teaching goals/process

3. Purpose/goal/expected outcomes

Another key EnPro document that facilitates the company's way of working is its Meeting Management Worksheet (figure 10), which EnPro employees use for every meeting, every day.

I hope you review these figures and documents carefully and take advantage of all there is to learn from how **EnPro is integrating the New Way of Being and New Way of Working necessary for Hyper-Learning into the company's daily way of working.**

In your Learning Journal I suggest that you write down your key takeaways from EnPro's example.

ENPRO'S PRACTICES

1. **Psychological safety:** Feeling free to take interpersonal risk and speak up.

2. **Community building:** Creating a safe place to be vulnerable and cultivate new behaviors.

3. **Sitting in a circle:** Being inclusive—no hierarchical leader position.

4. **Check-ins:** Inviting participants to share what's most present on their minds.

5. **"I" statements:** Sharing only from one's viewpoint with openness, authenticity, and vulnerability.

6. **Human-centered design:** Focusing on and empathizing with users to generate ideas and prototype.

7. **Prototyping:** Experimenting to iteratively learn.

8. **Deep listening/levels of listening:** Being fully present in the moment without controlling or judging.

9. **Open-mindedness:** Accepting new information with the curiosity to examine things from all angles.

10. **Mindfulness/self-management:** Seeking self-awareness, self-compassion, and self-acceptance.

11. **Courage:** Speaking up/taking action even when one is uncomfortable.

12. **Curiosity:** Seeking new information and experiences and exploring possibilities.

13. **Collaboration:** Thriving in environments where openness, trust, and curiosity are embraced.

Figure 9: EnPro's Practices

ENPRO'S PRACTICES

14. **Connecting with nature:** Spending time in nature to experience contentment, joy, and meaning.

15. **Gratitude:** Affirming the outside sources of goodness in one's life.

16. **Letting go:** Releasing all doubt, worry, and fear about a situation, person, or outcome.

17. **Meditation/sitting practice:** Scheduling regular time for meditation.

18. **Self-awareness:** Understanding and controlling one's emotions and actions.

19. **Solo reflection:** Reflecting on one's experiences and thoughts to learn about oneself.

20. **Journaling:** Keeping a record to explore the thoughts, feelings, and events in one's life.

21. **My voice:** Reflecting on how past experiences affect one's behavior today.

22. **Assessments:** Taking assessments to gain insight into how one thinks, feels, and acts.

23. **Pausing:** Taking time to thoughtfully consider and understand what one has heard before responding.

24. **Mood checks:** Checking in to determine the nature and sources of one's mood.

25. **I am not my idea/I have a possibility:** Separating the self/ego from the ideas one shares.

Figure 9 (cont)

ENPRO MEETING MANAGEMENT WORKSHEET

Meeting name, location, date: _____

Instructions:

In preparation for each meeting:

❑ Prepare and distribute agenda to include times, topics, objective, and owner/presenter

❑ Assign the following roles (meeting owner, "This is EnPro" guide, note taker, timekeeper)

❑ Review Active Listening Guidelines (end of document)

❑ Review Critical Thinking Questions (end of document)

❑ Review Post-Action Review (PAR) process and then complete at the end of the meeting

Meeting Purpose: _____

Meeting owner: _____

This is "EnPro" Guide: _____

Note Taker: _____

Timekeeper: _____

Complete Agenda:

Time	Topic	Objective	Owner/Presenter
	Centering	Encourage Mindfulness	
	Check-in	Initiate Connections	

PRE-MEETING PREPARATION
ACTIVE LISTENING GUIDELINES

❑ Prepare to listen:

   ❑ Center yourself

   ❑ Calm your emotions

Figure 10: EnPro Meeting Management Worksheet

ENPRO MEETING MANAGEMENT WORKSHEET

❑ Reminders:

    ❑ Listening is NOT about me

    ❑ Listen to learn

    ❑ I am NOT my idea

❑ Ask questions before you tell your opinion

❑ Place focus and concentration on understanding

❑ Reflect before you respond; "try on" the idea

❑ Be aware of your emotions and speaker's emotions

❑ Don't interrupt

❑ If you are not concentrating on the speaker, you may not be listening

CRITICAL THINKING QUESTIONS

❑ "What do you think?"

❑ "Do you have enough (quantity) credible (quality) evidence to make those assumptions, inferences or conclusions?"

❑ "Are we focused on the real issue/problem?"

❑ "Have we gotten to the root cause?"

❑ "Have we looked at the problem from different viewpoints?"

❑ "Do we have enough data to make a decision?"

❑ "Who disagrees with this course of action? Why?" (Warning sign if no one disagrees)

❑ "Have we eliminated all the unacceptable risks of this decision or course of action?"

❑ "Have we taken into account self-interest bias? Confirmation bias? Satisficing? Availability? Anchoring? Overconfidence? Loss aversion?"

❑ "How do you feel?"

Figure 10 (cont)

ENPRO MEETING MANAGEMENT WORKSHEET

POST ACTION REVIEW:

PROCESS (evaluate the collect process exhibited by the team)

❑ Did we accomplish our objective?

❑ Did we stress-test our thinking critically?

❑ What worked?

❑ What did not work or could have been done better?

❑ What should we do differently next time?

❑ What are our major learnings or takeaways from the meeting?

❑ Did the best ideas come to the forefront, did the best idea win, regardless of who it came from?

BEHAVIORS (observable behaviors exhibited by individual or team; be specific)

❑ Were we present?

❑ Did we follow our "This is EnPro" practices (i.e., centering, check-in, "I" statements)?

❑ Were we open-minded?

❑ Did we deeply listen to each other well?

❑ Did we ask questions and explore the topics with curiosity?

❑ Did we manage ourselves and be mindful of those around us?

❑ Did we practice being courageous? Did I/we feel safe to give my/ our voice in the meeting?

❑ Were we a collaborative community?

Figure 10 (cont)

CHAPTER 10

Hyper-Learning Practices

As we get further into the digital age, we all must ask ourselves two big questions:

1. **Can we adapt and evolve in ways necessary to stay relevant and flourish?**

2. **Can we and will we embrace a New Way of Being and a New Way of Working in order to become Hyper-Learners who have meaningful employment and the ability to add value to society in ways that technology alone can't?**

The first nine chapters presented a path forward—a way of increasing your chances of saying, "Yes, I can!" in answer to those big questions.

We have been on an active-learning journey together. In part 1, you learned about why and how to develop a New Way of Being (your Best Self) in order to Hyper-Learn, and you began your own journey toward cultivating Inner Peace, a Hyper-Learning Mindset, and Hyper-Learning Behaviors.

THE CHALLENGE/OPPORTUNITY

Based on my experience and feedback from companies and individuals (not rigorous scientific experiments), the top two reasons why people are unable to cultivate Inner Peace or become Hyper-Learners are (1) a lack of self-discipline and (2) trying to do too much too soon.

Self-Discipline

People start out with the best of intentions. Most begin their journeys using some practices and working on one or two behaviors, but then life gets busy at work and/or home and so they skip a day, and then over time they are skipping more days, and eventually they are skipping all days. This journey to a New Way of Being and a New Way of Working is a daily one. **In other words, you need to make your journey a top priority.**

Professors Anders Ericsson, Lyle Bourne Jr., and Alice Healy are world-class cognitive psychology researchers. Professor Ericsson studies expertise and *deliberate practice*, and Professors Bourne and Healy focus on the best ways to train people to learn new things. In full disclosure, I know all three of them. Dr. Bourne was my graduate psychology advisor and has been an *anam cara* (soul friend) for four decades.

Their research clearly indicates that learning something new or improving a skill requires practice, practice, practice in small bits or chunks and that you are more likely to be successful if you measure yourself daily.

Regarding measuring yourself, in my work, people have found having an accountability partner to be very helpful. I recommend such a partner at work and at home.

Another example comes from one of the leading executive coaches in the world, who disclosed in one of his talks that no matter where he is in the world, his accountability partner calls him nightly to check in on how he did that day on the behaviors he was working on.

What I have learned studying and working with people who are working on achieving their Best Selves is that having the self-discipline to be on the journey is, in and of itself, very meaningful and rewarding. You feel good being on the journey, and you face life with a more positive attitude.

Starting Small

The second reason many people abandon this journey is early frustration with a lack of meaningful results, often caused by trying to do too much too soon. You have to start small.

Here is what I recommend:

■ Start out with your Daily Intentions. Reflect on them daily. Take 10 to 15 minutes. Visualize behaving that way.

■ If you need to learn how to meditate, start out with 2 or 3 minutes and then over time work up to 5 minutes, then 10 minutes, then 20 to 30 minutes. Do not start out trying to do 20 minutes. You will get too frustrated. Use an app featuring one of the leading meditation experts, such as Jon Kabat-Zinn, Tara Brach, Jack Kornfield, or Sharon Salzberg.

■ Pick *one* additional behavior to start working on at work and home. Create a plan to change or adopt that behavior. Reflect on why that good behavior will help you and visualize doing your new behavior many times each day. Grade yourself every day in your Learning Journal.

■ Before every meeting, take 2 minutes to read over your Daily Intentions (using your phone or a 3″ by 5″ card). You need to create your own words. Here are some of my words as food for thought only:

- Take three deep breaths (actually do it).

- I am not my ideas.

- This is not about me.

- Smile and be kind.

- Listen to learn, not to confirm.

- Ask, don't tell.

- Be a positive life force.

- On your way home, mentally review how you did that day with your Daily Intentions:

  - Where did you make progress?

  - Where did you not behave as you wanted?

  - Think about how you felt when you behaved that way. What triggered you to act that way?

  - Record your results nightly in your Learning Journal.

  - At least weekly, talk about your results with your accountability partner or a trusted team member.

Remember that every person sharing a personal story in this book about his or her own journey began that journey in a very different place, but through years of daily hard work and self-discipline, they changed themselves. **Yes, you can change yourself—if you really want to!**

Reflection Time

I invite you to stop here and reflect on what we've discussed is this chapter so far. Have you ever started a self-improvement plan and then quit? Many people do that every year with their New Year's resolutions.

Why does that happen?

Have you quit a self-improvement plan in the past?

Did you get too busy? Did you forget? Could you not control your time? Did you get sick? Did a family member need your time? And on and on?

Many people I have worked with pick a time—either first thing in the morning or in the evening after personal home activities are done—to focus on self-improvement. Some people who commute on trains or buses do it on their commute home. The key is to pick a time. And make that time habitual! For example, my time is first thing in the morning when life is quiet. I can find 30 minutes or more every morning. And because my schedule allows it, I can usually also find 30 minutes every late afternoon.

> **Start small. Be patient. Reflect on how good**
> **you feel every time you work on your *self*.**
> **Experience that inner warmth.**

In this chapter, I want to share with you some Hyper-Learning Practices that you can use on a daily basis that will help you become a Hyper-Learner and help you implement your Hyper-Learning Mindset and Behaviors.

These Hyper-Learning Practices are in addition to the EnPro practices discussed in chapter 9.

GET COMFORTABLE WITH THE NEW, THE DIFFERENT, AND THE UNKNOWN

There are several practices that can help you do this.

Become More Childlike

Do you remember when you learned to ride a bicycle?

Think back to that time.

How did you feel? Scared? Excited? Both?

What did you do?

My guess is someone held the bike and helped you get on it or the bicycle had training wheels and you got on by yourself.

How did you learn to ride that bicycle?

My guess is you started trying to make it move. And my guess is you fell off the bicycle many times. (I fell off more than once.)

Then what did you do?

I venture to guess that it took courage, iterative learning (trying to ride, falling off, learning from your fall) and resilience—getting up and trying to ride the bicycle again, considering what you learned.

Young children's days are filled with exploration and discovery, experimenting with the unknown, and learning through trial and error.

Reflection Time

How is the discussion above relevant to our conversation?

Think about how children behave when they are young, say between the ages of two and eight, as compared to how you behave as an adult.

Do young children fear or worry about failure? Do you?

Are they concerned about making mistakes? Are you?

Are they concerned about looking bad? Being judged? Not being thought of as smart? Are you?

Are young children fearful of telling you what they think? Are you fearful of being totally honest at work?

Are young children spontaneous? Are you? Or are you guarded or cautious at work?

Are young children good explorers? Learners? Are you? Why not?

Are you spontaneous? An explorer? Fearless? Courageous? Why not?

How much time do you spend thinking about or worrying about what other people think of you?

I suggest that if you are in a work environment that is safe for you, you need to bring your childlike behaviors back. Awaken the child in you and embrace play when you feel safe to do so.

Actively Explore

Currently, your brain prioritizes or seeks:

- Efficiency

- Speed

- Confirmation of what you already believe

- Affirmation of your ego through cognitive and emotional self-protection

- Cohesiveness of your inner stories

All of that hinders Hyper-Learning.

In the digital age, humans must excel at the types of thinking and emotional engagement with other humans that will be hard for smart machines to do. That is generally imaginative, creative, innovative, and emergent thinking, all of which involve positive emotions and accessing and managing the unique inner voice of your subconscious.

In the digital age, you need to train your mind to better prioritize:

- Seeking novelty, exploration, and discovery—*not* primarily confirmation, affirmation, and cohesiveness

- Actively seeking disconfirming information that challenges what you believe

- Asking questions that lead to exploration and discovery (Why? What if? Why not?)

- Deferring judgments (saying, "Yes, *and*" not "Yes, *but*") in order to explore and discover

- Embracing differences and trying to make meaning of differences

- Embracing ambiguity by not rushing to the safety of making comfortable, speedy decisions

- Embracing the **JOY** of Hyper-Learning every day by continually learning, unlearning, and relearning and updating your mental models of how the world works

- Getting hooked on Hyper-Learning as opposed to being hooked on "knowing"

- Excelling at "not knowing" and knowing how to learn (That is the wilderness of Hyper-Learning. It is in the wilderness that we can learn and update our mental models.)

- Embracing the powers discussed earlier in this book:
  - The Power of Serenity
  - The Power of Humility
  - The Power of Positive Emotions
  - The Power of Slowing Down
  - The Power of Presence
  - The Power of Reflective Listening
  - The Power of Making Meaning
  - The Power of Exploration

- The Power of Reflection
- The Power of Emergence
- The Power of Owning You

Each day, write down in your Learning Journal what you explored, what you discovered, what you learned, and what you want to explore tomorrow. Consider forming an "explorer club" with trusted team members at work or trusted friends and share your explorations with each other weekly. Make exploration and discovery part of your New Way of Being.

Change Your Brain and Mind

To become Hyper-Learners, we all have to become proficient at updating our mental models. That means we all have to create new neuronal connections in our brains.

New neuronal connections result from intensely focusing on learning new things, new perspectives, and new habits and from mentally simulating new ways of behaving. Visualize, then do.

Norman Doidge is a leading research neuroscientist who for decades has been one of the leading experts of neuroplasticity—the brain's ability to structurally change throughout our lives. Research shows that we humans can actively help that process along. For example, Doidge and colleagues have built a technology-enabled app called Brain HQ, which is designed to stretch your brain with short exercises. They designed the app to help older people, but the skills it's designed to help the user develop are important for all of us.

Another way to build new connections in the brain is by intentionally thinking and acting differently. For example, by actually behaving like an explorer and seeking to learn something new we can change our minds and brains in ways that make exploration and new learning a habit.

There is also research that shows that we can learn new physical activities by mental simulation practices.[115] I interpret that to mean that we can rewire our brains in ways more conducive to, say, collaboration by mentally rehearsing how we want to behave in a meeting or in a collaboration exercise. We can mentally rehearse asking the right exploratory questions and trying to connect and relate to other people. That is a powerful tool. I find it so fascinating that this neuroscience is consistent with the teachings of some of the ancient philosophers who advocated deep reflection as a learning tool. For example, there is an ancient belief that you can overcome a fear of dying by mentally rehearsing how you want to physically act on your death bed and mentally simulating dying.

Reflection Time

Why not mentally simulate doing a desired behavior? Choose one of your desired Hyper-Learning Behaviors to visualize doing. Yes, right now, please.

Mental rehearsal becomes super powerful when the new things you do in and of themselves help you be a better learner and help you develop emotional and cognitive skills you don't have. For example, by mentally visualizing the act of reading another person's emotions and responding in ways that help you and the other person get in sync (as discussed in chapter 7) you can improve your ability to do it in the real world.

Mental rehearsal can also help you develop nonlinear thinking skills such as sense-making, storytelling, and divergent, emergent, innovative, and creative thinking. The way to develop those skills is by having the courage to try them and by not worrying about looking bad at the beginning of your learning process. In other words, you need to just start. Don't procrastinate or put it off. Just do something each day to learn and get better.

Here is another good example of what you could do to practice embracing the new and different in ways that can change your brain and mind: **take an improv training course**. The research shows that learning improv helps you communicate better emotionally with others. When I was creating the Leadership Institute at Emory University's Goizueta Business School 15 years ago, we intentionally designed a course to take students out of their daily comfort zones with four specific experiences: improv training, diversity training, learning the life of a homeless person, and an immersive experience at the U.S. Marines Leadership Center at Quantico, Virginia (students spent an evening and night as enlisted Marines and a day in officer leadership experiential training). The purpose was to put students in novel situations and activities requiring focus and engagement.

I suggest that you do more activities that take you out of your comfort zone and enable you to stretch yourself. That is what we all need to do. And you can do it yourself without going to Quantico.

Here is a simple thing to try. I love grocery shopping. I used to always start on the far-left aisle of Whole Foods here in Charlottesville. One day, I decided to start on the far-right aisle. Geez, you would think I had gone to another planet. It took me more than double the time to do my shopping because I had to think differently. Try it. See how your brain handles it.

Try writing your name with your nondominant hand. Try it multiple times over a week or more. What did you learn?

Try driving to work a different way every day. What did you notice?

To learn how to adapt to and flourish in a new world, we need to train ourselves to love going into the new and the different. Training ourselves on low-stakes novel tasks can build the confidence we need to truly thrive in the constantly changing and uncertain environments of the digital age.

Reflection Time

Do you recall the last time you ventured
into something new or different?

How did you feel?

What did you do?

How did you figure out what to do?

What happened?

What did you feel at the end of the event or action?

What did you learn?

The velocity of change in the digital age is high and constant. Think back to the Hyper-Learning Mindset chapter. What philosophical concept could help you become more comfortable in that kind of environment?

If you said impermanence, you are correct.

Thriving in a rapidly changing, uncertain environment starts with having the right mindset—an attitude that sets you up to seek novelty, explore the unknown, and be comfortable in ambiguous situations, the kind of mindset that helps you confront key questions like: What is changing? How is it changing?

A mindset that is comfortable with impermanence enables you to be curious about the answers.

Be Curious

It's curious people who will thrive as the digital age advances.

To pique your own curiosity, I suggest asking yourself the following questions frequently throughout the day (add them to your Daily Intentions):

- **What am I missing?**

- **What is new?**

- **What is different?**

These questions prime you to notice, sense, and discover the new and the different.

The goal is to learn to love the new, the different, and the unknown.

The goal is to love exploring and learning every day. The goal is to not end the day knowing only what you knew yesterday.

Be on the lookout for new insights.

The following Insight Discovery Questions can help:[116]

- What are we trying to do here? What kind of thinking should I be using?

- Is there any data here that contradicts or is inconsistent with what I believe? If so, what could that mean?

- Is there something new, unusual, or out of the ordinary present that I should think about? What could that data mean?

- Can I look at the data differently and produce a different answer?

- Is there a pattern here?

- If I define or reframe my question or problem differently, would that open up new alternatives or help me see more data or create a different pattern?

■ What in the data or exploration is surprising? Why is it surprising? What could it mean?

■ Could it be important? Why? Why not?

■ What do I feel? Why am I feeling that? What do I want to do with that feeling?

■ What is my body telling me? What do I need to do?

■ If I did this, what could happen? Visualize it. How did that feel?

■ What did I expect? What happened? What can I learn from that?

Use Tools Designed for Exploration and Discovery

You *can* learn to embrace the new and see the different, and I predict that if you do something every day to learn something new, you will get hooked on learning because it will be emotionally rewarding. It will generate the release of emotionally positive hormones that will give you a *learner's high.*

But to fully embrace the new and different, it helps to have tools to figure out the unknown.

One such tool is the process underlying scientific experiments, which is the *same* process that underlies such well-known business processes as Lean Startup, Effectuation Thinking, and Design Thinking. All of these processes share the same learning approach.

Think about it.

What is an entrepreneur trying to do?

What is an innovator trying to do?

What is a creative person trying to do?

Are they trying to find or create novelty through exploration or discovery, or are they trying to confirm what they think they know?

Okay, so what do entrepreneurs, innovators, and creative types actually do?

In many cases, they use a process designed for exploration and discovery, which is basically the scientific method:

1. First, they create a hypothesis (e.g., I believe if I do X, person Y will do Z. Or, if I do X, Z will happen).

2. They ask themselves:
   - What must be true for that to occur?
   - What would make my hypothesis false?

3. They design an experiment to test the hypothesis.

4. They find relevant data (e.g., through interviews or research) to test the hypothesis.

5. They ask themselves: What happened? What did I learn?

If you have a way of learning in new situations, a way of exploring that is low-risk, and a way of iteratively learning in small steps, change is no longer so scary.

Reflection Time

What are you going to do differently tomorrow
to get better at going into the unknown?

Do you agree that the scientific method is a tool
you can easily use daily to discover the new and
the different? To go into the unknown?

Please understand, I am just sharing what I have learned. I am not saying do it my way. Heavens, no! Remember you have a CHOICE! What I am suggesting is that you develop a process for exploring that is easy and low-risk. I am trying to stimulate thoughtfulness and action, not compliance.

Engage in Activities That Are New and Different—Break Your Routine Way of Being

(I've put an asterisk beside the ones I've personally tried.)

Which will you try?

- *Learn the scientific method. (This is a must do.)

- *Take improv training. (This stuff works.)

- *Take an art class. (This was a big "new" for me, and I want to do more.)

- *Take a dance class. (I was awful. It was not fun.)

- Take a martial arts class.

- Learn to play a musical instrument.

- *Learn to play a new sport.

- *Visit museums and learn about the creation of art.

- Do a maker's workshop. (Go make something.)

- Take a storytelling class.

- Take a writing class.

- *Play thinking games, such as chess or bridge. (I love bridge and want to do more this year.)

- Put yourself into very different environments via volunteer work.

- *Take daily walks in natural environments, intensely focusing on the foliage, the sounds, the colors, the sky, the stars. (I now try to do this every day.)

- Take a Design Thinking course.

- Take Andrew Ng's Coursera course on AI for Beginners.

- Do creativity exercises with your children.

Read Regularly

Do you remember what Charlie Munger said about reading?

Do you remember what Marvin Riley said about reading?

I recommend regularly reading in fields where you have little knowledge and in fields that add to your understanding of how the world works and how you tick. Focus especially on the areas of physics, biology, psychology, artificial intelligence, and emotional intelligence and read some novels or poetry.

Follow Thought Leaders on Social Media

Follow thought leaders and peruse their postings weekly. When you find a thought leader who helps you, look to see whom she or he follows. I recommend that every quarter you prune the list of people you follow, keeping the most helpful and trying some new ones.

Listen to Podcasts

I suggest listening to at least one podcast every week in which thought leaders present their views. Here are some leading podcasts to consider (try some and choose a topic weekly from a couple of different people):

- *Back to Work*

- TED Talks

- *The Tim Ferriss Show*

- Farnam Street's *The Knowledge Project*

- *StarTalk*, Neil deGrasse Tyson

- *Science Weekly*

- *Quirks & Quarks*

- *The Vergecast* (technology news)

- *a16z Podcast* (technology)

- *Planet Money*

Sometimes I go on YouTube and search for thought leaders to follow on podcasts. That has been helpful.

Keep a Learning Journal

Writing makes you think about what you really know and whether you can explain it in ways that other people can understand. In the case of fiction, writing helps you become creative and imaginative and more able to access and understand feelings and emotions.

I highly recommend continuing to keep a Learning Journal and writing down your learnings each day. That is what Ray Dalio did and from that journal came his book *Principles* and his investment strategies.

A Learning Journal is also good for writing down ideas or thoughts that arise from your subconscious. That can happen when you wake up or after you have taken a walk in nature or when you have done your physical workout. Or whenever they pop into your head.

Why not write your life story so far? An outstanding book to use in doing that is *The Path of the Everyday Hero* by Lorna Catford and Michael Ray. A couple of years ago I worked through the exercises between Christmas and New Year's Day. It was an illuminating and meaningful exercise that helped set a more focused course of action for the following years. It helped me look at my life and think deeply about when I was the best me. What was I most proud of? When was I the most courageous? Were there any consistent approaches that brought me inner joy? I wrote down a list of the things I had done that made me feel really good—that felt like the real me or that had a positive impact on others—and I found some consistencies.

What did I conclude? I concluded that when I went to Wall Street I became a very different person than I was before. My 20 years in investment banking were very rewarding in many ways, but on reflection, they were my years "in the wilderness" because I got caught up in the *success* game as opposed to being in the *purpose* game. One part of me took over my life, and I lost for a while the parts of me that brought great joy to my heart—my soul. In many ways, my story is similar to Marvin Riley's story when he shared with us his approach to life when he began his career and how he had to change. I, too, had to change to be true to myself.

This type of deep reflection practice can be very helpful in helping you center your sense of self—in helping you identify the uniqueness that you can bring to the world to find purpose and meaningful work.

Follow Leading-Edge Think Tanks

For no money, you can follow these institutions to read about their latest thinking and discoveries:

- Santa Fe Institute
- Brookings Institution
- McKinsey Global Institute
- Singularity University
- Oxford University Institute for the Future of Humanity
- Deloitte Center for the Edge
- Leading Edge Forum
- World Economic Forum
- Pew Research Center

- MIT Media Lab

- Yale Center for Emotional Intelligence

Use Templates Daily

Here are three templates that my students and consulting clients have found helpful.

Getting Ready to Collaborate and Listen Checklist

© Edward D. Hess 2020

1. Take deep breaths, then ask yourself:

- Am I calm emotionally? Take deep breaths until you are calm.

- Is my mind clear? Am I really ready to focus and be present? If not, take deep breaths and get ready.

- What is the purpose of this meeting? Exploration? Critical thinking? Feedback? Making a decision? Defining the problem?

2. Then say to yourself:

- Slow down. Don't rush to conclusions. Don't interrupt. Think, don't react.

- Listen to understand and learn. Don't be defensive.

- I am not my idea. This is not about me.

- My mental models are not reality, they are only my perception of reality.

- Being accurate is more important than being right.

- Collaborating is not a competition.

3. Then remind yourself:

- Don't interrupt.

- Don't think about your response while the other person is talking. Focus on listening.

- Don't get defensive.

- Reflect and make meaning together.

- Do no harm. Critique ideas, not people.

- Be a humble, empathetic, and caring listener.

- This is not about me.

- Ratio of inquiry to advocacy: 1:1.

- Ratio of positive to negative feedback: 3:1.

- People won't care what I believe unless they believe I care about them.

Critical Thinking Questions Checklist[117]

© Edward D. Hess 2020

1. What do you think?

2. Why do you believe that?

3. What assumptions are you making to get to that point?

4. What inferences are you making?

5. What facts must be true for that to be true?

6. How credible are the sources of those facts?

7. Do you have enough (quantity) credible (quality) evidence to make those assumptions, inferences, or conclusions?

8. What facts would disprove your assumption, inference, or conclusion? Did you look for them?

9. What other interpretations or meaning can you draw from the facts?

10. What alternatives did you consider? Pros and cons of each? Why did you choose X?

11. Are we focused on the real issue/problem?

12. Have we gotten to the root cause?

13. Have we looked at the problem from different viewpoints?

14. Do we have enough data to make a decision?

15. Who disagrees with this course of action? Why? (Warning sign if no one disagrees)

16. If we do this, what is likely to happen? What would that cause to happen? What could result then?

17. Is there something here that just doesn't make sense or feel right?

18. Have we illuminated all the unacceptable risks of this decision or course of action?

19. What is the probability we are correct? What are the big downsides if we are not correct? Have we mitigated or hedged the big downsides to nil?

20. Have we considered self-interest bias? Confirmation bias? Satisficing? Availability? Anchoring? Overconfidence? Loss aversion?

Unpacking and Stress-Testing Assumptions Checklist[118]

© Edward D Hess 2020

1. **State the belief clearly.**

2. **Use the "5 Whys" to illuminate what assumptions or inferences must be true for the belief to be true.**

3. **For each assumption, ask the following:**

   ■ What facts do we already know that confirm the assumption?

   ■ What facts do we already know that cast doubt on the assumption?

   ■ What specific facts would confirm the assumption?

   ■ What specific additional facts would disconfirm the assumption?

4. **For each specific additional fact that would confirm the assumption:**

   ■ Who knows those facts?

   ■ Where do we find those facts?

   ■ How many different confirming sources do we need?

   ■ How will we mitigate confirmation bias in our search?

5. **For each specific fact that would disconfirm or cast doubt on the assumption:**

   ■ Who knows those facts?

   ■ Where do we find those facts?

   ■ How many different disconfirming sources do we need?

Let's go back a moment. I have shared lots of ideas with you. You can't do all of them.

Remember, start small and be rigorous in daily execution and then add more activities when the new ones have become habitual.

Pick some personal practices that are going to help you be the person you desire to be at home and at work.

It should be clear by now that the goal here is for all of us to find a workplace where our Best Self can flourish. Only then will we be whole and only then will we have the chance to be all we can be. Only then can we bring our human uniqueness to work to make a meaningful contribution to something that we believe is meaningful.

As noted poet David Whyte stated:

"To have a firm persuasion in our work—to feel that what we do is right for ourselves and good for the world at the same exact time—is one of the great triumphs of human existence."[119]

CHAPTER 11

The Adam Hansen Personal Transformation Story

Adam Hansen and I met a couple of years ago on Twitter and LinkedIn. I started following him because he was an out-of-the-box thinker. Adam has an MBA from Indiana University and was a new product development manager and a director of new brands at Mars. After working as an innovation consultant for 10 years, he became a principal and vice-president of innovation at Ideas To Go, Inc. He is the co-author of *Outsmart Your Instincts: How the Behavioral Innovation™ Approach Drives Your Company Forward.*

Adam is a master innovator. He thrives on going into the unknown. His story has a lot of learning for all of us regarding how to seek the new and the different and explore the unknown.

Here is Adam's story in his own words.

My Journey to Ikigai

Why don't we spend more time doing what we love, focusing our energies on that and becoming better, and in the process being compensated fairly for our expanding capabilities, and find more and more ways to solve issues that the world clearly needs to be solved?

What's stopping us?

Here's what I love: I am a professional innovator. I love discovery, exploration, and creating novelty. I love going into the unknown, into the mystery. It's fascinating to start pulling together vague forms out of the chaos and seeing where something unique might go.

Here's what I've become better at: I've worked and learned how to discover insights that others miss and see opportunities that others might not see. Over the years I have had the honor of honing my craft and developing the skills to do that well.

I get paid fairly for creating new forms of value that my clients hadn't pulled together before. This work often gives them an important beachhead for further exploration and refinement, changing not just the line of products or services they offer but also their capacity to create new, unique, and relevant offerings again and again.

What's become clearer to me is that our world can be better to the extent that everyone learns and applies a simple innovation toolkit to their work and to their life. Personal innovation is a natural part of Hyper-Learning.

Ed asked me to share my personal journey to being an innovator. For me that was a Journey to Ikigai, or the four domains discussed above—I Love Doing It, I'm Good at It, I Can Be Paid Fairly for It, and The World Needs It. In this case, certainly, the journey itself is the reward. Sure, it takes some work, but clarity and focus on this journey are endurably satisfying, and put us on a trajectory of continuous learning and doing more and better.

To do this, I had to adopt a mindset and behave in ways that optimized my ability to go beyond the obvious and discover and create meaningful novelty. That required me to overcome fear and my ego in order to open myself up to the different, the new, and the maybe. Along the way, I had to learn how to optimize sensing and hearing others and listening to the creative intuitive part of me. I had to learn to behave in many of the ways that Ed writes about in this book.

When you have some clarity on your Ikigai, or life purpose, you also get clarity on what you need to learn, unlearn, and re-learn. My story has been a ceaseless, iterative, and satisfying learning story—I continue to learn and improve along the way as you will do. You do not need to be perfect to begin your journey because none of us will reach that stage. And the reality is that "done" or "enough for now" is better than "perfect." "Done" or "enough" will help you move out into the world, while "perfect" can easily keep you caught up in its own endless loop.

Life's too short not to love what we do, not to work on interesting topics that matter, with great people alongside us. I've been fortunate in this regard; I have always loved my work, and I don't believe that my experience should be the exception. I want to help everyone to have love as the animating force in all facets of their life, including work.

The concept of Ikigai gives us an important way to tie love to all you're doing in your career. When I first saw Ikigai (see figure 11) through some post on LinkedIn or Facebook sometime around 2013, it resonated nuclearly with me, as in the nucleus of every cell in my body began buzzing.

It hit me because, without having that precise framework in mind beforehand, I knew it's what I'd been working on for about 25 years. I got it immediately, began telling everyone I could about it, etc. I had all the evangelizing zeal of the new convert.

In pulling together the four domains and being thoughtful about their various intersections (e.g., how might we think about Passion, or the intersection of I Love Doing It and I'm Good at It) we can assess where we're growing and what might need some more loving effort. Each domain affects the other three, and having this simple framework gives us an ongoing way to get better at what we're already good at and love doing.

Ikigai shows how Passion, Profession, Vocation (or Calling) and Mission interconnect, why they're not merely broad synonyms, and how their important intersections can inform ongoing action for you.

WHAT MAKES LIFE WORTH LIVING

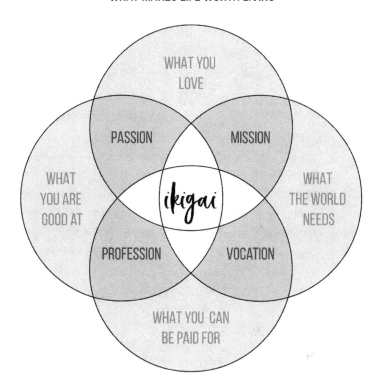

THE PROCESS OF ALLOWING
THE SELF'S POSSIBILITIES TO BLOSSOM

Figure 11: Ikigai

My Good Fortune

I have been fortunate several times in my life to be at the right place, at the right time, to hear the right thing and/or to have an important experience that reframed my thinking and moved me forward. I believe getting on the Journey to Ikigai increases these beneficial moments, as the focus it provides is narrow enough to make our exposure to new ideas and people relevant, while having four domains to nurture gives us ample variety and no shortage of productive pursuits.

One of these critical times was in grad school. I went to Indiana University for my MBA, in the marketing/product management track. Having my interest in innovation piqued during my undergrad work, I really looked forward to the New Product Development class I'd take during my studies. Little did I know what that class would mean to me, or how my professor would come to be such an important mentor and friend over the succeeding 30 years.

The professor, Tom Hustad, happened to be one of the seminal figures in innovation within academia and in the efforts of innovation academics to connect with practitioners in the marketplace. Tom was both the founding editor of the academic journal *The Journal of Product Innovation Management* and one of the founders of the Product Development and Management Association. He clearly loved innovation and didn't see it merely as an interesting topic for intellectual inquiry. Tom continues to see innovation as a noble effort in its practical advancement of serving people better and better. I was thrilled to have him as a professor.

It started to dawn on me that innovation could be more than part of my career, that it could be *the career*.

That came as amazing news to me. I remembered thinking with unusual clarity, "If I could do that for my whole career, why wouldn't I?"

How did that clarity come to me? A couple of thoughts:

Experience had already taught me that my subconscious is smarter than the strictly rational, calculating me. That makes sense—we've learned that a healthy subconscious is in part pattern recognition at the sub-attentional level—we know some things without being able to figure out why we know what we know. This innovation thing seemed like the obvious thing to occupy my attentions. I knew that without knowing entirely why. It was important that I was listening to my subconscious at this time.

Experience also hit me repeatedly with the insight that I wasn't going to get good at something without starting off being pretty bad at it. This seems self-evident, but we repeatedly ignore or forget it. I learned to relish the feeling of being inept in an interesting creative area for a while in service of learning and getting to where I could start creating decent work. For example, I started playing keys in a rock band when I was 13, being content to be bad at it for a while, along with my bandmates who were somewhere with me in the Bad Ballpark, getting just better enough over time to recognize and enjoy the progress. Our lack of proficiency was beside the point; being able to do the meager bit we could was tapping into the heedless thrill of rock! There was so much satisfaction in the effort itself, particularly when I realized that I was getting just enough better over time and could take on bigger and bigger challenges as I moved forward.

So, coming out of MBA school, I really wanted to work in an innovative, entrepreneurial atmosphere, and got my first paid gig as innovation manager at a great, aggressive, creative, small-kitchen-electrics manufacturer and marketer, where I would have all the responsibility a green kid could ever ask for. I was on my way. I got to see how early, half-baked (quarter-baked?) ideas could be iterated, built upon, and set the stage to drive uniqueness and new forms of relevance for our customers.

Four jobs after this first one in innovation and almost 30 years later, I have had great experiences I couldn't have hoped for, even with an active imagination. I've traveled the world for business (with my wife too infrequently, but sometimes), met so many people, and enjoyed the deep satisfaction of collaborating with other impassioned innovation geeks as clients and colleagues. I've had the experience and perspective from both the client side and the consultant side, and have been an important part of bringing 15 products from concept to market in a hands-on way, and midwifing several hundred early prototypes that led to over 200 launched products or services.

I didn't know enough 30 years ago to understand fully how satisfying this journey would be, but I had high hopes and didn't know enough to be jaded.

I still don't know enough to be jaded!

How Did I Get Here?

What mindset and behaviors help us move beyond the obvious and explore broadly, discover, and create meaningful novelty?

How can we navigate inevitable fear and ego demands in order to open ourselves up to the different, the new, and the maybe?

How might we learn to sense and hear others while listening to the creative intuitive part inside each of us?

What approach can we take to innovate innovatively, not resting on best practices from years before, but incorporating the increasing bounty of insights from the human sciences?

Throughout my journey, I've picked up some more tips that may help you with these questions. Each one alone is a helpful part of the puzzle; together they increase your odds of making progress on your Journey to Ikigai.

- **The idea of "enough."** You don't need all the answers. You don't need perfect clarity before taking action. "Enough" clarity, coupled with thoughtful action, will help you move forward and gain the additional clarity and momentum you will need. A fixation on perfection too early can paralyze you. It's often a very smart-sounding dodge that prevents you from acting. You simply cannot anticipate all the helpful questions or the insights that will come to you until you get moving and having the experiences necessary to formulate those great questions. The most important questions I've had within my journey are the ones I have now—I couldn't think of them earlier because I didn't know enough.

- **Simple prototypes.** Prototypes are only as good as the conversations they engender. They're a helpful shared space that converts the "adjacent possible" into the "tangible right in front of you." Thinking and talking in bigger abstractions is helpful very early on, but you have to start playing with actual possibilities and forms to reveal important considerations that don't come to you otherwise. And it's never been easier to assemble and test prototypes across the spectrum from early written product concepts through clunky "looks like" and "works like" prototypes to beta products and services for more hands-on testing with your target audience.

One thing you can do very early on is to assemble a free, simple Google Forms survey to get input. Write up a concept statement and ask even 50 people three to five questions about it. Your cost here? The time to write up your concept, the survey, and getting it through 50 completions. You might have to ask 100 people to get 50 to complete it, but, hey, with this Internet thing I keep hearing about, it seems pretty easy to start going after it.

- **Rich conversations.** Using prototypes is a great way to pull together questions and have conversations that move you forward. Another way to have really rich conversations is to pay attention to people you've connected with who have the magical combination of (a) enough in common with you and (b) enough difference from you to increase the likelihood of productive exchange.

  Use social media to be, y'know, social! In my experience, people love engagement and thoughtful questions. Try more to be interested, and not too concerned about being interesting. Build out the kind of social scene for yourself (be that via social media or in flesh-and-blood life) where such conversations are more likely. Find conversation partners you can trust, which I define as people who are curious, open, and intrigued by differences between you, and see these differences as great places to explore, not to argue about. Being curious and effective beats being "right," except perhaps in dire medical emergencies, where a premium on the right intervention is appropriate. I do hope that's a rare occurrence for you!

- **Innovation for all.** "Innovation" doesn't have to be in your job title for you to use the tools of innovation or to think like an innovator. In the incipient Age of Smart Machines, we'll all need to get better at innovation for our work and ourselves. Personal innovation must become the concern and practice of all of us. Innovation makes the school teacher, the small bakery owner-operator, the construction-company manager, and the city planner better. Through the rest of this century, the more we can democratize the tools of innovation, the healthier our society will be.

- **The self-sustaining nature of questions.** Questions are one of the most amazing phenomena we have. Answering one can easily turn into having three or four new ones that keep you curious and moving forward. Talk about a renewable resource! Later questions simply aren't available at the start. The new targets of your curiosity and attention aren't visible or even thinkable earlier. You need to advance so you can have new perspectives that your curiosity can play with and stoke the furnace of wonder.

- **Be at least as concerned about the risks of omission as the risks of commission.** Research shows that the regrets expressed near the end of life aren't nearly so much about "What I did" but "What I thought about, but didn't do." It's easy to understand why we focus too much on the risks of what we do versus what we don't do—it's easier to think through the tangible and actual, and difficult to think about the abstraction of what we don't do. But today, it's never been easier to pull together resources to give your ideas a shot. It's almost as easy to try it as it is to wonder about it. What's stopping you? What bets are you making about how long life is and vague notions about being able to try things later, in some unreal future?

- **Don't just be tolerant of ambiguity, actively seek it out.** Love the mystery and pulling together vague forms out of it, getting into some rough prototyping, and then learning, learning, learning. Anything meaningfully new was earlier a bunch of "uns"—unknowable, unthinkable, unimaginable, uncomfortable. It's enjoyable turning these "uns" into the knowable, thinkable, imaginable, and more comfortable.

- **Balance your concerns between validity (are we doing the right thing?) and reliability (are we doing things right?).** Validity often has a shorter shelf life than reliability, so I believe we need to think about it more than we commonly do. We can keep cranking out the consistent, but increasingly irrelevant, product far past its usefulness. Humans will still be better at judging validity than smart machines for a very long time. And it would be fascinating to watch the machines catch up.

- **Learn to love learning.** Once you find your Ikigai, you will want to keep learning, because you'll continue to see the difference between where you are and where you could be in terms of effectiveness in helping others. You'll want to test and expose your ideas to more people, understanding that they might make a difference for the right audience.

Where I'm Heading Now

A new area that has captured my imagination is at the intersection of behavioral science and innovation, which we call the Behavioral Innovation™ approach. Behavioral Innovation is based on the idea that the better understanding of how humans actually think and behave can lead to lessening the effects of resisting forces to innovation and increasing the power of those forces that help us move forward.

Within this important, generative intersection, we started out analyzing cognitive biases—nonconscious cognitive shortcuts that served our ancestors really well, but that often are a mismatch for the conditions we face now, especially when we're trying to do innovation right. We teach our clients how those cognitive biases tend to show up and how they can use some simple tools to lessen their effects, freeing up energy to move innovation forward more effectively and quickly. We wrote a book, *Outsmart*

Your Instincts: How the Behavioral Innovation™ Approach Drives Your Company Forward, to help our clients and anyone interested in doing innovation to gain more awareness and practical experience in doing innovation better.

Within my work at ITG and Behavioral Innovation, I am confident that I have enough interesting questions to keep me occupied for another 15 to 20 years. Ikigai can be a rich, satisfying journey that doesn't end, because you get better and better at it and find more to pursue.

My Wish for You

Today, Ikigai is my primary mindset. It is the framework that helps me continue to be passionate about innovation. It is the way I make meaning of my life.

Innovation is what I love, innovation is what I am good at, innovation is what the world needs, and I can earn a good living by doing innovation.

My wish for all is that you find what your Journey to Ikigai looks like and realize that it's an ongoing, iterative process. What lights you up as innovation does me? You should keep learning more about your life purpose throughout your life. Wouldn't it be great to do something meaningful about your life's purpose even during your final month alive? Why wouldn't you? I can imagine how vital and thriving our society would be if more of us were moving, still being generative, today, this month, this year, this decade, through the end of our lives.

Gratitude for this entire experience is the only rational response. There's enough wonder here to keep a person occupied for a lifetime. I love being with others who feel a responsibility not to squander the profound gift that we have of life, consciousness, loving relationships, and meaningful work. The net of our life's experience should be some tangible form of expressing "thank you." I believe that finding and staying on your Journey to Ikigai makes life as gratitude not merely a possibility but an eventuality.

Admittedly, pulling this all together is a bit like threading a needle while wing-walking across two Blue Angels aircrafts flying wingtip to wingtip, simultaneously attempting to translate Proust into Esperanto. There's every reason to believe the task is not doable.

Yet . . . why not try? What better use of our love and time could we imagine?

I sometimes get into a conversation with strangers while flying. I've learned to be respectful (meaning not nosy and not a conversation hijacker), and have noticed that most people are interested when they hear that I'm this thing called an innovation consultant. It regularly moves into a conversation about how much I love my work and how Ikigai has come together for me. As they express interest (did I mention that I truly do try to avoid foisting this line of thought onto them?), it's easy for me to start asking them Ikigai-related questions.

So, with that, my seatmate on the journey through this chapter:

- What part of your career do you enjoy/have you enjoyed the most? Why?

- Describe what it looks like when you're really immersed in something positive at work, please.

- How might you increase the amount of time you spend doing that or things just like that?

- What beliefs do you hold that tell you that you can't enjoy it more?

- What part of what you do in your work could be applied to great causes to help them move forward?

I'd love you to join the army of Ikigai Instigators, Imaginators, and Innovators.

What could you create with this amazing gift of life, love, and learning?

What could our world look like if 75 million more of us understood the concept and were actively pursuing their Journey to Ikigai?

I want to live in that world!

Onward and upward!

Reflection Time

1. A fabulous inspirational and aspirational story—do you agree or disagree? Why?

2. How does Adam's use of prototypes fit with the scientific method that we discussed in chapter 10?

3. Is doing a prototype the same as doing an experiment to learn?

4. How does Adam's having "rich conversations" fit with what you learned in chapter 8?

5. In my talks with Adam, he said something that was an eye opener for me:

"Doing prototypes is a way to create content to have rich conversations."

What does that mean to you?

6. What did Adam's fear of the "risks of omission" mean to you? What is he afraid of?

7. If Adam fears missing something, does that make it easier or harder for him to be open-minded? Curious? Willing to listen to different opinions?

8. How does Adam view questions?

9. Do you agree that Adam has laid out for us a nice approach to finding joy in the new, the different, and the unknown?

10. Please summarize that approach. What will you adopt?

11. Could his approach help you be a Hyper-Learner?

12. If so, how are you going to behave in order to do that?

Adam's story is the perfect way to end the book.

Adam, with a big HUG, thank you.

EPILOGUE

Well, my active learners, our journey is coming to an end as far as new material and stories are concerned.

My hope is that our journey together has been a meaningful beginning or a meaningful continuance for you.

The digital age is dramatically changing how we humans live and how we work.

In the digital age, the past is no longer a reliable predictor of the future.

We humans must learn to think differently and that means learning to behave differently.

We need to learn a New Way of Being and a New Way of Working.

We need to become Hyper-Learners.

Our challenge is made harder because the science of adult learning is clear—we are suboptimal learners in that we are wired for thinking efficiently and speedily. We are prediction machines based on our past experiences. We seek confirmation of our mental models, affirmation of our egos, and cohesiveness of our existing stories about how the world works.

Nonetheless, we must learn how to create, explore, discover, and innovate.

We must excel at being emotionally and socially intelligent.

We must learn to continually update our mental models.

We must learn to overcome the two big inhibitors to learning: our egos and our fears.

We must learn to excel at collaborating with other people, and that requires us to excel at reflective listening, being open-minded, and emotionally connecting with others in ways that build trust.

In other words, each of us must TRANSFORM to become a Hyper-Learner: a person who excels at learning, unlearning, and relearning at the pace of change.

Personal transformation is hard. But with the right mindsets, the right behaviors, and the daily use of the right practices, it is achievable. Hopefully, the personal stories by Susan, Marvin, and Adam provided evidence for you of that achievability.

That is what this book has been about—inviting you to join the journey to your Best Self in the pursuit of Hyper-Learning—embracing a New Way of Being and a New Way of Working so you can excel in the advancing digital age. I tried to make that invitation real and practical for you through the active-learning approach we took.

I hope you learned that:

HYPER-LEARNING IS EMOTIONAL AND BEHAVIORAL

Hyper-Learning is dependent upon having Inner Peace and behaving in ways that enable meaningful positive human connections. And it is dependent upon a Hyper-Learning Mindset and the daily use of Hyper-Learning Behaviors and Practices.

Hyper-Learning occurs best in work environments that are very humanistic and that encourage and facilitate mindsets, behaviors, and practices designed to foster an idea meritocracy, positivity, psychological safety, and self-determination. It occurs through Caring, Trusting Teams who are able to consistently have High-Quality, Making-Meaning Conversations that result in collective flow.

I want to close by discussing the **JOY that awaits you!**

THE JOY OF HYPER-LEARNING

This is what I have experienced:

- Hyper-Learners love learning!

- They love the processes of learning!

- They love the joy of helping others learn!

- They enjoy the challenge and the results of having High-Quality, Making-Meaning Conversations.

Hyper-Learners love:

- The creation of the new and the better

- The power of building on ideas

- The power of "Yes, *and*"

- The power of "Say more"

- The joy of getting in emotional sync with others

- The joy of being oneself openly

- The joy of discovery and being in a better place at the end of conversations

- The joy of being part of a Caring, Trusting Team

- The joy of having High-Quality, Making-Meaning Conversations

- The joy of attaining collective flow with others

Hyper-Learners embrace the magnitude of their ignorance, and through Hyper-Learning Behaviors, go into the unknown, embrace new opportunities, and become agile, adaptive, iterative learners who don't allow fear or ego to inhibit their learning.

Hyper-Learners understand that their biggest competition is themselves, and they are committed to daily rigor, self-discipline, intention, and the use of daily practices to improve themselves.

There is JOY in that process. You will feel good about yourself just by practicing the Hyper-Learning Behaviors and engaging in the practices that will make the behaviors become a habit, and you will see results at work and at home with team members, friends, loved ones, and others that you meet in passing.

I invite you to SEEK THE JOY.

I invite you to EMBRACE THE JOY.

I invite you to SHARE THE JOY.

$\sim$

WITH DEEP GRATITUDE TO SUSAN, MARVIN, AND ADAM . . .

. . . for sharing their journeys so openly. I hope you frequently reread their stories. Their stories will never get old and will serve as friendly reminders. They, like you and I, are human beings who are not perfect, who make mistakes, and who can always be better. What differentiates them, however, is that they have accepted all of that and invested their energies in the journey to their Best Selves, which enables them to embrace a New Way of Being and a New Way of Working and to empower their team members to do the same.

WITH DEEP GRATITUDE TO YOU

I am deeply grateful for your willingness and efforts to embrace an active-learning approach with me.

I truly hope that you will join the journey to your Best Self in order to become a Hyper-Learner.

We live in exciting and challenging times. May you have the courage to embrace those challenges with all your heart.

May you liberate your human uniqueness and find meaningful ways to flourish in this digital age.

May you achieve Inner Peace and the daily warmth of your heart connecting to other warm hearts.

May you be all that you can be in every moment and experience daily many micro-joys.

May you learn how to excel at Hyper-Learning and experience its JOY and MAGIC daily.

And may you have many meaningful relationships along with meaningful work.

~

From my heart to your heart, with a BIG HUG, I wish you all the best.

~

P.S. If you are interested in creating a Hyper-Learning community platform where you and I and other readers can share questions, challenges, and learnings and help each other on our journeys, please reach out to me on LinkedIn.

NOTES

1. McKinsey Global Institute, "The Future of Work in America: People and Places, Today and Tomorrow," July 2019, https://www.mckinsey.com/featured-insights /future-of-work/the-future-of-work-in-america-people-and-places-today-and -tomorrow.

2. Carl Benedikt Frey and Michael A. Osborne, "The Future of Employment: How Susceptible Are Jobs to Computerisation?" Oxford Martin School Working Paper, Oxford University, September 17, 2013, https://www.oxfordmartin.ox.ac.uk /downloads/academic/The_Future_of_Employment.pdf.

3. Yuval Noah Harari, *21 Lessons for the 21st Century* (New York: Spiegel & Grau, 2018), 266.

4. Ibid., 268–269.

5. Daniel Kahneman, *Thinking, Fast and Slow* (New York: Farrar, Straus, and Giroux, 2011), 3.

6. Chris Arygris, *Teaching Smart People How to Learn* (Boston: Harvard Business School, 2008), 26.

7. Barbara L. Fredrickson, *Positivity: Top-Notch Research Reveals the 3:1 Ratio That Will Change Your Life* (New York: Three Rivers, 2009), 191.

8. Jim Clifton and Jim Harter, *It's the Manager* (New York: Gallup, 2019), 11.

9. Gary Hamel, *What Matters Now: How to Win in a World of Relentless Change, Ferocious Competition, and Unstoppable Innovation* (San Francisco: Jossey-Bass, 2012), 37.

10. Ibid., 188.

11. John O'Donohue, *Anam Cara* (New York: Harper Perrenial, 1997), 143.

12. "Culture," EnPro Industries, https://www.enproindustries.com/culture.

13. See, for example, David Sloan Wilson, *Does Altruism Exist? Culture, Genes, and the Welfare of Others* (New Haven, CT: Yale University Press, 2015); Charles Daniel Batson, *Altruism in Humans* (New York: Oxford University Press, 2011).

14. Anil K. Seth and Karl J. Friston, "Active Interoceptive Inference and the Emotional Brain," *Philosophical Transactions of the Royal Society B: Biological Sciences* 371, no. 1708 (2016); Andy Clark, "Whatever Next? Predictive Brains, Situated Agents, and the Future of Cognitive Science," *Behavioral and Brain Sciences* 36, no. 3 (2013): 181–204.

15. Lisa Feldman Barrett, *How Emotions Are Made: The Secret Life of the Brain* (New York: Houghton Mifflin Harcourt, 2017), 65.

16. Christopher G. Lucas, Sophie Bridgers, Thomas L. Griffiths, and Alison Gopnik, "When Children Are Better (or at Least More Open-Minded) Learners Than Adults: Developmental Differences in Learning the Forms of Causal Relationships," *Cognition* 131, no. 2 (2014): 284–299; Alison Gopnik et al., "Changes in Cognitive Flexibility and Hypothesis Search Across Human Life History from Childhood to Adolescence to Adulthood," *Proceedings of the National Academy of Sciences* 114, no. 30 (2017): 7892–7899.

17. Milton Lodge, Charles Taber, and Brad Verhulst, "Conscious and Unconscious Information Processing with Implications for Experimental Political Science," *Cambridge Handbook of Experimental Political Science* (2011): 280.

18. Edward O. Wilson, *The Origins of Creativity* (New York: Liveright, 2017), 59.

19. Matthieu Ricard, *On the Path to Enlightenment: Heart Advice from the Great Tibetan Masters* (Boulder, CO: Shambhala, 2013), 128.

20. Jon Kabat-Zinn, *Mindfulness for Beginners: Reclaiming the Present Moment—and Your Life* (Boulder, CO: Sounds True, 2012), 1.

21. William James, *The Principles of Psychology*, vol. 1 (New York: Cosimo Classics, 2013), 424.

22. Kabat-Zinn, *Mindfulness for Beginners*, 152.

23. Daniel Goleman and Richard J. Davidson, *Altered Traits: Science Reveals How Meditation Changes Your Mind, Brain, and Body* (New York: Avery, 2017), 154.

24. Edward D. Hess and Katherine Ludwig, *Humility Is the New Smart: Rethinking Human Excellence in the Smart Machine Age* (Oakland: Berrett-Koehler, 2017), 84–85.

25. Robert A. Emmons, *Gratitude Works! A 21-Day Program for Creating Emotional Prosperity* (San Francisco: Jossey-Bass, 2013), 3–4.

26. Barbara L. Fredrickson, *Love 2.0: Creating Happiness and Health in Moments of Connection* (New York: Plume, 2014), 8.

27. John O'Donohue, *The Space Between Us: A Book of Blessings* (New York: Convergent, 2008).

28. Robert Kegan and Lisa Laskow Lahey, *Immunity to Change* (Boston: Harvard Business Press, 2009), 318.

29. Howard Kirschenbaum and Valerie Land Henderson, eds., *The Carl Rogers Reader* (New York: Houghton Mifflin, 1989), 302.

30. Carol S. Dweck, *Mindset: The New Psychology of Success* (New York: Ballantine, 2016).

31. Hess and Ludwig, *Humility Is the New Smart*, 38.

32. Albert Einstein, *The Ultimate Quotable Einstein*, ed. Alice Calaprice (Princeton, NJ: Princeton University Press, 2011).

33. Ibid., 177.

34. Ibid., 181.

35. Kirschenbaum and Henderson, *The Carl Rogers Reader*; Edward D. Hess, *Learn or Die: Using Science to Build a Leading-Edge Learning Organization* (New York: Columbia University Press, 2014).

36. Kirschenbaum and Henderson, *The Carl Rogers Reader*, 19.

37. Ibid., 28.

38. Ibid., 304.

39. William James, *Psychology: The Briefer Course* (Toronto: Dover, 2001).

40. Ibid., 194.

41. Ibid., 195.

42. Warren Bennis, *On Becoming a Leader* (Philadelphia: Basic Books, 2009).

43. Ibid., xxvi.

44. Ibid., 65.

45. Peter D. Kaufman, ed., *Poor Charlie's Almanack: The Wit and Wisdom of Charles T. Munger* (Virginia Beach, VA: PCA Publications, 2016).

46. Ibid., 6.

47. Ibid., 74.

48. Ibid., 54–56.

49. John L. Hennessy, *Leading Matters: Lessons from My Journey* (Stanford: Stanford Business Books, 2018).

50. Jonathan Haidt, *The Happiness Hypothesis: Finding Modern Truth in Ancient Wisdom* (New York: Basic Books, 2006).

51. Ibid., 222.

52. Ibid., 224.

53. Ray Dalio, *Principles* (New York: Simon & Schuster, 2017); Ray Dalio, *Principles for Success* (New York: Avid Reader, 2019); Ray Dalio, "What I Have for You," LinkedIn, June 17, 2019, https://www.linkedin.com/pulse/what-i-have-offer-you-ray-dalio-1f/; Hess, *Learn or Die*, 113–163.

54. Hess, *Learn or Die*, 117.

55. William B. Turner, *The Learning of Love: A Journey Toward Servant Leadership* (Macon, GA: Smyth & Helwys, 2000).

56. Ibid., 148.

57. Ibid., 149.

58. Twyla Tharp, *The Creative Habit: Learn It and Use It for Life* (New York: Simon & Schuster, 2006), 7.

59. Ibid., 22.

60. Viktor E. Frankl, *The Will to Meaning: Foundations and Applications of Logotherapy* (New York: Plume, 2014).

61. Ibid., 51.

62. Abraham H. Maslow, *The Farther Reaches of Human Nature* (New York: Penguin, 1976); Abraham H. Maslow, *Toward a Psychology of Being* (Princeton, NJ: Van Nostrand, 1962).

63. Maslow, *Toward a Psychology of Being*, 15.

64. Ibid., 65.

65. Mary Catherine Bateson, *Composing a Further Life: The Age of Active Wisdom* (New York: Vintage Books, 2010).

66. Ibid., 24.

67. Ibid., 243.

68. John C. Bogle, *Enough: True Measures of Money, Business and Life* (Hoboken, NJ: Wiley, 2009).

69. Arthur Herman, *The Cave and the Light: Plato Versus Aristotle, and the Struggle for the Soul of Western Civilization* (New York: Random House, 2013).

70. Ibid., 53.

71. Ibid., 56.

72. Ibid.

73. Ibid., 20.

74. Ibid., 23–24.

75. Lao Tzu, *Tao Te Ching*, trans. Stephen Mitchell (New York: Harper Perennial, 1988).

76. Ibid., 9.

77. Ibid., 67.

78. Epictetus and Sharon Lebell, *The Art of Living: The Classical Manual on Virtue, Happiness, and Effectiveness* (New York: Harper One, 1995).

79. Ibid., xii.

80. Ibid., 3.

81. Ibid., 75.

82. Seneca, *Letters from a Stoic*, trans. Robin Campbell (New York: Penguin, 2004).

83. Ricard, *On the Path to Enlightenment*.

84. Ibid., 128.

85. Ibid., 210.

86. Dalai Lama, *Beyond Religion: Ethics for a Whole World* (Boston: Mariner, 2012); Dalai Lama and Desmond Tutu, *The Book of Joy: Lasting Happiness in a Changing World* (New York: Avery, 2016); Dalai Lama, *How to Practice: The Way to a Meaningful Life*, ed. and trans. Jeffrey Hopkins (New York: Atria, 2002); Dalai Lama and Thubten Chodron, *The Foundation of Buddhist Practice* (Somerville, MA: Wisdom, 2018); Dalai Lama, *Practicing Wisdom: The Perfection of Shantideva's Bodhisattva Way*, ed. Thupten Jinpa (Somerville, MA: Wisdom, 2005).

87. Dalai Lama, *Beyond Religion*, xi.

88. Dalai Lama and Chodron, *The Foundation of Buddhist Practice*, 11.

89. Dalai Lama, *Beyond Religion*, 109.

90. Dalai Lama, *Practicing Wisdom*, 6.

91. Dalai Lama, *How to Practice*, 10.

92. Gary Hamel, *What Matters Now: How to Win in a World of Relentless Change, Ferocious Competition, and Unstoppable Innovation* (San Francisco: Jossey-Bass, 2012), 142.

93. Excerpted from Hess and Ludwig, *Humility Is the New Smart*.

94. Hess, *Learn or Die*.

95. Julia Rozovsky, "The Five Keys to a Successful Google Team," re:Work, November 17, 2015, https://rework.withgoogle.com/blog/five-keys-to-a-successful-google-team/.

96. Maslow, *Toward a Psychology of Being*, 55.

97. Excerpted from Edward D. Hess, "Leadership in the Smart Machine Age: The 4 Es," Darden Ideas to Action, September 20, 2016, https://ideas.darden.virginia.edu/leadership-in-the-smart-machine-age-the-4es; and "The 4 Es: The CEO Is the Chief Enabling Officer," Darden Ideas to Action, October 20, 2016, https://ideas.darden.virginia.edu/the-4-es-the-ceo-is-the-chief-enabling-officer.

98. Ray Dalio, "Principles," Bridgewater Associates, quoted in Hess, *Learn or Die*, 123.

99. Satya Nadella, *Hit Refresh: The Quest to Rediscover Microsoft's Soul and Imagine a Better Future for Everyone* (New York: HarperCollins, 2019), 4–6.

100. Jane E. Dutton, *Energize Your Workplace: How to Create and Sustain High-Quality Connections at Work* (San Francisco: Wiley, 2003), 16–17.

101. Paul J. Zak, *Trust Factor: The Science of Creating High-Performance Companies* (New York: AMACOM, 2017), 8.

102. Rozovsky, "The Five Keys to a Successful Google Team."

103. Fredrickson, *Love 2.0*, 51.

104. Ibid., 10.

105. Bogle, *Enough*, 163.

106. Julia B. Bear and Anita Williams Wooley, "Role of Gender in Team Collaboration and Performance," *Interdisciplinary Science Reviews* 36, no. 2 (June 2011).

107. Ibid.

108. Kirschenbaum and Henderson, *The Carl Rogers Reader*, 135–138.

109. Joseph Henrich, *The Secret of Our Success: How Culture Is Driving Human Evolution Domesticating Our Species and Making Us Smarter* (Princeton, NJ: Princeton University Press, 2016), 329.

110. William Isaacs, *Dialogue: The Art of Thinking Together* (New York: Currency, 1999), 117.

111. Edgar H. Schein, *Humble Inquiry: The Gentle Art of Asking Instead of Telling* (Oakland: Berrett-Koehler, 2013), 3.

112. Kirschenbaum and Henderson, *The Carl Rogers Reader*, 20.

113. Isaacs, *Dialogue*, 84.

114. Joseph Jaworski, Gary Jusela, and C. Otto Scharmer, "Coming from Your Inner Self: Interview with W. Brian Arthur," April 16, 1999, https://www.presencing.org/aboutus/theory-u/leadership-interview/W_Brian_Arthur.

115. Norman Doidge, *The Brain That Changes Itself* (New York: Penguin, 2007), 196–214.

116. Hess, *Learn or Die*, 80.

117. Hess and Ludwig, *Humility Is the New Smart*, 103–104.

118. Hess, *Learn or Die*, 82–84.

119. David Whyte, *Crossing the Unknown Sea: Work as a Pilgrimage of Identity* (New York: Riverhead Books, 2001), 4.

ACKNOWLEDGMENTS

As you can imagine with a life of over seven decades, I have many more people whom I should acknowledge for their gifts to me along my life journey than I can do here. With deep gratitude:

To my parents, who instilled in me the love of learning, to always do the right thing, and to have the courage to go out in the world to discover and learn. They brought books into my daily life at a very young age. It was through reading books that I discovered a world bigger than me and bigger and different than my small hometown in rural Georgia. And they encouraged me to have the courage go out into that world and to find my place doing good for others.

To my teachers and mentors who saw something in me and with a helping hand and heart inspired me, guided me, listened to me, and gave me growth opportunities: Tom Aiello, Dean Maryam Alavi, David Bonderman, Professor Lyle E. Bourne Jr., Dean Robert F. Bruner, Professor Kim S. Cameron, Professor Richard D'Aveni, Professor Edward W. Davis, Professor Charles M. Davison Jr., Professor Robert Drazin, Professor James R. Freeland, Coach Ray Graves, Coach Charles Grisham, Professor Al L. Hartgraves, Professor Sydney Jourard, Professor Robert K. Kazanjian, Professor Robert D. Landel, Professor Jeanne M. Liedtka, Jack McGovern, Peter J. Norton, Coach Fred Pancoast, Dean Deryck Rensburg, Dean Thomas S. Robertson, Dean Peter Rodriquez, Professor Antonin Scalia, Professor Jagdish Sheth, Professor Sankaran Venkataraman, Ira T. Wender, and Jack White.

To the many leaders from whom I have learned, including Bradbury H. Anderson, William R. Berkley, John Brown, Tom Cousins, Ray Dalio, Michael L. Eskew, Marvin Riley, John Gabbert, Herb Kelleher, Fernando Merce, Admiral (Ret.) Gary Roughead, Sean P. Ryan, Richard J. Schneiders, Horst Schultze, John Schwieters, and William B. Turner.

To Jeevan Sivasubramaniam and Neal Maillet of Berrett-Koehler, who asked me to write this book, and to the entire team at Berrett-Koehler for being a joy to work with and being consummate caring professionals.

To my fabulous research associate Katherine Ludwig, whose high standards, love of learning, and contributions to my work over the last seven years have made my work so much better and whose friendship has allowed us to collaborate and have the joy of experiencing many High-Quality, Making-Meaning Conversations.

To the Batten Institute at the Darden School of Business for its financial support of my work and to its executive director Sean Carr for all his support over the years.

To my administrative assistant Kathy Kane, who for over 13 years has brought joy and positivity into my life as well as her expertise, high standards, and good judgment in shepherding my work.

And with all my love and gratitude to my wife, Katherine, whose love and caring compassionate support of my career and her patience during my writing of 13 books has been an immeasurable gift from her heart that has given me the courage to be.

INDEX

accountability: Daily Intentions for, 159; feedback for, 156; in teamwork, 132

active inference, 28

active-learning, 19

active listening, 247–248

adult learning, 6–7, 208, 290

advocacy, 147–149

Altered Traits (Goleman/Davidson), 42

ambiguity, 284–285

amygdala, 44

Anam Cara (O'Donohue), 17, 182

ancient philosophers, 58, 64

anxiety, 135

apologies, 213–214

Argyris, Chris, 7

Aristotle, 79–80

arrogance, 83

Arthur, W. Brian, 224–225

artificial intelligence, 101

The Art of Living (Epictetus), 82

assumptions: checklist, 274f; in digital age, 217; failure and, 212; from judgment, 82–83; reflecting on, 219

attitude. *See* Hyper-Learning Mindset

authenticity, 69, 137

authority, 64, 65

automatic responses, 33

autonomy, 99, 174–176

auto-pilot, 32

Barrett, Lisa Feldman, 29

Bateson, Mary Catherine, 77–78

Bayesian probability, 28

behavior. *See* Hyper-Learning Behaviors

Being. *See* New Way of Being

Bennis, Warren, 67–68

Berkley, Bill, 99, 100; on change, 101; leadership of, 107–109; success for, 104; teamwork for, 103; technology for, 102. *See also* W. R. Berkley Corporation

Berkley, Rob, 99, 100; failure for, 103; leadership of, 107–109; participation for, 104; status quo for, 101–102; teamwork for, 102. *See also* W. R. Berkley Corporation

Berkshire Hathaway, 68

Best Self: brain-body-mind connection for, 33; Daily Intentions for, 12; defining, 70; in digital age, 205; emotions for, 50; focusing on, 192–193; at home, 168f, 172; Inner Peace and, 23, 83, 134, 200; journey to, 54–55, 133, 294; meditation for, 46; at meetings, 210; New Way of Being and, 5, 11, 250, 291; New Way of Being for, 165, 205; striving for, 19–20, 41; at work, 182; in workplace, 161, 171, 275

biology, 27

bodies: body language, 189; body scans, 46; brains and, 28–30; emotions and, 193; minds and, 32–33; quiet bodies, 26, 47–49, 122–123

Bogle, John, 194

Bourne, Lyle, Jr., 8, 185, 251

brains: amygdala, 44; bodies and, 28–30; Brain HQ, 258; intellectual capacities, 60; mental chatter from, 142–143; minds and, 32–33; neuroscience of, 258–261; plasticity of, 29–30, 60; predictions by, 32, 35; priorities of, 256; sensations and, 31–32; tasks for, 30

break times, 39, 68–69, 79, 82

breathing, 48–49, 51–52

Bridgewater Associates, LP, 46, 71, 173

Brown, Richard P., 48–49

Buddhism, 41, 46–47, 72, 76–77, 84–87

business. *See* workplace

calm-and-connect response, 189–190

caring, 185–186, 194–196; psychology of, 198; trust and, 200–204, 201f, 211

Caring, Trusting Teams: collective intelligence for, 197–198; creating, 185–188; in digital age, 16–17, 170; emotions in, 188–194; High-Quality, Making-Meaning Conversations with, 18, 165; New Way of Working and, 16, 179–180, 198–200; workshops for, 200–204, 201f
case studies, 13
Catford, Lorna, 267
Catmull, Ed, 62–63
The Cave and the Light (Herman), 79–80
centering, 141–143
challenges: in communication, 144–145; in digital age, 101, 250–254; from egos, 73–74; in learning, 290–291; for status quo, 94, 106, 116t; at workplace, 37
change: Berkley, B., on, 101; childlike mindset for, 254–256; from conversations, 8; core concepts for, 64; in culture, 165–166; curiosity for, 261–263; from Daily Intentions, 119; diagnostics for, 13; in digital age, 261, 290; engagement for, 265–266; in environment, 6; exploration for, 256–258; goals for, 262; for humans, 2–3, 5; in Hyper-Learning Behaviors, 131–133, 198; Hyper-Learning Mindset and, 4–5, 12, 57–59, 64–65, 92, 258–261, 282; in identity, 39–40; for Inner Peace, 40–41; knowledge and, 63; leadership and, 161–162; from love, 292; in meetings, 199–200; from mental rehearsal, 259–260; personal transformation and, 158; psychology of, 131–133; reflection and, 19, 253; for Riley, 155–156, 268; self-discipline for, 250; technology and, 1–2, 107–109; vulnerability and, 52–53; in workplace, 166–167, 167t–168t, 171–172
Chapman, Gary, 144
Chappell, Delane, 73

checklists: for assumptions, 274f; for collaboration, 270f–271f; for critical thinking questions, 272f–273f; for goals, 57, 159; for Hyper-Learning Behaviors, 133, 203–204; for listening, 270f–271f
childlike Hyper-Learning Mindset, 254–256
choice, 24
client-centric counseling, 58, 66
coaches, 140
Coca-Cola Company, 72, 74
cognition: cognitive psychology, 32–33; decision making, 3; emotions and, 48; engagement and, 16; information and, 6–7; in workplace, 9
Cognitive Behavior Therapy, 46–47
coherent breathing, 48–49
collaboration: calm-and-connect response in, 189–190; collective intelligence and, 197–198; competition and, 39; diagnostics for, 125–126; in digital age, 185–186, 199; effective, 31, 38, 95–96, 106, 114t–115t, 190; emotions from, 183; engagement and, 204; at EnPro Industries, 241, 242f–243f; for humans, 93; learning and, 3, 9, 16–17, 166; listening and, 270f–271f; reflective listening for, 291; research on, 259; rules of engagement for, 204, 223; teamwork and, 70, 199–200
collective flow, 18, 170, 193, 221–224
collective intelligence, 185, 197–198
"Coming from Your Inner Self" (Arthur), 224
command and control, 138–139, 145–146, 166
commission, 284
commitment, 230
common purpose, 187
communication: challenges in, 144–145; for expertise, 133; by leadership,

107–109, 140–141; in learning, 58, 185; positivity in, 150; for social connections, 33; trust and, 182; in workplace, 178. *See also* High-Quality, Making-Meaning Conversations
competence, 13, 177
competition, 39, 293
complacency, 5
Composing a Life (Bateson), 77
computer science, 69
concepts, 64–65
confirmation bias, 10, 217
connecting, 125–126, 193–194
conscious minds, 30–31
consciousness, 65
consistency, 89–90
continual learning, 232
conversations: change from, 8; collective flow in, 221–224; connection list for, 220t–221t; emergent thinking in, 224–225; in Learning Journals, 209; purpose of, 206–208; questions in, 214–216; reflection on, 20, 206, 217–219, 222–223; reflective listening in, 217–220; rich, 283, 288; teamwork and, 225–226; understanding from, 17–18. *See also* High-Quality, Making-Meaning Conversations
core concepts, 64
courage, 70, 94, 97t, 106; embracing, 180; at EnPro Industries, 241, 241f, 243f; Hyper-Learning Behaviors and, 97t, 112t; at WRBC, 97–98, 97t
creativity: *The Creative Habit*, 76; *Creativity, Inc.*, 62–63; imagination and, 91–92
critical thinking, 61; *Critical Thinking*, 62–63; questions, 248, 272f–273f
Csikszentmihalyi, Mihaly, 71
culture: change in, 165–166; cultural principles, 230–232; of dual bottom lines, 235; leadership and, 106; people-centric, 100, 170, 179, 227–228;

reflection on, 232; of teamwork, 106–107
curiosity, 94; for change, 261–263; at EnPro Industries, 240f, 241, 243f; intellectual, 70

Daily Intentions, 12, 49; for accountability, 159; for Best Self, 12; change from, 119; consistency for, 89–90; Hyper-Learning Mindset and, 131; Hyper-Learning Practices, 252–253; questions in, 79; visualization of, 252; workshops, 55–56
Dalai Lama, 55, 85–87
Dalio, Ray: Hyper-Learning Behaviors of, 46, 71–72, 157, 182; *Principles*, 62–63, 72, 267
data, 212
Davidson, Richard J., 42
Deadly Ps, 73
Deci, Edward L., 174
decision making, 3, 106, 113t, 139
deep breathing, 48, 51–52
deep listening, 239–240, 239f, 242f
deep-thinking, 140–141, 267–268
defensive reasoning, 7–8, 36–38
deliberate practice, 251
diagnostics: for building trust, 130–131; for change, 13; for collaboration, 125–126; for Hyper-Learning Mindset, 124–125; for learning, 128–130; for positive emotions, 123–124; for quiet bodies, 122–123; for Quiet Egos, 120–121; for quiet minds, 121–122; for reflective listening, 127–128; for workplace, 175–177
Dialogue (Isaacs), 213
digital age, 294; assumptions in, 217; Best Self in, 205; Caring, Trusting Teams in, 16–17, 170; challenges in, 101, 250–254; change in, 261, 290; collaboration in, 185–186, 199; collective flow in, 170; collective

digital age (*continued*)
  intelligence in, 185; engagement in,
  14; Hyper-Learning Mindset for,
  10–11, 31, 256–258; Hyper-Learning
  Practices in, 250, 260, 275; incentives
  in, 169–170; learning in, 5; New Way
  of Being in, 91; New Way of Working
  in, 91; skills in, 166; Smart Machines
  in, 284; tasks in, 15; technology for,
  2–3, 61, 91–92; thinking in, 256; trust
  in, 191; workplace in, 3–4
dignity, 208, 212–214
direct reports, 176–177
discipline, 160
discovery: exploration and, 255,
  263–265; Hyper-Learning Mindset
  for, 277; Insight Discovery Questions,
  262–263
distractions, 153–154
diversity: gender, 186, 197, 231–232;
  inclusion and, 234–235; in teamwork,
  186, 225–226
Doidge, Norman, 258
down time, 49
dual bottom lines, 18–19; culture of, 235;
  for humans, 230; reflection on, 231,
  236; theory of, 233–234
Dutton, Jane E., 188–189
Dweck, Carol, 59–60, 229

echo chambers, 155–156
Economic Complexity Theory Group, 224
economics, 18–19
Edmondson, Amy, 178
effective collaboration, 31, 38, 95–96,
  106; for Google, 190; Hyper-Learning
  Behaviors and, 114t–115t
efficiency, 10; for humans, 28; shortcuts
  for, 29; at workplace, 139–140
effort, 58
egos, 7, 11; challenges from, 73–74; fears
  and, 292; goals for, 40; Inner Peace
  and, 35–36, 38–39; Quiet Egos, 26,

38–39, 94, 120–121; for Riley, 154–155;
  sharing and, 215
Einstein, Albert, 65–66
Elder, Linda, 62–63
elitism, 178
embracing, 180
emergence, 25, 225
emergent thinking, 52, 224–225
Emmons, Robert A., 45
Emory University, 72
emotions, 11; for Best Self, 50; bodies
  and, 193; in Caring, Trusting Teams,
  188–194; cognition and, 48; from
  collaboration, 183; connections with,
  33; emotional intelligence, 94;
  engagement with, 31; Hyper-Learning
  Behaviors and, 34, 291; Inner Peace
  and, 31–32, 50–52; internal qualities
  and, 23–24; management of, 91;
  positive, 25–26, 50–52, 123–124,
  173–174, 192; recognition of, 212–213;
  from storytelling, 136–137; sub-Hyper-
  Learning Behaviors and, 13; teamwork
  and, 188–191; thinking and, 16
empathy, 70, 155
enabling: High-Quality, Making-
  Meaning Conversations, 212–220,
  221t–222t; for Hyper-Learning
  Mindset, 119; inhibiting and,
  220t–221t; leadership and, 169,
  179–181; psychology of, 170
Energize Your Workplace (Dutton),
  188–189
engagement, 180; for change, 265–266;
  cognition and, 16; collaboration and,
  204; collective flow and, 18; in digital
  age, 14; with emotions, 31; with
  gratitude, 44–45; Hyper-Learning
  Behaviors and, 59; with Inner Peace,
  23–26, 54; from leadership, 189–190;
  with others, 70; rules of, 186–188, 204,
  223; in teamwork, 187–188; thinking
  and, 3; vital, 71; at workplace, 102

enlightenment, 84–85

Enough (Bogle), 194

EnPro Industries, 18–19, 134–135, 152; CEO speech at, 233–236; collaboration at, 241, 242f–243f; cultural principles at, 230–232; Hyper-Learning Behaviors at, 237–241, 238f–241f; Hyper-Learning Practices at, 244, 245f–246f; meeting management worksheets at, 244, 247f–249f; people-centric culture at, 227–228; values at, 228–229. *See also specific employees*

entrepreneurs, 263–264

environment: change in, 6; for meetings, 145–146; psychology of, 153–154; for workplace, 14–19, 158

Epictetus, 82–83

Ericsson, Anders, 251

evidence, 106, 110t–117t

evolution, 3–6, 27

excellence, 229

excelling, at otherness, 180

experience, 20, 212

experimentation, 61–62

expertise, 6, 133

exploration, 255–258, 261, 263–265

failure, 103; assumptions and, 212; fear of, 105; humility and, 235–236; learning from, 137; trial and error, 255

fears, 7; actions and, 132; egos and, 292; psychology of, 179; trust and, 154; in workplace, 174

feedback, 156, 283

feelings, 27

fight-or-flight response, 189

The Five Love Languages (Chapman), 144

flow, 221–222. *See also* collective flow

forgiveness, 213–214

foundational Hyper-Learning Behaviors, 132

Frankl, Viktor E., 76–77

Franklin, Benjamin, 79

Fredrickson, Barbara, 8, 173–174, 189, 192

Garlock Group, 228

gender diversity, 186, 197, 231–232

Gerbarg, Patricia L., 48–49

Gibran, Kahlil, 71

Gladly, Cris, 144

global employment, 14

goals: for change, 262; checklists for, 57, 159; for egos, 40; for High-Quality, Making-Meaning Conversations, 221–225; for humans, 66; for Hyper-Learning Behaviors, 55, 220, 220t–221t; for learning, 38–39; noble goals, 160; psychology of, 81, 153–155; teaching, 244

Goizuetta Business School, 72, 260

Goleman, Daniel, 42

good fortune, 279–281

good Hyper-Learning Behaviors, 187–188

Goodrich Company, 228

Google, 173, 178, 190, 283

gratitude, 293; engagement with, 44–45; for Hansen, 286; Hyper-Learning Practices for, 146–147; journals, 44, 121; meditation and, 39; teamwork and, 39; training and, 47

growth Hyper-Learning Mindset, 59–60, 89, 106

guiding values, 140

Haidt, Jonathan, 70–71

Hamel, Gary, 15–16, 172

Hansen, Adam, 14, 289; good fortune for, 279–281; gratitude for, 286; Ikigai for, 276–278, 279f, 286–288; tips from, 282–285

Harari, Yuval Noah, 4–5, 78

Harvard Business School, 152

The Healing Power of the Breath (Brown/ Gerbarg), 48–49

Healy, Alice, 251
Hennessy, John L., 69–70
Henrich, Joseph, 212, 219
Herman, Arthur, 79–80
Hess, Ed, 144, 150
hierarchies, 144, 173, 178
High-Quality, Making-Meaning
    Conversations, 205–206; with Caring,
    Trusting Teams, 18, 165; enabling,
    212–220, 221t–222t; goals for, 221–225;
    workshops for, 209–212, 225–226
high-quality human connections,
    188–191
history, 27
Hit Refresh (Nadella), 182
honesty, 198
how-to-learn skills, 128–130
humans: auto-pilot for, 32; change for,
    2–3, 5; collaboration for, 93; defensive
    reasoning by, 7–8; development for,
    181; dual bottom lines for, 230;
    efficiency for, 28; evolution and, 3–6;
    goals for, 66; high-quality human
    connections, 188–191; human
    development, 18–19; human dignity,
    208, 212–214; humanistic psychology,
    77; Hyper-Learning Behaviors of,
    12–14; Hyper-Learning Mindset for,
    12; idea meritocracies for, 169; identity
    for, 35; Inner Peace for, 11–12; joy for,
    183–184; judgment by, 217–218;
    laziness for, 6–7; learning for, 20;
    management of, 15–16; micro-
    moments for, 192–193; by predictions,
    28–29; psychology of, 206–207; science
    of, 6–11, 28–33, 92; Smart Machines
    compared to, 285; smart technology
    for, 167; suffering for, 77, 86; survival
    for, 2; talking for, 17; teamwork for,
    165–166; thinking for, 27
Humble Inquiry (Schein), 214
humility, 25; failure and, 235–236;
    Humility Is the New Smart, 40–41,

131–133; in leadership, 69, 138; Quiet
    Egos and, 94
Hustad, Tom, 280
Hyper-Learning. *See specific topics*
Hyper-Learning Behaviors, 249; change
    in, 131–133, 198; checklists for, 133,
    203–204; Cognitive Behavior Therapy,
    46–47; courage and, 97t, 112t; of
    Dalio, 46, 71–72, 157, 182; effective
    collaboration and, 114t–115t; emotions
    and, 34, 291; engagement and, 59; at
    EnPro Industries, 237–241, 238f–241f;
    evidence-based decision making and,
    113t; foundational, 132; goals for, 55,
    220, 220t–221t; good, 187–188; of
    humans, 12–14; Hyper-Learning
    Behavioral innovation, 285–286;
    Hyper-Learning Behavioral science,
    285; Hyper-Learning Mindset and,
    91–92, 107, 282–285; inspiration and,
    171–172; learning, 93–98, 97t, 165;
    practical guidance for, 19–20;
    psychology of, 101–105; reflection for,
    98–99, 105, 109, 118, 259; reflective
    listening and, 111t; resilience for, 117t;
    SDT for, 106; self-management of,
    110t; status quo challenges and, 116t;
    sub-Hyper-Learning Behaviors, 13,
    239–241, 239f–241f; workshops for,
    93–98, 97t, 119, 237–238; at WRBC,
    99–101, 106–109. *See also* diagnostics
Hyper-Learning Mindset: for Aristotle,
    79–80; for Bateson, 77–78; for Bennis,
    67–68; break times for, 68–69, 79, 82;
    change and, 4–5, 12, 57–59, 64–65, 92,
    258–261, 282; childlike, 254–256;
    Daily Intentions and, 131; for Dalai
    Lama, 85–87; for Dalio, 71–72;
    diagnostics for, 124–125; for digital
    age, 10–11, 31, 256–258; for discovery,
    277; for Einstein, 65–66; enabling for,
    119; for Epictetus, 82–83; for Frankl,
    76–77; growth, 59–60, 89, 106; for

Haidt, 70–71; for Hennessy, 69–70; for humans, 12; Hyper-Learning Behaviors and, 91–92, 107, 282–285; impermanence and, 224, 261; for leadership, 227; lifelong learning Hyper-Learning Mindset, 59; for meetings, 63; NewSmart, 60–63; for New Way of Being, 209; for personal transformation, 291; for Plato, 80–81; reflection for, 63, 255–256; for Rogers, 66–67; for Seneca, 83–84; theories for, 59–63; for Turner, 72–75; workshops for, 88–90

Hyper-Learning Practices: Daily Intentions, 252–253; in digital age, 250, 260, 275; at EnPro Industries, 244, 245f–246f; for gratitude, 146–147; Learning Journals, 267–268; for personal transformation, 135–136, 146–147; podcast listening, 266–267; reading, 266; reflection on, 264; routines and, 265–266; self-discipline, 251; for self-improvement, 254; think tanks, 268–269

idea meritocracies, 15–16, 106, 157–158, 169, 173
identity: change in, 39–40; defensive reasoning and, 36–38; for humans, 35; innovation and, 102; neuroscience of, 42; NewSmart Identity, 40–41; self-image in, 36; for success, 131
Ikigai, 276–278, 279f, 285–288
imagination, 30, 65, 91–92, 172
immersion, 225
impermanence, 89, 224, 261
incentives, 169–170
inclusion, 234–235
inference, 28
influence, 165–166
information: cognition and, 6–7; processing, 30; seeking, 38; sharing of, 144–145

inhibiting, 220t–221t
Inner Peace, 200, 294; acts of gratitude for, 44–45; Best Self and, 23, 83, 134, 200; change for, 40–41; egos and, 35–36, 38–39; emotions and, 31–32, 50–52; engagement with, 23–26, 54; from enlightenment, 85; for humans, 11–12; meditation for, 41–44; methodology for, 59; minds and, 30–33, 45–47, 205; personal transformation and, 14; philosophy of, 83; quiet bodies and, 47–49; reflection for, 26–27, 34, 36–38, 52–53; science of, 27–28; workshops for, 55–56

innovation, 16, 70; by entrepreneurs, 263–264; experimentation for, 61–62; Hyper-Learning Behavioral, 285–286; identity and, 102; *The Journal of Product Innovation Management*, 280; for personal transformation, 283–284; psychology of, 143–144, 276–277, 280–281, 286–287; questions for, 103; social intelligence for, 92; strategies for, 92, 99, 103–105; from teamwork, 105
inquiry, 147–149, 214
Insight Discovery Questions, 262–263
inspiration, 171–172, 179–180
instincts, 27, 276
integration, 158–159
integrity, 95
intellectual capacities, 60, 66, 92
intellectual curiosity, 70
internal noise, 25–26
internal qualities, 23–24
interrupting, 219–220
investing, 68
Isaacs, William, 213, 218, 219
Isen, Alice, 173–174

James, William, 42, 67
jobs. *See* workplace
Joffrey Ballet, 76

The Journal of Product Innovation Management (Hustad), 280
journals, 44, 121. *See also* Learning Journals
joy: for humans, 183–184; of learning, 292; micro-joys, 51; psychology of, 293
judgment, 66; assumptions from, 82–83; of hierarchies, 173; by humans, 217–218; by leadership, 149; learning and, 214; mind-wandering and, 45; psychology of, 42

Kabat-Zinn, Jon, 42, 46
Kahnemen, Daniel, 6
Kegan, Robert, 57
knowledge, 63

Lao Tzu, 81
laziness, 6–7
leadership: change and, 161–162; command and control, 138–139, 166; communication by, 107–109, 140–141; culture and, 106; during disruption, 100; distribution of, 146; enabling and, 169, 179–181; engagement from, 189–190; expertise and, 6; humility in, 69, 138; Hyper-Learning Mindset for, 227; influence and, 165–166; judgment by, 149; *Leading Matters*, 69–70; learning from, 118, 135–136; *The Learning of Love*, 73; in Marines, 260; in meetings, 143–144, 193–194, 226; Native American, 208; for New Way of Being, 100; for New Way of Working, 100; organizational leaders, 7; patchwork quilt approach for, 78; performance and, 173; in problem-solving, 147–148; reflection on, 236–237; student, 72; studies, 67; thinking and, 266; trust with, 172; workshops on, 233–236
learning: active-learning, 19; adult, 6–7, 208, 290; from authority, 64; break

times for, 39; challenges in, 290–291; collaboration and, 3, 9, 16–17, 166; communication in, 58, 185; competition in, 293; from concepts, 64–65; confirmation bias and, 217; continual, 232; diagnostics for, 128–130; in digital age, 5; from failure, 137; goals for, 38–39; how-to-learn skills, 128–130; for humans, 20; Hyper-Learning Behaviors, 93–98, 97t, 165; inhibitors, 60–61; joy of, 292; judgment and, 214; from leadership, 118, 135–136; learner's high, 263; *The Learning of Love*, 73; *Learn or Die*, 46, 71, 152, 157–158; lifelong learning Hyper-Learning Mindset, 59; love of, 285; from mistakes, 87; motivation and, 59–60; from observations, 94–96, 109, 110t–117t; from others, 9; people-centric cultures and, 179; from personal transformation, 134–135; proactive, 6; quality of, 2; from questions, 94; from results, 62; science of, 7–10; smart technology for, 3; strategies for, 264–265; suboptimal, 9–10; in teamwork, 143–144; templates for, 269, 270f–274f; training and, 119; unlearning, 67; from warning signs, 133; from wisdom, 57; from writing, 88
Learning Journals, 34, 60; collective flow in, 222–223; conversations in, 209; Hyper-Learning Practices, 267–268; for observations, 239–241; reinvention in, 4–6; trust in, 191, 198–199
Lebell, Sharon, 82
legacies, 70
lifelong learning Hyper-Learning Mindset, 59
life purpose. *See* Ikigai
listening, 218; active, 247–248; collaboration and, 270f–271f; deep, 239–240, 239f, 242f; interrupting when, 219–220;

in meetings, 26; personal transformation from, 147–149; podcasts, 266–267; as respect, 137–138; for wisdom, 78. *See also* reflective listening

LKM. *See* loving-kindness meditation

logotherapy, 77

love, 74–75; change from, 292; *The Five Love Languages*, 144; of learning, 285; *The Learning of Love*, 73; *Love 2.0*, 8, 189, 192; platonic, 144–145, 151; purpose and, 160; *Real Love*, 47; at workplace, 147

loving-kindness meditation (LKM), 46–47

Ludwig, Katherine, 40–41, 60

Macadam, Steve, 233

machines, 15

management: direct reports for, 176–177; of humans, 15–16; inspiration by, 179–180; *The Journal of Product Innovation Management*, 280; meeting management worksheets, 244, 247f–249f; self-management, 106, 110t, 240f, 241, 243f

Marley, Bob, 156

Maslow, Abraham H., 77, 179

"Matins" (O'Donohue), 55

Mead, Margaret, 77

meaningful relationships, 181–183, 187, 193

meditation: for Best Self, 46; centering and, 141–143; deep breathing in, 48; gratitude and, 39; guided, 46; LKM, 46–47; in meetings, 142; mindfulness, 39, 41–44, 46; research on, 43–44

meetings, 26, 45; Best Self at, 210; change in, 199–200; environment for, 145–146; Hyper-Learning Mindset for, 63; leadership in, 143–144, 193–194, 226; meditation in, 142; meeting management worksheets, 244, 247f–249f; for Native Americans, 208; values in, 223; visualization techniques for, 133

mental chatter, 142–143

mental models, 8, 68, 211

mental rehearsal, 259–260

mentorship, 157

methodology: for Inner Peace, 59; quantity, 61; scientific method, 62–63, 89, 264

micro-joys, 51

micro-moments, 192–193

mindfulness meditation, 39, 41–44, 46

minds: Inner Peace and, 30–33, 45–47, 205; natural tendencies of, 24–25, 67; quiet minds, 26, 45–47, 121–122; subconscious, 30–31, 35

mindset. *See* Hyper-Learning Mindset

mind-wandering, 30–31, 42, 45

mistakes, 61–62, 87

modern philosophy, 57

modern thinkers, 58, 64

money, 81

motivation, 59–60

Munger, Charlie, 68, 266

mutual conversations. *See* High-Quality, Making-Meaning Conversations

Nadella, Satya, 182

Nakamura, Jeanne, 71

Native American leadership, 208

natural tendencies, 24–25, 67

negativity, 51–52

Nero, 83

nervous systems, 48

neuroscience, 28–29, 42, 258–261

NewSmart Hyper-Learning Mindset, 60–63

NewSmart Identity, 40–41

New Way of Being, 2, 5, 11, 250–251, 290–291, 293; attitude for, 131; for Best Self, 165, 205; Best Self and, 5, 11, 250, 291; in digital age, 91; exploration for, 258; Hyper-Learning Mindset for, 209; leadership for, 100; storytelling for, 134; in workplace, 244

New Way of Working, 2, 5, 11, 250–251,
    290–291, 293; Caring, Trusting Teams
    and, 16, 179–180, 198–200; in digital
    age, 91; leadership for, 100; storytelling
    for, 134; in workplace, 244; workplaces
    and, 14–19
noble goals, 160

observations: learning from, 94–96, 109,
    110t–117t; Learning Journals for,
    239–241
O'Donohue, John, 17, 55, 182
"Odyssey of the Mind," 147–148
omission, 284, 288
On the Path to Enlightenment (Ricard), 84
open-mindedness, 94, 239, 239f, 242f
organizational leaders, 7
otherness, 180
Outsmart Your Instincts (Hansen), 276,
    285–286
oxytocin, 189, 192

participation, 104
passion, 172
Pasteur Institute, 84
patchwork quilt approach, 78
The Path of the Everyday Hero (Catford/
    Ray), 267
Paul, Richard, 62–63
people-centric cultures, 100, 170, 179,
    227–228
perception, 29, 146–147
perfection, 282
performance, 71; competence and, 13;
    experience and, 20; leadership and,
    173; trust and, 16–17
personal transformation, 14; ambiguity
    for, 284–285; change and, 158; good
    fortune for, 279–281; Hyper-Learning
    Behavioral innovation for, 285–286;
    Hyper-Learning Mindset for, 291;
    Hyper-Learning Practices for,
    135–136, 146–147; Ikigai for, 276–278,

279f, 285–288; innovation for,
    283–284; learning from, 134–135;
    from listening, 147–149; from
    meditation, 141–143; meeting
    environment and, 145–146; reflection
    for, 150–151, 160–161, 288–289; for
    Riley, 152, 156–158, 161–162; security
    and, 144–145; self-image and, 149–150;
    simple prototypes for, 282–283; from
    storytelling, 139–140; team learning
    for, 143–144; thinking and, 140–141;
    from vulnerability, 136–139. *See also*
    Hansen
philosophy: ancient philosophers, 58, 64;
    of Buddhism, 41, 46–47, 72, 76–77,
    84–87; of human development, 18–19;
    of idea meritocracies, 15, 16; of Inner
    Peace, 83; modern, 57; science and, 11;
    Stoic, 46–47, 72, 76–77, 82, 86; Tao, 81;
    theories and, 64
Pixar Animation Studios, 62
plasticity, of brains, 29–30, 60
Plato, 80–81
platonic love, 144–145, 151
podcasts, 266–267
popularity, 73
position, 73
positive emotions, 25–26, 50–52;
    diagnostics for, 123–124; oxytocin
    and, 192; research on, 173–174
positive psychology, 158; research on, 50;
    for workplace, 173–174
Positivity (Fredrickson), 8
positivity resonance, 50–51, 192–193
possessions, 73
post action review, 249
practical guidance, 19–20
practices. *See* Hyper-Learning Practices
Prasangikas, 86
preconditions, 209–210
predictions, 28–29, 32, 35
prejudice, 73
presence, 25

Presencing Institute, 225
pride, 73
Principles (Dalio), 62–63, 72, 267
privacy, 140
proactive learning, 6
probability, 28
problem-solving, 147–148
promotions, 154
prototypes, 282–283
psychological safety, 106, 234–235, 237, 243f; trust and, 190; in workplace, 178–179
psychology: of arrogance, 83; of authenticity, 137; of caring, 198; of change, 131–133; client-centric counseling, 58, 66; coaches for, 140; cognitive, 32–33; of echo chambers, 155–156; of enabling, 170; of environment, 153–154; of fears, 179; of flow, 221–222; of goals, 81, 153–155; humanistic, 77; of humans, 206–207; of Hyper-Learning Behaviors, 101–105; of innovation, 143–144, 276–277, 280–281, 286–287; of joy, 293; of judgment, 42; logotherapy, 77; of love, 144–145; meditation and, 41; of perfection, 282; positive, 50, 158, 173–174; of recognition, 141; of SDT, 169; of self-image, 36–37; of smartness, 60–61; of smiling, 51; social, 70; of thinking, 84; of vulnerability, 159; of willingness, 40
purpose: common, 187; of conversations, 206–208; expected outcomes and, 244; love and, 160

quantity methodology, 61
questions, 65, 79; in conversations, 214–216; critical thinking, 248, 272f–273f; about Ikigai, 287–288; for innovation, 103; Insight Discovery Questions, 262–263; learning from, 94; self-sustaining nature of, 284; for

storytelling, 149–150; teamwork and, 148
quiet bodies, 26, 47–49, 122–123
Quiet Egos, 26, 38–39, 94, 120–121
Quiet Minds, 26, 45–47, 121–122

Ray, Michael, 267
reading, 68, 266
Real Love (Salzberg), 47
recognition, 141, 146–147, 212–213
reflection, 19; on assumptions, 219; change and, 19, 253; on conversations, 20, 206, 217–219, 222–223; on culture, 232; deep-thinking and, 140–141, 267–268; on dual bottom lines, 231, 236; on exploration, 261; for Hyper-Learning Behaviors, 98–99, 105, 109, 118, 259; for Hyper-Learning Mindset, 63, 255–256; on Hyper-Learning Practices, 264; for Inner Peace, 26–27, 34, 36–38, 52–53; on leadership, 236–237; for personal transformation, 150–151, 160–161, 288–289; on respect, 229; on teamwork, 191, 195–196, 198–199, 202–203; on workplace, 168, 171–172, 184
reflective listening, 25, 31, 38, 106; for collaboration, 291; in conversations, 217–220; diagnostics for, 127–128; Hyper-Learning Behaviors and, 111t; questions for, 214; strategies for, 95–97
regulation, of negativity, 51–52
relatedness, 174–177
relating, 125–126
relationships, 181–183, 193, 213–214
reliability, 285
research: on collaboration, 259; on collective intelligence, 197; by Google, 178; on gratitude, 45; on meditation, 43–44; on mind-wandering, 42; on positive emotions, 173–174; on positive psychology, 50; on workplace, 71
resilience, 95, 106, 117t

respect, 137–138, 212–214, 229
results, 62
review, 249
Ricard, Matthieu, 41, 84
rich conversations, 283, 288
Riley, Marvin, 14, 74, 179, 233–237, 266;
    change for, 155–156, 268; childhood
    of, 153–154; egos for, 154–155;
    integration for, 158–159; personal
    transformation for, 152, 156–158,
    161–162. *See also* EnPro Industries
risks, 284, 288
Rogers, Carl, 58, 66–67, 88, 198, 217
Roman empire, 83–84
routines, 265–266
rules of engagement, 186–188, 204, 223
Ryan, Richard, 174

safety: psychological, 106, 178–179, 190,
    234–235, 237, 243f; in workplace,
    228–229
Salzberg, Sharon, 47
Santa Fe Institute, 224
Scharmer, Otto, 225
Schein, Edgar, 214
science: of adult learning, 290; of
    amygdala, 44; cognitive psychology,
    32–33; of evolution, 27; of humans,
    6–11, 28–33, 92; of imagination, 30; of
    Inner Peace, 27–28; of learning, 7–10;
    of nervous systems, 48; neuroscience,
    28–29, 42, 258–261; philosophy and,
    11; of positivity resonance, 50–51;
    scientific method, 62–63, 89, 264
SDT. *See* self-determination theory
The Secret of Our Success (Henrich), 212
security, 81, 144–145
self-determination theory (SDT): for
    Hyper-Learning Behaviors, 106;
    psychology of, 169; skills and, 235; for
    workplace, 174–175, 178; workshops
    for, 175–177
self-development, 157

self-discipline, 250–251
self-image, 36–37, 149–150
self-improvement, 254
self-management, 106, 110t, 240f, 241, 243f
self-measurement, 251
Seneca, 83–84
sensations, 28, 31–32, 34
serenity, 25
sharing, 215
shortcuts, 29
simple prototypes, 282–283
skills: in digital age, 166; how-to-learn,
    128–130; SDT and, 235; for smart
    technology, 132
Smart Machines, 284–285
smartness, 60–61
smart technology: for humans, 167; for
    learning, 3; machines for, 15; skills for,
    132; Smart Machines, 284–285; for
    workplace, 1–2, 4
smiling, 51, 193–194
social connections, 33, 197
social intelligence, 3, 92, 94
social media, 266, 283
social psychology, 70
The Space Between Us (O'Donohue), 55
status quo: for Berkley, R., 101–102;
    challenges for, 94, 106, 116t
Stemco, 228
Stoic philosophy, 46–47, 72, 76–77, 82, 86
storytelling, 70; emotions from, 136–137;
    for New Way of Being, 134; for New
    Way of Working, 134; personal
    transformation from, 139–140;
    questions for, 149–150
stress, 141–142
stress-testing, 274f
subconscious minds, 30–31, 35
sub-Hyper-Learning Behaviors, 13,
    239–241, 239f–241f
suboptimal learning, 9–10
success: for Berkley, B., 104; diversity for,
    186; identity for, 131

suffering, 77, 86
survival, 2, 27
Sweeney, Susan, 14, 74, 134–135. *See also* personal transformation

talking, 17
Tao philosophy, 81
tasks, 15, 30
teamwork: accountability in, 132; for Berkley, B., 103; for Berkley, R., 102; caring for, 194; collaboration and, 70, 199–200; collective intelligence of, 197–198; connecting for, 193–194; conversations and, 225–226; culture of, 106–107; diversity in, 186, 225–226; emotions and, 188–191; engagement in, 187–188; flow for, 222; gratitude and, 39; for humans, 165–166; innovation from, 105; learning in, 143–144; positivity resonance for, 192–193; preconditions for, 210; questions and, 148; reflection on, 191, 195–196, 198–199, 202–203; trust for, 185–186, 198; trusting teams, 17–18; in workplace, 205–206; workshops for, 200–204, 201f. *See also* Caring, Trusting Teams
Technetics Group, 228
technology: artificial intelligence, 101; for Berkley, B., 102; change and, 1–2, 107–109; for digital age, 2–3, 61, 91–92; for feedback, 283; machines, 15; Smart Machines, 284. *See also* smart technology
telling, 214–215
templates, for learning, 269, 270f–274f
10 powers of Inner Peace, 25
Tharp, Twyla, 76
theories: dual bottom line, 233–234; for Hyper-Learning Mindset, 59–63; philosophy and, 64. *See also* self-determination theory
thinking: choice in, 24; critical, 61–63, 248, 272f–273f; about decision

making, 139; deep-thinking, 140–141, 267–268; in digital age, 256; emergent, 52, 224–225; emotions and, 16; engagement and, 3; for humans, 27; leadership and, 266; modern thinkers, 58, 64; psychology of, 84; sensations and, 34; think tanks, 268–269; wisdom and, 64
Tibetan Buddhism, 84–87
Tolstoy, Leo, 158
Tower of Care and Trust, 200–202, 201f
training: feelings, 27; gratitude and, 47; learning and, 119; mental rehearsal as, 259–260; for quiet minds, 26
transformation. *See* personal transformation
transparent honesty, 198
trust: authenticity and, 69; building, 130–131; caring and, 200–204, 201f, 211; communication and, 182; in digital age, 191; fears and, 154; with leadership, 172; in Learning Journals, 191, 198–199; performance and, 16–17; psychological safety and, 190; for teamwork, 185–186, 198; *Trust Factor*, 190; trusting teams, 17–18
Trusting Teams. *See* Caring, Trusting Teams
Turner, William B., 72–75

understanding, 17–18
unlearning, 67

validity, 285
values, 187, 223, 228–229
Vanguard Mutual Funds, 194
visualization, of Daily Intentions, 252
visualization techniques, 133
vital engagement, 71
vulnerability, 52–53, 136–139, 159

warning signs, 133
Whyte, David, 275

willingness, 40
The Will to Meaning (Frankl), 76
Wilson, Edward O., 30
wisdom, 41; learning from, 57; listening for, 78; reading and, 68; thinking and, 64
work. *See* New Way of Working
workplace, 107; anxiety at, 135; autonomy at, 99, 174–175; Best Self in, 161, 171, 275; challenges at, 37; change in, 166–167, 167t–168t, 171–172; cognition in, 9; command and control at, 145–146; commitment in, 230; communication in, 178; diagnostics for, 175–177; in digital age, 3–4; efficiency at, 139–140; *Energize Your Workplace*, 188–189; engagement at, 102; environment for, 14–19, 158; fears in, 174; hierarchies at, 144; High-Quality, Making-Meaning Conversations in, 211–212; humanizing, 161–162, 165–166, 169–171, 179–181; idea meritocracies for, 173; love at, 147; meaningful relationships at, 181–183; mentorship at, 157; negativity at, 51–52; New Way of Being in, 244; New Way of Working and, 14–19; New Way of Working in, 244; people-centric

cultures at, 100; positive psychology for, 173–174; promotions at, 154; psychological safety in, 178–179; reflection on, 168, 171–172, 184; research on, 71; rules of engagement in, 186–188; safety in, 228–229; SDT for, 174–175, 178; smart technology for, 1–2, 4; teamwork in, 205–206; Tower of Care and Trust for, 200–202, 201f; workforce equality, 231–232; at WRBC, 92, 118
workshops, 87, 107; for Caring, Trusting Teams, 200–204, 201f; Daily Intentions, 55–56; for High-Quality, Making-Meaning Conversations, 209–212, 225–226; for Hyper-Learning Behaviors, 93–98, 97t, 119, 237–238; for Hyper-Learning Mindset, 88–90; on leadership, 233–236; for SDT, 175–177; strategies for, 194; for teamwork, 200–204, 201f
W. R. Berkley Corporation (WRBC), 13, 241; courage at, 97–98, 97t; Hyper-Learning Behaviors at, 99–101, 106–109; workplace at, 92, 118
writing, 68, 88

Zak, Paul J., 190

ABOUT THE AUTHOR

Ed Hess is Professor of Business Administration, Batten Faculty Fellow, and Batten Executive-in-Residence at the University of Virginia Darden School of Business. He spent more than 20 years in the business world as a senior executive at Warburg Paribas Becker, Boettcher & Company, the Robert M. Bass Group, and Arthur Andersen.

He joined academia in 2002 as an Adjunct Professor of Organization and Management at the Goizueta Business School at Emory University where he was the founder and executive director of the Center for Entrepreneurship and Corporate Growth and of the Values-Based Leadership Institute. In 2007, he joined the Darden faculty as the first Batten Executive-in-Residence. He teaches Innovation courses in the Darden MBA and EMBA programs; has taught in over 25 Executive Education programs at Darden, IESE (Barcelona), the Indian School of Business, Georgia Tech, and AVT Denmark; and regularly consults with businesses and governmental agencies.

He is the author of 13 books, over 120 practitioner articles, and over 60 Darden cases dealing with growth, innovation, and learning cultures, systems, and processes. The common theme of his work is high individual and organizational performance.

His book *Smart Growth* was named a Top 25 business book in 2010 for business owners by *Inc.* magazine and was awarded the Wachovia Award for Research Excellence. His book *Learn or Die* was an Amazon best-seller and was awarded the Wells Fargo Award for Research Excellence. His most recent best-selling book, with co-author Katherine Ludwig, is *Humility Is the New Smart: Rethinking Human Excellence in the Smart Machine Age* (Berrett-Koehler, 2017).

Hess's work has been featured in *Fortune* magazine, *European Business Review, Harvard Business Review, SHRM, Fast Company, WIRED, Forbes, Inc., Huffington Post,* the *Washington Post, Business Week, Financial Times,* and more than 400 other global media publications as well as on CNBC's *Squawk Box*, *Fox Business News with Maria Bartiroma*, *Big Think*, WSJ Radio, Bloomberg Radio with Kathleen Hayes, Dow Jones Radio, MSNBC Radio, Business Insider, and Wharton Radio.

His recent speaking activities have centered around two themes: Modernizing Capitalism: Saving the American Dream and Hyper-Learning: Human Excellence in the Digital Age.

Also by Edward D. Hess

Humility Is the New Smart
Rethinking Human Excellence in the Smart Machine Age
By Edward D. Hess and Katherine Ludwig

Your job is at risk—if not now, then soon. Smart machines, led by artificial intelligence, will take over millions of jobs. Smart machines will know more data and analyze it faster than any human and be free of the emotional, mental, and cultural baggage that so often mars human thinking. Edward Hess and Katherine Ludwig offer a new game plan guided by humility called NewSmart: learning how to excel at doing the things machines can't do well—critical and innovative thinking and high emotional engagement with others. The key to success is not to be more like the machines but to excel at the best of what makes us human.

Print paperback, ISBN 978-1-5230-8929-1
Print hardcover, ISBN 978-1-62656-875-4
PDF ebook, ISBN 978-1-62656-876-1
epub ebook, ISBN 978-1-62656-877-8
Digital audio, ISBN 978-1-62656-879-2

Berrett–Koehler Publishers, Inc.
www.bkconnection.com   800.929.2929

Dear reader,

Thank you for picking up this book and welcome to the worldwide BK community! You're joining a special group of people who have come together to create positive change in their lives, organizations, and communities.

What's BK all about?

Our mission is to connect people and ideas to create a world that works for all.

Why? Our communities, organizations, and lives get bogged down by old paradigms of self-interest, exclusion, hierarchy, and privilege. But we believe that can change. That's why we seek the leading experts on these challenges—and share their actionable ideas with you.

A welcome gift

To help you get started, we'd like to offer you a **free copy** of one of our bestselling ebooks:

www.bkconnection.com/welcome

When you claim your **free ebook**, you'll also be subscribed to our blog.

Our freshest insights

Access the best new tools and ideas for leaders at all levels on our blog at ideas.bkconnection.com.

Sincerely,

Your friends at Berrett-Koehler

Certified

Corporation